The Economics of Wealth and Poverty

By the same author

The Calculus of Consent: Logical Foundations of a Constitutional Democracy (with James M. Buchanan) (University of Michigan Press, 1962)

The Politics of Bureaucracy (Public Affairs Press, 1965)

The Organization of Inquiry (Duke University Press, 1965)

Toward a Mathematics of Politics (University of Michigan Press, 1967)

Private Wants, Public Means: An Economic Analysis of the Desirable Scope of Government (Basic Books, 1970)

The Logic of the Law (Basic Books, 1971)

Modern Political Economy: An Introduction to Economics (with Richard B. McKenzie) (McGraw-Hill Book Company, 1978)

Trials on Trial: The Pure Theory of Legal Procedure (Columbia University Press, 1980)

The Economics of Income Redistribution (Kluwer-Nijhoff Publishing, 1983)

The Economics of
Wealth and Poverty

Gordon Tullock
Holbert R. Harris University Professor
George Mason University

DISTRIBUTED BY HARVESTER PRESS

First published in Great Britain in 1986 by
WHEATSHEAF BOOKS LTD
A MEMBER OF THE HARVESTER PRESS PUBLISHING GROUP
Publisher: John Spiers
Director of Publications: Edward Elgar
16 Ship Street, Brighton, Sussex

British Library Cataloguing in Publication Data

Tullock, Gordon
    The economics of wealth and poverty
    1. Income distribution
    I. Title
    339.5'2   HC79.I5

ISBN 0-7450-0141-6

Typeset in Times Roman, 10pt. by Gilbert Composing Services

Printed and bound in Great Britain by
Robert Hartnoll (1985) Ltd., Bodmin, Cornwall

THE HARVESTER PRESS GROUP
The Harvester Group comprises Harvester Press Ltd (chiefly publishing
literature, fiction, philosophy, psychology, and science and trade books);
Harvester Press Microform Publications Ltd (publishing in microform
previously unpublished archives, scarce printed sources, and indexes to
these collections); Wheatsheaf Books Ltd (chiefly publishing in economics
international politics, sociology, women's studies and related social
sciences); Certain Records Ltd, and John Spiers Music Ltd (music
publishing).

Ye Shall Know the Truth
and
the Truth Shall Make You
(at least moderately)
Charitable

Contents

Acknowledgements

I am grateful to the following publishers and individuals for permission to reproduce the articles which appear in this volume: *Southern Economic Journal* for 'Reasons for Redistribution'; Western Economic Association International for 'Charity of the Uncharitable'; *Kyklos* for 'The Cost of Transfers' and 'More on the Welfare Cost of Transfers'; Edgar K. Browning and *Kyklos* for 'On the Welfare Cost of Transfers'; Columbia University Press for 'Giving Justice'; *New York University Law Review* for 'Giving Life'; University of Chicago Press for 'Inheritance Justified'.

1 Introduction

During most of the last 40 years, redistribution of income and wealth has been a major activity of governments. It has also been a major subject of discussion among economists, but the amount of formal analysis has been limited. Further, what analysis there was, was very largely an effort to determine how equally income was distributed both before and after the redistribution.

In addition to this, the rather traditional economic field of income distribution, of course, continued active. In fact, it expanded considerably due to the realisation that human capital was an important variable, and hence, there were studies of the return on human capital and its effect on the distribution of income. Sometimes these studies were carried on in the context of income redistribution.

Nevertheless, there was relatively little work on the economics of redistribution itself. My point in discussing this approach by other economists is, more or less, to excuse the fact that I too did very little during most of this time on income redistribution. Like other economists, I was interested in the subject but tended to think it essentially a matter of morals or values which could not be analysed. I, of course, still think that the ultimate decision on the amount of equalisation is a matter of individual values, but I now think that, nevertheless, a good deal of research can be done. As I have now produced a book on the subject,[1] it seemed timely to put together what I had previously written in the field of income redistribution and related topics. Hence, this book. I am happy to say that none of these papers deals with efforts to measure the degree of equality in society before or after redistribution, although there are some references to measures made by other people.

Perhaps I should, however, begin by making a few remarks about my own value situation. Basically, I started out with, I think, the standard view. That is, I thought that we should help the poor. I had no determinate idea as to how much we should help them, but would have been willing to say that particular payments were too much or too little. I now realise, of course, that these judgements, like most value judgements in this area, were perfectly arbitrary, but I don't think that when I was in college studying law I was aware of this.

At that time, I don't think that I had any feeling at all about whether help to the poor should be done by government or private charity. Later, I came for a time to think that it should be mainly dealt with by private charity, but I was cured of that by Milton Friedman, of all people.

1

This rather normal, badly thought-out set of values is, I think, standard in this field. In my case it received a very severe blow when I joined the foreign service and went to China and later Korea. I immediately found myself in very poor countries which were both made even poorer than usual because of war. I was surrounded by people who, literally, were on the verge of starvation. Further, in China one saw on the streets people with various conditions which obviously required medical treatment. They weren't being treated because they couldn't afford it. There were also in China a certain number of professional beggars, who had been deliberately crippled as small children by their parents, in order to increase their appeal as beggars. The number of the latter was quite small because since the overthrow of the Manchu Dynasty in 1911, crippling of this sort had been illegal. The enforcement of these laws had been made difficult by the continuing civil war but, nevertheless, this phenomenon which used to be very common in China had become a rarity. But there is a difference between being a rarity and not being there at all.

Granted the sort of standard American values which I have described above (i.e. we should help the poor but without any clear idea of how much) this was a rather shocking situation. It was perfectly obvious that my income, if I chose to redistribute it, dropping myself to, let us say, an average Chinese income (at the time, that would have been about the average world income) would have permitted me in almost any year to save from starvation something in the order of 50 to 60 human beings. This would, of course, have involved a sharp reduction in my own living standard, but it is very hard to argue that I, in any real sense, deserved a higher income than the world average. Of course, my superiors in the foreign service would have probably had me shipped home as mentally unstable if I had made such a redistribution. Nevertheless, the problem was a real one, and one which I found quite disturbing.

To give but one extreme case, I was in Seoul immediately after the war, at a time of very great poverty. Outside the window of my office in the American embassy there were the ruins of what, I take it, had been a house. In any event, the ruins consisted primarily simply of a fireplace and a little bit of chimney. A gang of about eight or nine street boys had made this into their 'house' . Specifically, at night they would sleep huddled together into the fireplace. Obviously, only one or two of them could actually get into the fireplace, even though they were quite small, but by clumping with the fireplace on one side it was possible to keep warmer at night.

I was, at the time, living in a small, dilapidated government furnished house, but it was obvious that if I had invited them into my house and given them, let us say, one half of it, they would have been massively better off yet still much worse off than me. Needless to say, again, this would have led to my being shipped back to the United States. I could, however, think of no objective reason why I deserved the difference in our income. Further, even if I did deserve the difference in our income, standard moral principles would have implied that I should have made large gifts to them.

Another aspect of the problem, which I found at the time surprising, was that an awful lot of these people were cheerful. This street gang, which I never had any personal contact with, used to get little bits of wood and cook something for their breakfast every morning. I presume it was not very good food, but I was looking down from the third floor and couldn't make any close examination. On several occasions I watched them having their breakfast, and they were clearly quite cheerful and happy about the whole thing. Further, in China itself I discovered that, on the whole, the Chinese seemed to be reasonably happy. This would have given me a very strong feeling that money does not bring happiness, were it not for the fact that, of course, money at least gave me a standard of medical care that they did not have, and illness is positively painful. Still, the ability of human beings to make the best of a bad deal was quite impressive.

I should say that I now feel that these observations about their happiness are, to a considerable extent, deceptive. The 'Reduction of Cognitive Dissonance', discussed further below (Chapter 3) leads people frequently to underplay their own problems. All of these people would have much preferred the kind of food, housing, clothing, medical care, etc. that I had, although whether they would have laughed louder at jokes in my social environment than in their own social environment is dubious. As a matter of fact, the Chinese have, over the centuries, rather specialised in those two cheapest of all 'luxuries', good manners and an elaborate social life. No doubt they get a great deal of satisfaction out of them. They would get more satisfaction out of them, however, if their real resources were greater.

As I said, all of this bothered me. Obviously, inspecting my own preference function, I was not willing to impoverish myself in order to prevent a lot of real suffering and death among a number of other people. That would have been true even if the Department of State would not have shipped me home if I had. The problem was made somewhat more severe by the fact that actually giving people money, whether to beggars on the streets or a more regular pension arrangement, was positively dangerous. For example, suppose I had decided to help this small group of boys by taking them into my home and providing them with food, it would have been dangerous because, in essence, the demand was infinite. I would immediately have found myself deluged by other people with equally good claims who would want my aid also. It was decidedly unpleasant to be known to beggars in either China or in Korea as a person who made gifts to them. I discovered this the hard way, and after the first month or so, never gave anything to any street beggars.

Another problem here was that most of my colleagues didn't seem to be bothered by the matter. In general, their political position was well to the left of mine, and they were in favour of equality, and so on, but they didn't seem to find the fact that their income was so very much higher than that of the Chinese or Koreans indicated that they should do anything. They were, on the whole, content to live that way, perhaps to make small contributions to various local charities which could offer a reasonable guarantee that you would not, as a result of the gift, be deluged by people waiting outside your door to demand money as soon as you came out.

Indeed, in many cases, these people seemed to develop an antagonism against the poor of the native population. Rather than feeling sorry for them, they felt irritated and would actually make remarks as if their poverty was, in some way, a reflection on the people themselves. This is particularly true of those of my friends, particularly wives of the foreign service officers, who did occasionally make gifts to beggars on the street. As a result of these gifts, they found themselves continuously having to fight off eager solicitors for more money. This, quite reasonably, irritated them and they tended to express their irritation in terms of criticism of the beggars. I, myself, found the matter annoying and stopped making gifts to beggars. I never, however, felt that the beggars were other than very unfortunate people who were doing their best in a terrible situation.

All of this led me to a good deal of thought and effort to reconsider my own value preferences. I came to realise something that I think most people do not realise, and that is that although I was in favour of giving money to the poor, I didn't want to give very much to them, and the basic reason I didn't want to give very much to them was very simple. I wanted to spend the money myself. In other words, my preference function (this was before I knew much economics) put much more weight on my consumption than it did on the consumption of the poor, although it did not give zero weight to the consumption of the poor. In essence, I realised that all of my life I had been saying things about helping the poor which were not really in accord with my preferences.

I should say that, as far as I know, this reaction on my part to the problem was unique. Most of the people continued being, let us say, mildly socialist and in favour of equality, while neither wanting themselves to give money to the Chinese population to the point where there was something even remotely close to equality between their own income and the Chinese, or wanting the American government to do so. My realisation that there was substantially nobody in the United States who was poor by world standards was an unusual evaluation of the situation. Most people continued making statements about the desirability of equality and helping the poor, and in fact, making only rather modest sacrifices to that end. They were also in favour of their government making only rather modest gifts to the poor.

This problem continued to bother me, both when I was in the foreign service and later. I observed, for example, that the American government was, by international standards, quite generous in making gifts to the poor parts of the world. These gifts, however, were very modest if you compared them with the amount that the American people could have given, or the amount that would be necessary if any serious thought had been given to the objective of equalising income between all human beings. They were also quite modest if you compared them with what the American government gave to American poor, who already had much higher living standards than the peoples of India or Africa. Further, inspecting on my own preference function, I found that I was not particularly opposed to the American government's programme. Indeed, I tended to be rather opposed to our foreign aid programme, but that was, essentially, not because I objected to giving money to foreigners, but because of the extremely inept way in which the money was normally dispersed.

Nevertheless, it was clear to me that what we were doing, if it was in accord with the popular preference and in accord with my own preference, more or less, was radically different from the official rationalisations used for it. Although our slogans imply that we should regard any human being as good as another, our practice is intensely nationalistic.

Further, if we look at the transfers in the United States, we find that the bulk of them do not go to the poor. But that is a matter which will be dealt with further below. Nor is this, in any sense, a special characteristic of Americans. The European welfare states in practice normally make a greater distinction between foreigners and their own citizens than we do. This is particularly remarkable because some of them, through guest-worker policies, have a number of foreigners actually working inside their country. With the notable exception of West Germany, these exploited foreigners do not have anywhere near the same welfare privileges as the citizens. Indeed, the treatment of the Turks in Zurich is very similar to the treatment of blacks in Johannesburg. This does not, of course, prevent the Swiss from being very critical of the South African government.

After I ceased to be a foreign service officer and became an economist, my primary work did not involve this particular problem. Nevertheless, I continued reading quite extensively about international matters and, hence, a radical distinction between the way the welfare state treats it own citizens and the way it treats impoverished foreigners was always in the front of my mind.

I kept thinking about the general problem during most of this period, but to no great consequence. There was a period during this time when I came to the conclusion that charity, on the whole, should be removed from the agenda of government activity and be private. I changed my mind about this partly because of the rather technical problem which is discussed in my first article on the subject, 'Information Without Profit'.[2] More importantly, however, I had the good fortune to be at the conference at Wabash College in which Milton Friedman read the lectures which eventually became his book *Capitalism and Freedom*.[3] In that book, he presents a valid economic argument for government provision of aid to the poor and downtrodden. The argument I found convincing and, ever since then, I have been in favour of government aid to the poor.

As I began learning more about the subject, however, I began to have doubts as to whether the government of the United States, or for that matter, the other welfare states, were actually much interested in the poor. 'The Charity of the Uncharitable' (Chapter 3) looks into some of the reasons why I began having doubts of a theoretical nature.

In the late 1970s, I became more interested in the economics of helping the poor and I also, by that time, had begun to have more definite ideas about it. These more definite ideas led both to a number of papers, some published and some not, and my book, mentioned above. What basically happened here is that I came to the conclusion that the personal preferences which I had found in myself as a result of examining my own behaviour in the Orient are, in fact, the personal preferences of most people. The reason that the Americans do not spend a larger part of their national income to help the very poor in other parts of the world is simply that they want to spend the money on themselves. They are charitable, but not very. By a rough rule of thumb, people are willing to give away up to 5 per cent of their own income to help others not in their family, but not more.

There are, of course, occasional saints who will, literally, impoverish themselves to help others. There are, also, occasional people who are so self-centred that they don't give away any money or other resources at all. The government system, like private charity, must adjust itself to the preferences of the people and, hence, does give relatively little to the poor, but does not give nothing to them.

The bulk of income redistribution tends to be back and forth within the middle class in terms of political organisation. In other words, it is given to people who want it, and have the political power to get it. Thus, redistribution is sometimes rationalised on the grounds that it helps the poor,[4] but basically, it is people making use of the government to improve their own wealth. The motives are selfish, not charitable. It is an example of rent-seeking, and I've included in this book one paper on this (Chapter 8).

I cannot blame people who behave this way. It is a perfectly ordinary pattern of behaviour. Still, one of the major points of this book is that that is what we do. We are not as charitable as we would like to think we are.

In general, my position on redistribution is unorthodox. The lack of orthodoxy, however, interestingly, refers only to what is said about redistribution, not to what is done. There is a vast literature in the field, but almost all of it implies that we should be giving far more money to the poor than we are. Almost all of it totally ignores our tendency to redistribute large amounts of money to well-organised groups, such as the farmers, the Gray Panthers, and the like. In practice, although we do indeed give funds to the poor, particularly to the American poor, we give far more to well-organised pressure groups.

Turning to the actual content of the book, Part I is devoted to our reasons for the policies we now follow. It fits into the general literature here in that it points out that our behaviour is frequently not in accord with our professions. It differs sharply from this literature in that it is not an argument that we should change our behaviour. Further, I suggest that we should change our language because I believe that our behaviour more accurately represents our actual feelings than what we say does. This is more or less the reverse of the usual approach. Amartya Sen[5] presents a new and radical interpretation of famines. He argues—and there is no doubt he is right in at least some cases—that the problem in famine is not a shortage of food, but a shortage of purchasing power. There is plenty of food, but the poor can't afford to buy it. From this he deduces that we should make certain that they can afford to buy the food in bad times. This is a very superior example of what I might call the normal approach. The difference between our moral aspirations and our actual activity is pointed out and it is urged that we do something about it. Note that in this, as in most such cases, the actual reform proposed is rather modest since the cost of providing food in famines would be a mere trifle in the American budget.

My approach, if I had been writing the book, might have been the same on facts, but my evaluation would have been different. I would have pointed out that what we claimed were our principles were not the principles we were working on and simply left it at that. I would not have delivered a moral lecture. Indeed, in at least one of the cases he discusses, the Bengal famine during 1943, I believe was deliberately induced by the imperial government of India for essentially political reasons. Personally, I find this kind of political activity extremely distasteful, but I try to avoid imposing my own values on the reader in this matter.

In a way, my position is much more radical than Sen's. His falls into the general tradition of analysis of poverty combined with a moral lecture. I avoid the moral lecture. If the reader feels strongly about these matters, he is free to use his own value system to evaluate them.

In any event, the first three chapters, simply look into our practice and the probable real motives behind it. Chapter 3, 'The Charity of the Uncharitable', was published some time ago and indeed has been republished twice since then. Chapter 1, 'Reasons for Redistribution', was published in a somewhat reduced and shortened form as my Presidential address to the Southern Economic Association; Chapter 2, 'The Objectives of Redistribution', was prepared for a private conference and has never been published before. The three, in a way, set the tone of the book and indicate fairly clearly the difference between my point of view and that held by most students in the field.

Part II deals with some problems in the organisation of aid to the poor and downtrodden. Chapter 4, 'Information Without Profit', has been reprinted in several places and deals with, quite literally, the extreme information problems that any charitable organisation, private or public, faces. Most discussions in this area tend to overlook these information problems, although no one has raised any questions about the accuracy of my analysis.

This particular article has a somewhat interesting history. The journal, *Public Choice*, started out as a single-issue collection of papers which were then circulating through the invisible academy, but which were difficult to publish because of their subject-matter. It was a personal entrepreneurial activity with my original plans being that I would pay for it out of my own pocket.[6] Under the circumstances, I could put anything I wanted in it. All of the articles except this one are in the field we now call public choice. Since I wanted to put this one in however, I could hardly give the book a name which confined it to analysis of the political system. Thus, the not very attractive name, 'Papers on Non-Market Decision-Making', was chosen and when it was discovered that it would be possible to convert this single publication into a series, that name was retained for the two succeeding issues

At this time, various names were being canvassed for this new discipline, which involves a combination of economics and politics. For example, 'Polonomics' or 'Synergistics'. As a result of my choosing 'Papers on Non-Market Decision-Making', the actual decision was put off for a couple of years and then the name 'Public Choice' chosen. My selection of a particularly bad title gave us the opportunity to have a better title in the future.

The rest of Part II comprises an article that I published, together with Browning's criticism and my reply. I believe it was revolutionary in its time, although now of course it looks orthodox. Economists had, for a long period of time, thought that transfers were essentially a costless activity because the welfare triangles were obviously small. The debate changed the orthodoxy, although to this day, we do not have accurate measures of the actual costs. They are in any event bigger than the welfare triangles.

Part III contains two previously unpublished papers both of which offer suggestions for technical improvements in the way that we redistribute income. The last, Chapter 10 'Demand Revealing, Transfers, and Rent Seeking', was written for this book and demonstrates that the demand-revealing process can be used for income transfers without excessive cost. It also provides an analysis of cases in which we would rather that the income transfer did not occur, such as payments to well-organised pressure groups, and demonstrates that they would be much harder with demand revealing than they are under present circumstances. Since demand revealing would be, to put the matter mildly, a radical change in our present circumstances, it may seem that it is not worth the trouble discussing it. Nevertheless, radical changes have occurred in the past, and if this is an improvement, we should at least think about it.

Chapter 8, 'Local Redistribution', deals with a problem in which the orthodox opinion is almost certainly wrong, the error of which has already been pointed out by earlier writers. Since the previous work of Pauly and Buchanan,[7] however, has been very largely ignored, it seemed worthwhile presenting it again in forceful language. The original contribution of this particular article is the discussion of concrete institutional structures which would make it possible for the theoretical suggestions of Pauly and Buchanan to be carried out.

'Aid in Kind' (Chapter 9) is simply a technical investigation of the rather common tendency of welfare states to make some of their aid to the poor in the form of such things as free medical care or subsidised housing. In this respect, it is a step forward from the existing literature but mainly in a technical sense. There are no radical proposals for change although, like substantially all economists, I prefer payments in cash to payments in kind.

Part IV deals with a number of specific technical problems in redistribution. In each case, my position is different from the current orthodoxy, but also in each case, I believe that the problem with the current orthodoxy has been a tendency to permit emotions to overcome logic. Indeed, it is not that the defenders of the orthodox position make logical errors, they simply pay no attention to some of the basic problems.

Chapter 11, on public defenders, is a clear-cut example. I have been unable to find anywhere in the very extensive legal and political literature on public defenders any solution to the problems that I raise. People who actually administer the provision of free legal aid to the poor must be reaching practical solutions, but there is no evidence that there is a formal decision on the matter or that different agencies reach the same practical solution.

Chapter 12 deals with an area where there has been immense discussion. Calabresi and Bobbitt, when they wrote their book *Tragic Choices*, set off a major outburst of interest in the problem. My paper reproduced here was originally a review in the *New York University Law Review*,[8] of that book with, of course, reference to the discussion to which it had given rise. If I am correct—and Calabresi more or less confirmed this to me in private correspondence—the basic problem here is that we, as basically charitable citizens, do not like to think about situations in which we permit people to die simply because the amount which we would need to spend on keeping them alive is too great.

This leads to the adoption of organisational structures, the basic purpose of which is to conceal from us the decision we are in fact making. Obviously, we cannot make decisions about these institutions either, because that would raise the same kind of mental tension. But having raised this problem, I regret to say, I have no solution for it. Perhaps some of the readers can do better than I have.

There has been very little discussion of inheritance in the technical economic literature. In spite of this, most peoples tend to feel that inherited wealth is undesirable and confiscatory taxes justifiable. Chapter 13, 'Inheritance Justified' challenged this view and immediately set off quite an active discussion. I think, technically, the argument that confiscatory taxation injures some people and benefits no one is invulnerable. There are, of course, many people who feel that there are overriding social values which require limitations on inheritance. My argument here will be thought irrelevant by them.

Part V deals with two conditions which may lead to poverty. Chapter 14, 'Population Paradoxes', is the only paper in this volume which I made a serious, but unsuccessful effort to have published. I would say that the reason it was not published is that the paradoxes pained the population experts to whom the work was sent. The readers may feel that they were right and I was wrong, but in any event, that is my opinion. If I am correct the paper raises a very serious problem which the standard literature on population has simply ignored.

The final chapter is a rather unusual thing to come from someone from the University of Chicago. It argues that, to some extent, the market lacks a stabilising mechanism. Thus, we can expect depressions and booms together with sharp fluctuations in specialised markets. When I was a small child, I visited Florida immediately following the collapse of the great Florida boom of the 1920s and I saw many examples of a macro fluctuation which had not been stabilised by the market.

There is a distinct resemblance to the work of Leijonhufvud and that of Clower. It differs mainly in pointing to a specific mechanism and in arguing that there are many cases in which the macro failure is not one of the whole economy going up and down more than it should, but of some special segment of it, like the Florida land prices in the 1920s, deviating from their long-run pattern.

The book as a whole superficially seems to be a fairly severe criticism of our present practice in the field of charity. Actually, I do not intend to criticise our practice, but our theoretical discussions of it. As an economist, I think that what people want is better represented by what they do than by what they say. In the field of redistribution, there is a vast gap between what people say and what they do. I would suggest that this gap be closed, not by changing our actions, but by changing what we say. Let us frankly admit that we are only moderately charitable, and that we are quite nationalistic. Let us further frankly admit that our political system and, indeed, all known political systems are susceptible to rent seeking, with the result that they engage in a lot of income transfers for which the only argument is that the recipients want the money. This may not be a very encouraging point of view, but at least it is beginning from which we can do valid research. If we want to improve our situation, we must begin by recognising what the situation is.

NOTES

1. *Economics of Income Redistribution* (Hingham, Mass. Kluwer-Nijhoff, 1983). There is a sort of condensation of this book, *Welfare for the Well to Do* (The Fisher Institute, 1983).
2. See 'Information Without Profit', Chapter 4, below.
3. *Capitalism and Freedom*, Milton Friedman (Chicago: The University of Chicago Press, 1962).
4. Benjamin Franklin once said, 'What a help it is to be a reasoning being, because it permits us to rationalise anything we wish to do.'
5. Amartya Sen, *Poverty and Famines: An Essay on Entitlement and Deprivation* (New York: Oxford University Press, 1981).
6. A small foundation grant came in at the last minute with the result that I did not have to do so.
7. Mark Pauly, 'Income Distribution as a Local Public Good', *Journal of Public Economics*, vol. 2 (February 1973), pp. 35–58. James M. Buchanan, 'Who Should Distribute What in a Federal System?', in *Redistribution Through Public Choice*, ed. H. Hochman and G. Peterson (New York: Columbia, 1974).
8. 'Avoiding Difficult Decisions', a review article of *Tragic Choices*, by Guido Calabresi and Philip Bobbitt. In the *New York University Law Review*, vol. 54, no. 1 (April 1979), pp. 267–79.

Part I
Why Redistribute?

1 Reasons for Redistribution*

If I am correct, redistribution is a slogan behind which there is really very little rational thought. Most, albeit not all, people seem to be in favour of redistribution, but I am unable to find any significant agreement among them as to what they mean by the term or how much redistribution there should be. Most people who present arguments for redistribution normally either present very confused arguments or, in those cases where they are not confused, they in fact refuse to apply their own line of reasoning. Further, no real-world redistribution system even remotely resembles the kind of redistribution which would be called for by, let us say, Rawlsian reasoning. This is not to say that one could not present arguments of redistribution, even arguments for the particular pattern of redistribution we see before us. It is only to say that people who favour redistribution have not done so.

I believe the explanation for the non-rationalised characteristic of redistribution is simply that for most people it is either a private good in the sense that they hope to receive redistribution, or it is a public good. The individual for whom redistribution is a public good—the wealthy man who feels that the poor in India should be helped, for example—has little or no motive to think carefully about the project, because of the usual arguments for poor information in political procedures. We shall see below that these arguments are even stronger in this case than they usually are. The person who hopes to benefit from redistribution has reasons for thinking about the distribution programme, of course, but in general he is better advised not to state publicly his true motives for favouring particular redistribution programmes. Hence, the public debate on the subject shows very little thought and a good deal of emotion.

I hope that the rational consideration with respect to redistribution which I propose to discuss below, leads to an improvement in clarity in this field, if it does not lead to any change in policy. I am attempting to find out what views on redistribution are held publicly in the hope that this will make it possible for me to provide a better discussion than I can on my present, rather feeble base. But before talking about various technical aspects of redistribution, let me very briefly take you on a tour of South Africa.

The South African economy is a complex one and I do not want to go

---

*This paper was later shortened considerably and used as my Presidential address for the Southern Economic Association, and first published as 'The Rhetoric and Reality of Redistribution' in *Southern Economic Journal*, Vol. 47, April 1981, pp. 895–907.

through it in detail. Basically, there are two white groups, the Afrikaaners and the English-speaking, with the English-speaking group making up about 40 per cent of the whites and being markedly more prosperous than the Afrikaaners; together they comprise 20 per cent of the total population. The remaining 80 per cent of South Africans are mainly black, although there are two other groups—Asians and coloureds who get special treatment and whom I shall not discuss here. The blacks' income is very low, probably in the order of 20 per cent of the whites'. In part this reflects a much lower level of skill and other kinds of human capital on the part of the blacks, but in part it also represents discrimination. The most important aspect of the discriminatory system is the confining of about half the black population to what used to be called the native reserves and are now called homelands where they engage in subsistence agriculture at very low returns.[1] The blacks who live in the cities are subject to discrimination and are classified in a number of different categories which affect their employment opportunities, but in general their income is probably closer to that of the whites than that of the 'Homeland' blacks.

Redistribution is, however, what I would like to talk about. The government of South Africa has an active programme for income redistribution, a part of which is referred to as income redistribution and part of which is hidden under other titles. The main recipients of these income redistributions are the Afrikaaner population, about half of whom are employed by the government. The government farm programme takes care of a large part of the remaining Afrikaaner population. In addition, the so-called poor whites, defined (more or less) as whites whose income is no more than three times the black average, are recipients of direct welfare payments of the type we are accustomed to in the United States and Europe.

It should not be said that the blacks themselves are totally ignored. There are welfare programmes directed to both the blacks and the whites to provide them with education, etc. There is a net transfer of tax funds from the white population to the black. It is, however, utterly trivial compared with the transfers that occur within the white population. Further, it is by no means obvious that the blacks gain from the whole system since various redistributional arrangements, particularly in agricultural areas among the white population, raise the price of food and this may more than compensate for the rather small direct transfer to the black. There is also the fact that the aid to the black community is largely administered by white civil servants and it may well be that the gain to that small part of the white population involved in this work is as great as the net profit that blacks make on the redistributional activities which aim at benefiting them. ·

I find that most people on hearing about this system tend to get rather indignant. As a matter of fact, however, it is roughly the system that is used by all democratic countries, if you simply realise that the blacks in South Africa are not citizens. It very closely resembles the attitude of Switzerland or Sweden to their so-called guest-workers. The government of Sweden, for example, does not permit all Turks to enter Sweden and take jobs, and once they arrive in Sweden they are paid less than Swedes, partly because their human capital is less, but they are also subject to various discriminatory rules on the type of jobs they may take. Sweden, of course, engages in a large-scale income redistribution within their population and has a foreign aid programme. The foreign aid programme is comparatively small, and among its beneficiaries surely are those Swedes who are administering it. The only difference between Sweden and South Africa is that some people regard the blacks in South Africa as citizens of South Africa,[2] but do not regard the Turks as citizens of Sweden.

There is an apparent radical difference in the way in which we redistribute to people who are regarded as citizens and those who are not.[3] We are indignant with South Africa for treating people in two different ways and restricting the immigration of some of their blacks to their major cities, but we are not particularly indignant with the Americans for treating people differently when one group are the Mexicans. Indeed, the American-Mexican problem is very similar to that of South Africa with respect to the blacks. American cities, like South African cities, have a certain number of the discriminated-against Mexican group present legally, and a large number who are there illegally. Our attitude towards these illegal Mexicans is again very similar to the South African attitude towards the illegal blacks. We alternate between trying to get rid of them and feeling sorry for them. In both cases, if they are caught they can be removed (deported from the United States, and signed out in South Africa) by administrative officials without a court intervention, although once again in both cases it is possible to have the administrative decisions reviewed by a court.

The reason for sharply limiting the immigration of Mexicans, Jamaicans, Asians etc. are exactly the same as those used in South Africa to keep out the blacks. We do, however, keep out far more of them. The average major city in South Africa has about three blacks for every white, while only something like 4 or 5 per cent of the population of the average American city is non-American. The fact that we keep more out than do the South Africans, however, certainly is no argument that we are morally superior.

It is notable that the South Africans, having observed this particular oddity in the western moral system, have been attempting over recent years to convert South Africa into a situation in which the blacks are foreigners and hence their being kept in subordinate positions, or even kept out of the major cities, would therefore be in conformity with western practice. The great indignation that this has aroused indicated that there is something further in this distinction that they have not fully understood.

Another example of redistributionist muddle concerns the dismantling of the European empires. Let us consider only the British case, because in some ways it is the most extreme example. When a socialist party took control of the government in London, the inhabitants of India were as much subjects of George VI as were the inhabitants of Britain. It is true, strictly speaking, that they were subjects of the Emperor rather than the King, but this was really not a distinction of much importance. A socialist government, interested in helping the poor, should have noticed that of the population subject to its control, something like 85 per cent were much more poor than anybody living in Britain, in fact, many of them were on the verge of starvation. Hence, it should have made immense transfers to this portion of the population. As democrats it would also have been sensible for them to agree that the Indians should send representatives to Parliament in proportion to their population. Needless to say, this prescription was not only not implemented, it was not even thought of. I talked at the time to a few British socialists about this and they showed a certain amount of embarrassment, but characteristically argued that the Indians did not want to be put in complete control of the British government which is what such a voting method would provide. They wanted independence. This was clearly simply a rationalisation.

It is, I suppose, clear that the reason that the empires were dismantled rather than granting to the subjects full citizenship was a simple selfishness on the part of the population of the central metropolitan power. It would have caused an immense drop in the living standard of the English, the French, the Portugese, the Dutch and the Belgians if they had simply integrated the colonies into the whole society with an equal role.[4]

Why, then, other than for selfishness did the colonial powers not make large transfers to their colonial subjects, once they came under the control of socialists? Why not permit them to vote? Indeed, why do we not permit foreigners to vote? We pass a number of Bills in our Congress which are of great interest and importance to foreigners—the foreign aid programme is perhaps the most significant example—but we do not permit them to vote on it. When I talk to people about this issue, the normal, immediate reaction is one of complete incredulity that I should raise it. When I point out, however, that for most egalitarians (and I usually talk about this subject only with egalitarians) it is contrary to their own ideas of equality to make distinctions on accidents of birth or geography, they normally simply become embarrassed and turn away. One particularly clear-cut example of this occurred when I visited New Mexico. A liberal member of the faculty of the university there, obviously intending to embarrass a visiting conservative, asked me if I thought the illegal Mexicans in the state should be permitted to vote. I was, of course, to say no, thus indicating how backward and contrary to advanced modern thought I was. Instead, I said that I saw no reason why mere position on either side of an arbitrary line should make any difference, and asked him whether he thought the Mexicans in Mexico should be permitted to vote in the New Mexican elections. He paused, looked somewhat shaken, said, I never thought of that, but I suppose we should let them vote, and then quickly changed the subject. I am sure he had the whole incident erased from his memory by a little later that afternoon.

Why don't we permit Mexicans to vote in those American elections where something directly concerning them is involved? The only answers that one can find are simply that we believe in nationalism in a strong sense, which most moderns deny, or that we are selfish. We realise that they would use the vote to obtain money from us and, even though we talk about egalitarianism, we don't really want to have our income reduced that much. South Africa again is a clear-cut case. The white South Africans, as I have mentioned above, do make some transfers to blacks, but egalitarianism in South Africa would mean transfers of something in the order of 80 per cent of the wealth of the whites to the blacks. They may be interested in equality, but not that much. We are the same.

The point of the above discussion is not to urge that we make large transfers to the poor who happen not to be American citizens, or that we permit them to vote. It is to point out that the standard explanations for egalitarian behaviour do not fit the real world. Those Americans who are receiving grants of various sorts from the American government on the grounds that they are poor, are uniformly higher in income than the world average. In other words, if we had a really egalitarian programme, almost every single American who now is being aided by the state would in fact be taxed in order to transfer what little he has to people who have even less. Obviously, that is not our policy. Furthermore, most people who tell you that they are interested in equality are shocked when it is proposed.

Rawls' book is a particularly clear example of this kind of thing. As almost everyone knows, he turns to the original position in which you do not know who you are and then discusses the type of policy you would propose. He does not, however, discuss whether you know you are a citizen of the United States, Italy, India, etc. If you actually do not know who you are, and you think therefore the likelihood of your being a citizen of India or of Communist China is as great as the likelihood of your being an American citizen, you would be in favour of very drastic transfers of funds away from the American citizens.[5] The best policy would be removing at least two-thirds of the present after-tax income of American citizens and giving it to the poorer parts of the world, and very likely 80 per cent would be a more reasonable figure. Swedes, even if members of the socialist party, or members of the British Labour Party, etc., all would find themselves impoverished.

In all of the published discussion of Rawls' book by people who favour income redistribution, I've only seen this matter discussed once. Beitz,[6] talks to some extent about such redistribution, but his discussion seems to be based on the theory that we should only redistribute to poor foreigners if their poverty is caused by a lack of raw materials in their country. He does not suggest an 80 per cent of income transfer to them. But with this exception, income redistribution is implicitly, but almost never explicitly, confined to within the nation-state. In most cases there are people within the nation-state who are not made subjects of redistribution. The blacks in South Africa and the bulk of the Arabs of Israel are particularly clear examples, but there are others. The guest-workers in most European countries, the illegal immigrants in the United States, and for that matter legal immigrants to the United States whose status is such that they can still be deported if they become public charges, are examples. Really, however, the distinction is as to location on the map, which is as arbitrary a distinction as I can name.

The rules followed by substantially every wealthy country in the world is to restrict immigration in order to provide to their labourers a small amount of protection from competition.[7] This is, of course, a distinction which increases the total inequality in the world. There are, then, elaborate welfare schemes in almost every wealthy country in which only people within the boundaries of the country—and in general only citizens who are within the boundaries—can share. These schemes probably also increase total world inequality, although that is not absolutely certain.

To see the increasing inequality caused by these schemes, consider Figure 1.1. I have drawn here on the vertical axis income and on the horizontal axis we simply have people designated by name. They are arranged from left to right on the horizontal axis with the people with the highest incomes on the left. (The actual shape of the line I-I which shows the income of each individual arranged in this way would be a fairly complex curve, but for simplicity I have drawn it in as a straight line.) Let us suppose now that a club of millionaires, i.e. everyone to the left of the vertical line, became concerned by the fact that some millionaires are only just millionaires while others have 10, 15 or 20 million dollars. They therefore set up a redistribution programme which changes the income distribution to the left of point M as shown by line R-R. The result of this redistribution, however, is a reduction in the total efficiency of the economy and in consequence the income received by the people who aren't millionaires (i.e. those to the right of M) is also reduced, as is shown by the dashed line. The post-income distribution then is shown by line R, a vertical drop at M and then the dotted line whereas before it was I-I.

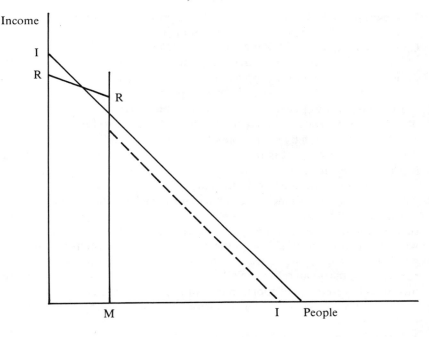

Figure 1.1

The income distribution is thus certainly lower for the lower-income groups and probably more unequal for society as a whole. When I have presented this proposition orally to various groups of economists they have agreed that the consequences that I specify occur, but some of them have thought that it might lead to more income equality. This would be purchased at the cost of lowering the incomes for substantially everyone except the poorer millionaires.

The question of whether this increases or decreases the income equality seems to me unimportant, but to some people it might be thought to be important. One of the criticisms of Rawls' book has been that he attempts to maximise the income of the citizen who is worst off. This has been criticised by various people on the grounds that an increase of the income of a wealthy man by 5 dollars might be accompanied by an increase of the poorest man by 1 dollar, and these critics feel that that would be undesirable. I have great difficulty in having much sympathy with this criticism, but it has been made.

The point of Figure 1.1 is that equalisation of income within the upper-income groups, i.e. the citizens of the United States, Italy, Germany, etc., is roughly equivalent to our equalisation of income among the millionaires.

By lowering the efficiency of the world economy it lowers the income of the poor people who may live in such countries as India and Communist China. Thus equalisation of incomes in the United States is probably a way of increasing the degree of inequality of incomes in the world and certainly impoverishing the poorer people in the world, which means in essence that their death rate which is already high, will rise further.

I should perhaps pause here to say a little bit about the efficiency effects of equalisation. They are debated to some extent, but so far as I know the debate is always won by the people who argue that equalisation will lead to a lower total income. It is not obvious, however, that maximising world income is the thing we would want to do. We must be careful about offsetting equalisation against efficiency.[8]

Changing a person's income by an income tax lowers the marginal return on effort for him and at the same time lowers his wealth. In general we think that people who are wealthier, tend to work a little less hard than people who aren't so wealthy, although the empirical evidence on this is not very good. On the other hand we would anticipate that people would work harder is the marginal return on effort was greater. Thus, for people whose income is lowered by a proportional income tax, it is not clear whether their work effort would be increased or lowered. Further, the empirical evidence is also not clear.

Income redistribution, however, also includes giving money to the poor. They receive what is the equivalent to a negative income tax of some sort (i.e. their income is supplemented) but the supplement is so arranged that it either declines as their earned income rises or is cut off entirely at some point. In either event, in their case the income effect raises their income which would tend to mean that they would work less hard and the reduction of a marginal return on their effort also would mean that they are likely to work less hard. Thus, the people who receive the transfers will work less vigorously than they would had the transfers not been paid to them.[9]

The empirical evidence on the declining work effort of people who are receiving some transfer is not as voluminous as we would like; but it is clear. For example, the negative income experiment seems to indicate the withdrawal of labour power of about 15 per cent from the market when the negative income experiment was introduced. Since the people who were receiving the negative income payments had to a considerable extent been eligible for other transfers before, this is not a measure of the reduction in labour offerings caused by the negative income tax, but the difference between that and a somewhat less generous programme. Our efforts to measure the reduction in efficiency by the other types of relief and welfare programmes have on the whole not been very successful because of the rather disorderly nature of these programmes. It is, however, clear that they do reduce the total product of the economy. It has been suggested, for example, that a good deal of unemployment is caused by unemployment benefit. Employment of people over the age of 63 and under the age of 72[10] is very markedly lower than it was before the social security programme was introduced. We have all also heard of welfare cheaters and at least some of the loud indignation is well justified.

But so much for the inefficiency effects of equalising income transfers. A brief discussion is necessary here because of the demonstration that equalising incomes within an upper-income group (for example, the citizens of the United States) tends to lower the incomes of the poorer parts of the population (for example, the citizens of India or Communist China).

Why then do we observe so much interest in equalisation of the incomes of Americans and so little interest in equalising world incomes? Note that there is some interest in equalising world incomes, we do indeed make gifts to various foreign countries as the South Africans make transfers to their blacks. We also make some transfers to the illegal immigrants in the United States.

In order to understand these phenomena, it is essential that we consider the actual motives behind income redistribution. Here I should say that I have spent several years attempting to find a coherent discussion of the motives behind income redistribution among the writings or in the oral expressions of proponents of it. One of my techniques was to read a paper before a number of audiences composed of economists almost all of whom would at least purport to be in favour of income equalisation. In it I raised the question of why we gave only very small amounts of money to the very poor people in the world and quite a lot of our co-nationals who are very much wealthier than these poor people. I never found an answer to this question even from people who were highly motivated for equality.

Two of them, Les Thurow and an English left socialist whose name I didn't get, showed considerable embarrassment about the question and then eventually took refuge in political possibilities saying that it was difficult enough to get equalisation within the United States/England rather than working on equalisation in the world as a whole. We must concede that their political judgement about the difficulties of getting equalisation for the world as a whole are correct, but if it is difficult, it must be difficult because it is an unusual desire. Surely, there would be no great difficulty in getting the citizens of the United States to make large payments to the poor of Bangladesh if their actual motive is literally to reduce the amount of inequality. It would simply be necessary to point out to them that the people who live in Harlem are immensely better off than the people who live in the Sahel. The fact that these two well-intentioned people had given up on the problem indicates that their judgement of the actual motives of people who are willing to vote for income redistribution was that they are really not interested in treating all humans alike.

But these two were my prize exhibits. Most of the people with whom I raised this question either refused to answer it at all or took the view that it was perfectly obvious that, let us say, the Canadians should not transfer money to India. They couldn't imagine why I raised the question. They then might rearrange their previous remarks about eliminating poverty because all human beings are equal to say that they are eliminating poverty in the sense that all Canadians are equal. In these cases, however, I then said (as part of my experiment), 'You meant that the Wogs and Gooks and other lesser breeds without the law can be permitted to starve quietly in their villages'. They invariably rejected the implication vigorously. The inconsistency of their position did not lead them to reconsider, but merely to terminate the conversation.

A particularly interesting example occurred in Puerto Rico, where a communist[11] attacked the visiting American lecturer (myself) by saying the United States should transfer more money to Puerto Rico. I immediately replied that Puerto Rico was well above the average world income level and should transfer large sums of money to Bangladesh, which at the time was in the middle of its post-independence disaster. He responded by saying, 'Transfer money to Bangladesh?', paused briefly and then said, 'You don't understand, they are used to their present way of life'. I responded, 'You mean that if everybody in the village dies of starvation they think it is a local custom and don't mind?' This terminated the discussion.

In judging these conversations, it should be kept in mind that I have a good deal of experience. They were far from my first attempt on the subject but they frequently were the first trial by the people on the other side.

These two accounts are typical of my experience. No one seems to have any explanation for this matter based on the kind of reasons that are normally given for income redistribution. As I shall explain below, if one takes a more realistic view of the motives of income redistribution then it is not at all impossible to explain it.[12] But it is possible that some reader may have a better explanation. If so, I would appreciate his telling me what it is. I should say here that I rather anticipate that a good many people will say simply that my line of reasoning is absurd, but without communicating wherein that absurdity lies. I would appreciate anyone who thinks that this line of reasoning is absurd or erroneous kindly explaining to me why. It is possible that I am wrong. I don't think I am, but it is possible and certainly if I have made a ghastly error here. I am unlikely to recover on my own without the aid of my betters who realise what the error is.

It should be said here that there is a rather dishonest way of avoiding the whole problem. One can allege that what is important is relative poverty and not real poverty.

Poverty can be defined objectively and applied consistently only in terms of the content of relative deprivation. That is the theme of this book. The term is understood objectively rather than subjectively. Individuals, families and groups in the population can be said to be in poverty when they lack the resources to obtain the types of diet, participate in the activities and have the living conditions and amenities which are customary, or are at least widely encouraged or approved, in the societies to which they belong. Their resources are so seriously below those commanded by the average individual or family that they are, in effect, excluded from ordinary living patterns, customs and activities.[13]

The problem with this is that I have never found anyone who will stick to it. Thus, the statement that poverty is relative poverty, that what is important is that you don't feel poorer than your neighbours, does not withstand investigation.

Let us consider a few obvious examples. Our first is Newport in the 1890s. Poor Mr. Smith's yacht is only 95 feet long and the shortest other yacht on the sea off Newport is 150 feet long. He is, by the relative poverty definition, a deprived person and should, of course, receive government aid. Let us contrast his situation with a man whose name is Wong. He lives in a village in the Sahel and every single person in the village is now dying of starvation. There is, of course, no poverty in this village, because relatively they are all in the same position. Indeed, perhaps we should argue for transfer from this village where poverty has been abolished to Mr. Smith.

Suppose that you happen to be near Mr. Wong's village and happen also to have a camel caravan with food. The food, however, would only be enough to save the life of 90 per cent of the villagers. Clearly, you should not take the food to the village, because your arrival would immediately create an impoverished class of 10 per cent of the population.

This particular definition of poverty has interesting and most striking consequences for the American aid programme. This aid, as you no doubt know, is aimed at abolishing or at least reducing poverty. Simply raising the wealth of a country is not likely to serve this goal because, of course, it will raise the wealth of the wealthy too. But the contrary activity, having our armed forces destroy all material wealth in, let us say, Peru, would indeed abolish poverty.

As you can no doubt deduce, I have never run into any relative poverty man who would stick to his argument when pressed. I usually characterise this school of thought as one which believes that if everybody has a toothache, it doesn't hurt. The view that a person in Harlem who does not have a colour TV feels worse about it than the citizen of a Sahel village who is watching his child die, but knows that child death is very common in his village, and that he is not worse off than the other villagers, is a really extraordinarily heartless one. To repeat, I have never found anybody who

is actually willing to maintain it, although I have found people who refuse
to discuss the problem.

It should be said here that there was, for a while, some evidence which
supported the toothache theory. There were polls taken around the world
which implied that people's satisfaction with their position in life was
affected almost not at all by their absolute wealth but very heavily by their
wealth as compared to their neighbours. The Gallup organisation,
however, obtained funds to rerun these experiments and the results of their
rather careful work have demonstrated that although people's satisfaction
is indeed affected by comparison of their own wealth with that of their
neighbours it is also affected by their absolute wealth.

Gallup explains the difference between their results and the previous
results as derived from the rather technical way in which the problem was
presented. In fact, however, I think this technical difference (the difference
between a stair and a ladder) was relatively unimportant and the problem
was that the earlier poll asked individuals to compare their well-being
with that of other people in a somewhat similar situation to their own and
the latter poll permitted comparison with people in other countries, etc. It
may be, of course, that the time-lag is important here also. People today,
living in South India, have a better idea of the difference between their
living standard and the living standard of the Americans than they did 20
years ago. Indeed, the whole relevance of the relative deprivation argument
would collapse if we simply assume that people all over the world are
informed by movies and TV about upper-class American living standards.

This argument implies, and indeed sometimes it is directly stated, that
progress is either undesirable or at least neutral. The invention of a cure for
cancer would not reduce poverty. The immense reduction in transportation
cost which occurred recently, and which probably will continue to occur,
has not reduced poverty. The man who used to vacation in Brighton and
envy his neighbour's trip to Paris now holidays in Spain and envies his
neighbour's trip to Rio. His situation has not improved.

Earlier, I spoke of Rawls and the fact that his line of reasoning simply
avoids the problem of international comparisons of income. This is, I
think, probably the most blatant and obvious defect in his reasoning. I can,
of course, understand why he did treat the problems this way. Living in the
Harvard community he was going to be given a great deal of kudos for
having invented a new rationalisation for equality; but if this new
rationalisation implied that his friends and neighbours should have their
income reduced significantly, he would be given the silent treatment. If he
had specifically considered the situation in which behind the veil you don't
know what country you are going to turn up in, he would not have received
all those favourable reviews. On the other hand, if he had said directly and
openly, I am going to assume that behind the veil of ignorance you know

you are going to be an American citizen, he would have been regarded as a heartless racist. His technique was tactful and adroit.

As a minor aspect of this problem, a member of the Virginia Polytechnic Institute philosophy department, Professor Carson, does believe that international equality is important, and Rawls should take it into account. He has succeeded in obtaining substantially no interest in his point of view. People do not in general disagree with him, but they also don't talk about it. This is in keeping with the general picture we have drawn above.

There is, however, another defect with the Rawlsian procedure. Behind the veil of ignorance I would not only take into account the possibility that I might be born un-American, I would also consider the possibility that I might have some other grave misfortune, particularly a serious injury or a serious illness. In a way we are, in fact, behind the veil of ignorance with respect to these things. We all know that terminal cancers are a normal risk of life. Science is making progress, but not very much, and a lengthy and lingering death by an unpleasant form of cancer is something which we all know can happen to us, and which we also know is more or less a simple matter of luck. In other words, with respect to this particular problem, we are behind the veil of ignorance.

There is, of course, no reason why a programme could not be put in hand to tax the healthy for the purpose of not simply providing medical attention to those who are ill—something which many people are in favour of—but actually to provide exceptional facilities for the ill with the result that their net well-being is raised either to the same level as that of people who are well, or at the very least as high as is feasible. Seriously ill cancer patients could be taken to Hawaii where they would be put in a hospital located on a beach served by topless nurses and have symphony orchestras play while they eat meals prepared by famous chefs.

That this programme probably sounds as silly to you as it does to me, does not affect the relevance it has to the discussion. If we really had a Rawlsian attitude, we would be in favour of such programmes. The fact we are not indicates that Rawls has not properly accounted for either our or his own preference function.

I have found substantially no discussion of efforts to transfer enough money to people who are severely ill or badly injured, so that their net utility is equal to the average citizen. Indeed, in a number of cases there are direct statements that this should not be taken into account. We are to equalise everyone's utility is so far as the disutility that a person suffers does not come from disease or deformity. Why this exception should be made is not clear. It seems contrary to the line of reasoning normally proposed, which is that everyone should be made equal regardless of their natural talents, etc.[14]

What I am doing is showing that there are a number of ostensible reasons for being in favour of income redistribution which are not false, but that the people who offer them are not, in fact, willing to apply them outside a very narrow area. What we observe is a feeling that a certain amount of income equalisation in the United States is desirable (or at least it is desirable to advocate it), together with an incoherent set of reasons for such redistribution. Part of my research in this area has been financed by the National Science Foundation. In one of my grants I said that I proposed to investigate the reasons for income redistribution by various methods which involved asking people what their reasons were. This particular grant proposal attracted a very negative referee comment, and one of his negative comments was that obviously this part of my research was nugatory and I would have to begin by working out a theory of why redistribution is desirable.

This was rather odd, granted the fact that the question was directed to me. It is, however, typical. One of the intellectual activities of the modern intellectual is to provide rationalisations for income equalisation. The fact that the reasons he gives do not actually fit his behaviour or his desires is largely ignored. What we have is a desire either to redistribute income or alternatively at least to talk about redistributing income without any coherent explanation for this activity. This leads to a certain amount of intellectual tension and a very vigorous grasping at straws, such as Rawls' book.

Let us then turn to what I believe are the actual motives behind income redistribution in most modern societies, and indeed in the most ancient societies. One special motive which should be mentioned in passing, is carrying out religious duties. A number of religions require specific charitable acts for salvation. The Bible, although not very specific about it, nevertheless argues strongly for the desirability of helping the poor. The individual who takes gifts to the poor because he thinks he will burn in hell if he does not, is not actually being charitable, albeit the effects of his act are the same as if he were charitable.

Highly religious communities have traditionally had quite elaborate charitable activities. It should be pointed out, however, that in most cases in which highly religious communities have collected large amounts of money, (the Moslems with the WACF, the Mormons, the Roman Catholic Church in the Middle Ages, etc.) the bulk of these funds have not gone to help the poor, but to build elaborate cathedrals, maintain the hierarchy of the Church, issue propaganda on the Church's doctrine, etc. Nevertheless, a good deal of the money has always helped the poor. Indeed, it seems likely that societies of this sort actually help the poor more than we do now.

But it should be pointed out that even with the sanction of hell fire, and strong religious belief, formal tithing arrangements have never called on people to be very charitable. The net effect of being a Mormon in the

United States today is that you are supposed to put about 16 per cent of your income into the various programmes of the Church. The amount is, of course, tax deductible so the actual contribution is smaller. Under the Moslem rule it is 2.5 per cent; most Protestant Churches take 10 per cent. All of this is no doubt desirable, but these are not large transfers, granted what is said about them. Willingness to spend 10 per cent of your income on saving your soul by charitable donations while you spend 90 per cent selfishly may be admirable, but it is nevertheless 90 per cent selfish.

Here we must, if we are going to talk rationally about redistribution, begin by saying that the Church is not out of line in talking to an immense degree about charity but actually taking only 10 per cent. Most people in discussing income redistribution are extremely charitable. It is the amount they actually give away which is modest.

Some time ago there was a member of the political science department who could without any doubt at all be listed as a sloppy liberal. He was very much in favour of all redistributional programmes; felt the poor should be helped, etc. In the course of several long conversations (he was a neighbour) he revealed to me, that he thought that means-testing should be eliminated from most programmes, because it wasn't fair for people in his income bracket not to get the various free services given to the poor. On my pointing out that his point of view was contrary to his announced belief in progressive income redistribution, he agreed that it was but repeated that the present system was unfair to people in his income bracket. I should perhaps say that he also on one occasion told me that he felt that private charity was immoral. All income transfers should be done by way of the government. This permitted him to be very charitable in his language and attitudes, while making no sacrifices at all because, of course, his political effect was nil. Note, I am not accusing this man of conscious lying. He wasn't that bright. He was, however, in the true sense of the word a hypocrite.

This kind of hypocrisy, albeit in less aggravated form, is widely found among the population as a whole. Another colleague of mine, in the Polytechnic's political science department, expressed the view that he would be willing to have very large parts of his income go to prevent starvation in India, but, of course, he was not willing to spend it on institutions which wasted it on administrative costs. He was here somewhat misinformed. He thought that all of the institutions which you can turn to transfer money to the poor people in India would spend 60 per cent of your transfer on themselves. When I explained to him that there were also institutions called banks, and that by simply getting the names of some poor people in India he could arrange to transfer funds to them at a negligible cost, he laughed and changed the subject. In this case I should perhaps say that the man is not only in the political science department, but a perfectly genuine church minister. He gives sermons on Sunday on the desirability of charity and tells his classes about it. I believe also that, by American standards, he is a charitable man, probably making much more sacrifice of his own living standard to help others than most people do. Nevertheless, these sacrifices are strictly limited and much below the ones that he theoretically approves of.

But to return to our main subject which is the real motives for income redistribution. I think there is no doubt at all that the most important single such motive is the desire of the recipients to receive the funds. Note, that I am not criticising the recipients for having this desire; I like to receive transfers myself and so does everyone else I know. It is not making invidious distinctions to say that the people who in fact receive transfers want to receive them, nor that they will work towards obtaining them and, hence, can be one of the motivating forces. Indeed, it would be very surprising if this were not so.

The only issue then that is raised by the view that they are the major source is simply the word 'major'. The evidence for this is I think very strong, however, First, most of the transfers in most societies, democratic or dicatorial, do not go to the poor. They go to people who for one reason or another are politically well-organised. As an academic I am particularly well prepared to testify to this point because like most academics I spend my time making a transfer from the average taxpayer who supports the university system to a group of students, all of whom have been selected for having better than average general talents. They are therefore people who would have higher than average incomes even without any educational advantages, and the taxpayer is compelled to subsidise their receipt of an education which further raises their lifetime incomes. This is a clear-cut case of regressive income transfer with which all academics are familiar. It is, after all, how they make their living.

But this is by no means a deviant case. The Department of Health and Human Services is very largely engaged in transferring funds back and forth within middle-class areas in accordance with various political pressures. It does indeed make some payments to the poor but these are relatively modest. Indeed, if all its transfers were concentrated on the poor, the poor would cease to be poor and might even become members of the upper class.

While we are on the subject of the Department of Health and Human Services we might mention the largest single transfer activity in our society, the social security scheme. It should be said to begin with that the social security administration is characteristically advertised not as a transfer mechanism, but as an insurance scheme in which you pay your contribution during your working lifetime and then are paid back when you retire. If this were all there were to it, there would indeed be no transfer, and the social security scheme should be removed from all consideration of transfers or aid to the poor in our society. It would, of course, be true that the older people who were receiving the funds had less income than the young people who were paying in, but this would no more be a transfer from the well-off to the poor than the payment which implicitly goes from those policy-holders of fire insurance whose houses have not burned down to those whose have.

But this is not all there is to be said about social security. There is actually built into the system two transfers, one small and a second gigantic. Both of these transfers are probably progressive, but the larger one is in essence progressive by accident. In fact, it is a transfer from a group of people who do not have votes to a group of people who do.

Let us begin with the smaller transfers. Assume that the social security remains unchanged at its present basic structure for a long enough time so that a person who entered as a young person taking his first job, finally retires and dies. Within his generation there would be a very large payment made by all individuals during their working life and an equally large receipt by all of them when they retired.[15] Within this group, however, those who have the higher incomes while they were working would find that the total pension they receive will not repay them for their investment, while those who had the lower incomes would find that they received more than they put in.

The actual measure of this transfer is quite difficult due to the complicated nature in the social security arrangements. For example, there is a significant transfer from families in which both the husband and wife work to families in which only one works or in which there is only one person. Secondly, there is a significant transfer to civil servants and army personnel who get very much larger amounts out than they put in. Civil servants and army veterans are not among the poor of the population. This transfer is probably, although not certainly, regressive. The major progressive part of the programme involved quite substantial transfers to the poorer part of the population, however. Note, by the way, that any person whose income comes entirely from property is not a member of the system and hence does not participate. A wealthy man, on the other hand, who was on the board of directors of a couple of companies, and hence was very much a part-time employee, might take a profit out of the system.

An immense transfer which has been associated with the social security administration, however, has been a transfer from future generations to the present (immediately past?) generation.[16] Assume that you are in a society in which there is no social security system and the current general structure of the social security is suddenly imposed. Further, and only temporarily, let us assume that the economic growth of society is as high as the rate of interest. This means that almost everyone makes a net gain. The pay will be highest for elderly people who would immediately begin receiving pensions without making any payments. Other age cohorts will gain roughly in terms of their age. The 50-year-olds would have to put in 12 or 15 years of paying taxes, but the return that they will receive will be equivalent to what they would have received had they been saving the full amount of their payments from the time that they first started working and had invested it at the interest rate which, remember, is temporarily held to be equal to the rate of social growth.

Similarly the 21-year-olds would receive in pensions an amount which is slightly higher than the actual present value of the payments they will make through the rest of their working lives. Even the 18-year-old youngest voters would gain because the average working life includes some work before the age of 18 and they would not pay taxes on that part of their lifetime income but will receive a repayment which will include the average amount of work below the age of 18 as part of its base. There is a qualification to this rather simple picture due to the fact, as I have said before, that there is a progressive transfer in the social security system itself. Someone who was young and who had a fairly high income throughout his life might find out that he paid in more than the present actual value of what he received. The small group of people who would suffer in this way would actually suffer only a small decrement in their lifetime income.

Who, then, pays this transfer? The answer is that it is a modification of the Ponzi scheme, but with legal compulsion to make it work. The members of the first generation who receive these large payments receive them from people who enter the system later. Keeping our current set of assumptions, the latter generations all receive back amounts[17] equal to the actual value that they put in as long as the system continues. Thus, as long as the system continues no one is injured and it is always true that the existing population would be very badly injured by termination. The continuing transfer from those now working to the retired all works out actuarily except in the first and last generation. Further, since the future generations in general will be wealthier than the present generations, the net effect can be called a transfer which is of a progressive nature as a continuing matter by those who are not too critical.

There are two serious problems with this. One is that the rate of growth is unlikely to be as high as the effective interest rate, with the result that people entering the system actually pay in more than they get out. It seems likely, however, that with the amounts of interest in fact available to the average person, that only younger people are injured by this and that at any given point in time the majority of the population would favour continuing the system.

The second problem is, of course, that this system leads to much less capital accumulation than would a fully-funded system. Suppose, for example, the government simply compels people to buy insurance policies with the same net return as the present social security pensions. For any individual now entering the system this would be better, in the sense that it would cost him less because he would receive interest on his initial payments and because capital investment in society would go up with the result that his labour income would rise. Individuals whose income came from capital would, of course, suffer to some extent because the return on capital would be lowered by this sharp increase.

Whether the social security system reduces the total investment to anywhere near this extent, given that insurance purchase is not compulsory, is a much-debated question and one into which I do not want to enter now. Most good economists agree that there is at least some reduction in capital investment as a result of the scheme.

Thus, we have a system which benefited the first generation and which will remain in existence as long as possible because it is always in the interest of the majority of the population to keep it going even though once it has reached an equilibrium it no longer benefits them. The last generation, or the generation which has been in existence when the system is cut back for some reason, will suffer severely.

But does this resemble the American system? The answer is yes. The programme before 1977 was expanded not all at once in one fell swoop, but step by step. Each time it has been expanded there has been a group of people over 40 who gained, and the losses are clearly well-concealed and perhaps non-existent. Further, politically, the drive behind this has almost entirely come from older people which is an indication that the purpose is not to help the poor but to help certain people who are very anxious to be helped and who are willing to vote in terms of whether congressmen helped them or not. Since 1977, the programme has suffered a very considerable number of minor cuts and one quite major cut.[18] Which way the future will go is by no means obvious.

As further evidence that the scheme is not basically a charitable one, motivated by the desire of young people to help impoverished old people, but a desire by old people to help themselves, it should be pointed out that it was actually inaugurated by Prince Bismarck in Germany. Bismarck has never been noted for a desire to be charitable to the poor and downtrodden, although as a traditional aristocrat he doubtless felt it his duty to engage in a certain amount of paternalistic activity.

There is a further bit of evidence here. If I ask people the advantages of the social security scheme as opposed to letting people save money themselves, I invariably get the reply that a number of people wouldn't and that we would then have to take care of them. This is indeed, as far as I can see, the strongest single intellectual argument ever offered for the social security system, namely, that it makes it unnecessary for those of us who are provident to take care of the improvident.

This argument may conceivably be true, but note what it says: first, that without the social security we would be called upon to make transfers to the poor. We force them to save money which they don't want to save in order to avoid this transfer for ourselves. In other words, the standard argument for the social security system is that it reduces the amount of transfers actually made to the poor. In fact, the bulk of the transfers goes to people who are reasonably well-off one way or another.[19] This is reinforced by the fact that those poor people who are so poor that they actually receive financial aid from the state of one sort or another have the social security payment which they receive deducted from that amount so that the net effect is that having paid social security payments all of their life they end up receiving no more than they would had they, let us say, been living in Korea until their retirement and hence made no payments at all to the American government or social security system.

All of this is not atypical. Public opinion polls show clearly that the one and only part of the social welfare system which is unpopular are the direct payments to the poor. (I should say here that in talking to people about this I usually find that once I tell them how small those payments actually are they suddenly become in favour of increasing them!)

But so much for the drive to redistribute simply because the recipients want it. This is an immense phenomenon in all modern welfare states, but it is theoretically at any event a relatively simple motive. Let us now turn to some other motives, most of which are much less important than the desire to receive transfers, but which nevertheless do have an effect on redistribution. Note, that although I have given pride of place to redistribution to people because they want it, because I do think that is the most important motive, I do not have any clear idea as to the relative importance of the motives I am going to discuss below, and hence have put them in random order.

The first of these additional motives is undeniably charity. No one who looks at human behaviour can deny that most human beings are willing to make at least some transfers to people who are less well-off than they are out of purely charitable motives. Presumably this would affect their vote as well as their private actions. Note, however, that what data we have, seem to indicate that the amount they will give away is really quite small. The amount of talk about charity is great, but the amount that is actually given is small. Further, this amount does not seem to have changed very much with movement from the old-fashioned puritan-capitalist state in the mid-nineteenth century to the welfare state of today. This latter is based on a study by Liebergott[20] which shows that there has been sort of minimum income in the United States for a long time and that this has remained roughly speaking, a fixed fraction of the wage of the average working man.

There is in the literature an argument[21] that government redistribution would be larger than private redistribution because of the neighbourhood effect. The explanation can be seen on Figure 1.2. We assume a three-person society composed of one poor person and two well-off people. The two wealthy people each have a 'demand' for charity to the poor person shown by the line CC. The line P shows the cost of providing loaves of bread to the poor person in order to avoid his dying of starvation. Each individual well-off person would be willing to purchase bread for the poor person as far as point 0. If both of them are individually purchasing the bread and they are informed of each other's gifts the outcome is indeterminant, but it looks likely that the individual would receive only quantity 0. How the cost would be distributed between the two wealthy persons is not clear.

Suppose, however, that the two wealthy people get together and form a collective organisation. For each of them, then, the cost of buying a loaf of bread for the poor person is only P'. With the same demand for charity as they had before they will jointly purchase 0'. They will be better off and so will the poor person.

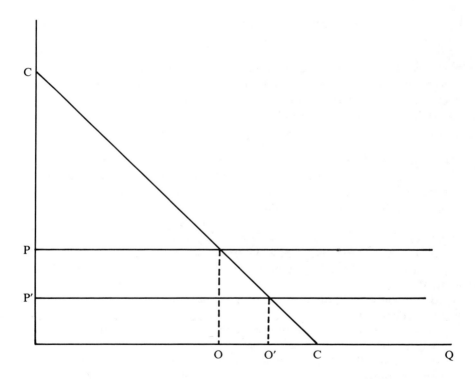

Figure 1.2

Let us turn now to my second genuine motive for redistribution which is simply envy. I should say that most people who are in favour of redistribution of income very strenuously disavow envy as one of their motives. I regret to say that I do not believe them. In redistribution literature there is at least as much discussion of the vicious spending habits of upper-income people as of the poverty of the poor. Partly this comes from simply intellectual misunderstanding, but more accurately I think it is an expression of annoyance and irritation with the rich which comes from envy. For example,

The chief conclusion of this report is that poverty is more extensive than is generally or officially believed and has to be understood not only as an inevitable feature of severe social inequality but also as a particular consequence of actions by the rich to preserve and enhance their wealth and so deny it to others. Control of wealth and of the institutions created by that wealth, and therefore of the terms under which it may be generated and passed on selectively or for the general good, is therefore central to any policies designed to abolish or alleviate the condition.

Once again I do not wish to blame people for being envious. I frequently find myself envying those who have more than I do and I am not surprised at being envied by people who have less. Envy is no doubt a deadly sin, but it is equally no doubt widely present in the human race. That it leads to redistributive attitudes is obvious, although in this case the redistribution, of course, is only away from people who have more than you have.

The combination of charitable motives and envy, I think, jointly leads to another explanation for income redistribution which in my opinion is largely a rationalisation of these two motives. It is frequently said, for example, by Henry Simons, the man who taught me economics, that it is desirable to have a greater degree of equality within the society simply because wide variance is in, and of, itself undesirable. I may be wrong in believing that this is simply a rationalisation of the two motives of charity and envy, but I don't think so. In any event, once again, this desire to have a greater degree of equality would normally appear to terminate at the national boundaries but I have never found an advocate of egalitarian policies who will actually stand up and be counted as arguing for such a break.

I have only one more argument for income redistribution, but if any of my readers have others I would appreciate their sending them to me. This one is the insurance motive. I realise that there is at least some prospect that I will become impoverished in the future. Since I am risk-averse, I am willing to put up at least some resources now to provide myself with insurance against this.[23] One way of organising such an implicit insurance policy is some kind of a state floor under incomes.

The question of whether this kind of income insurance could be provided by private insurance companies is somewhat open. The problem would, of course, be adverse selection of risks with individuals having—or at least thinking they have—better judgement than the insurance company as to what type of income they will receive in the future. It is not clear whether this type of adverse selection of risk would make the provision of such insurance by private companies impossible, but it certainly would make it difficult, and it is arguable that a government programme would do better because, being compulsory, it would eliminate this particular problem. The problem that individuals with this kind of insurance would tend to work less hard, would, of course, be characteristic of both models, but the individual himself would carry the principal cost of this through his premium payment, and if he voluntarily chose the programme we could assume he was better off. A compulsory system would, of course, deprive us of any way of determining whether individuals were better off under income insurance than without, but it certainly is quite possible that they would be.

This argument is relatively invulnerable to refutation on any other than empirical grounds. Further, it is very hard to think of a way to perform the empirical investigation to prove whether it is true or false. It has another advantage. It alone of all the arguments we have produced so far applies to justification for the break at the national boundary or at the ethnic boundary in countries where one ethnic group is in control. You know that whatever else happens you remain an American citizen unless you voluntarily choose to cease to be one,[24] just as a South African knows that his skin colour is not going to change. Therefore, if you favour income redistribution for this reason you need suffer no embarrassment about your unwillingness to include the citizens of Mexico in the distribution scheme.

It should perhaps be said in passing that all insurance policies have some equalising effect on net wealth. I mentioned the fire insurance policy before, but health insurance, life insurance, and for that matter marine insurance on super-tankers all have the characteristic of leading to a somewhat more equal wealth distribution than would exist without the insurance. Income insurance would be simply one example.

The other thing to be said about income insurance is that I very rarely run into it in the literature. Note, I said rarely, it is not totally absent, but it does not seem to be a major argument offered for income redistribution by those who are in favour of it. I discovered that when I asked ordinary citizens about their reasons for favouring income redistribution (if they do) that this answer comes up somewhat more frequently than it does in the formal literature, but still it is not very common.

The general theme of this chapter so far has been that the usual reasons given for income redistribution are muddled and not in accord with the

Part I

actual income redistribution that we observe. The actual motives imply a
very large volume of transfers in the society which don't necessarily help
the poor, some probably minor transfers to the poor for charitable motives
together with another unknown component of transfers to the poor because
the poor want it and transfers away from the wealthy regardless of whether
these transfers are beneficial or not, i.e. taxes may be put on the wealthy
which are high enough so that the total revenue that is derived by the
majority of the population for spending these taxes would be higher if the
taxes were lowered.

Why all the confusion? The answers I think are fairly simple. Let us begin
with the transfers to people who simply want them. On the whole it is
unwise for them to say that their gain is the reason that the transfer should
be implemented. This is not in general a good political ploy. The people who
receive the transfers can no doubt be expected to figure that out and hence
they will become allies where we propose this kind of transfer, but it is best
to keep other people confused.

Thus, Dr Townsend, proposing the famous Townsend plan during a
period of great depression, offered it primarily as a way of curing the
depression and the very large transfers to the elderly which he proposed are
merely a step towards that end. As he had expected, the elderly who were in
favour both of ending the depression and receiving large sums of money in
general pressed for the plan. The rest of the population as it turned out were
not confused enough so it could get through, but it seems quite likely that
the Townsend plan episode was one of the reasons that the social security
scheme was enacted later.

In this the programme is similar to almost all efforts to redistribute funds
to people which are initiated or argued for by the recipients. They have a
strong motive for concealing their real motive from the general public and
if possible also from themselves and hence they are rarely candid in their
explanations.

But to return to the other reasons for transfer. Considering the
desirability of acquiring accurate information about them on the part of
the voter, we immediately realise that it is very weak.[25] An individual who
purchases something or other for his own use almost immediately has
brought to his attention any defects of that commodity. If he purchases
something for someone else (i.e. engages in a charitable act) however, the
defects of his purchase will be felt by that other person.

If we turn to envy his motives for being well-informed are no greater.
Here he is attempting to injure someone and the act which he undertakes in
order to injure them is in general in and of itself a source of satisfaction. The
actual injury, unless it occurs directly in his sight, is not something from
which he gets much satisfaction because he doesn't have much information
about it.

Here again he will be irritated if he finds out that he has not been successful. Indeed, the general attention of the media to loopholes and tax evasion seems to indicate that the general irritation which he feels if the object of his envy escape his malice is stronger than his irritation if charitable funds are in his view wasted. Nevertheless, once again he does not have very strong motives for becoming informed of the actual results and it is hard to do.

With respect to the insurance motive which, as I have pointed out above, does not seem to be very much in the forefront of the minds of most people engaged in this activity, the individual would have strong motives for being well-informed if there were a private market in income insurance and he were considering whether or not to purchase it. Once it becomes a public matter, however, the usual public good argument against becoming well-informed applies. Of course, the public good argument against being well-informed applies also to people who are interested in income redistribution for the motives I have listed above. In these cases, however, there is an additional argument for being badly informed. The individual who is considering whether there should be an increase in the appropriation for the local police force would not be well-informed because of the public good argument. If he is considering an increase in the appropriations for the charitable contributions the public good argument is reinforced by the fact that he himself is not going to benefit directly or be injured by the results of the appropriation.

My theme has been that the arguments for income redistribution are chaotic. It is widely believed that income redistribution is desirable and I have said nothing here which indicates that that belief is false, but the discussions of the subject tend to involve a great deal of muddle and inconsistency. Further, we do not observe people behaving in a way which would be implied by the arguments in so far as their arguments are clear enough to imply anything. This does not, of course, indicate that income redistribution is undesirable, merely that the intellectual discussion of it is very poor. It seems to me that proponents of income redistribution should make an effort to clean up their act.

NOTES

1. Although the living standard is undeniably low it did not impress me that their life is all that unpleasant. The native reserves are usually fairly pretty, the climate is pleasant and the work requirements of the rather primitive form of subsistence agriculture are low. Thus, the citizens of the reserves are better off than inhabitants of a Chinese or Indian agricultural village. This does not, of course, mean that they are well off.

2. Legally they are not.
3. West Germany, interestingly enough, treats those guest-workers who actually get into Germany much the same as its own citizens, but it is, I believe, unique in this respect.
4. The United States faced some of the same problems with the first colony it gave independence, the Philippines. But, of course, the population of the Philippines was small enough so that although representatives and senators could have played a significant role in our Congress, they would not have dominated it the way the empires I have discussed above would have been dominated by the former subject people if they had extended the vote to them.
5. Rawls, John, *A Theory of Justice* (Cambridge, Mass.: Harvard University Press, 1971).
6. Beitz, Charles R., *Political Theory and International Relations* (Princeton, N.J.: Princeton University Press, 1979).
7. There are people who argue that this does not actually benefit the labourers.
8. See, Arthur Oken, *Equality and Efficiency, The Big Tradeoff* (Washington, D.C.: The Brookings Institution, 1975).
9. There is a partial and possible offset to this having to do with the extremely poor people, such as those living in South India, Communist China, etc., who may actually not have enough income to maintain reasonably good health. They might work harder if their income was raised. The problem does not arise with respect to American citizens, however. There are Americans who are poor because their health does not permit them to work very hard, but in most cases they are not suffering from a disease, such as malnutrition, which can be easily cured with a small increase in income.
10. Over the age of 72, social service payments are paid regardless of your income.
11. I am not insulting him, he was very proud of being a communist.
12. There is a small sub-section of people who are able to explain current income redistribution, but they are in general people who are not particularly interested in redistribution at all. They quite directly introduce distinctions among different groups of human beings, with the result that those who are closer to you are treated better than those who are farther away. I believe this is a correct statement of human motives as I shall explain below, but is not an argument that is used by proponents of income equalisation.
13. Peter Townsend, *Poverty in the United Kingdom: A Survey of Household Resources and Standards of Living* (Berkeley and Los Angeles: University of California Press, 1979), p. 31.
14. Of course, in many cases this does not mean true equality, but that the inequality should be reduced. This leads to the same conclusion.
15. With true stability of everything, the receipt would be the same as the amount paid out, i.e. there would be no interest payment. If we assumed the economy continues to grow this period, however, there would be an implicit interest payment equivalent to the rate of growth of society.
16. There is a much more detailed discussion of this point in my *Economics of Income Redistribution* (Boston, Mass.: Martinus Nijhoff, 1981).
17. Once again with the exception of those injured by the transfer from upper-income to lower-income groups.
18. See my *Economics of Income Redistribution*, for a more thorough discussion.
19. In many cases their asset situation has been adjusted to take advantage of the social security, but they would have no difficulty in providing for their retirement if that had been necessary. There are, of course, many individual

cases, for whom this is not true, and for whom charitable provision might well be made if the social security system did not exist.

20. Stanley Liebergott, *Wealth and Want* (Princeton, N.J.: Princeton University Press, 1975), pp. 53–69.
21. I first read this in Friedman's *Capitalism and Freedom*, but I here use an apparatus for explaining it which is somewhat different from his.
22. Townsend, op. cit., p. 893.
23. As far as I know, I am the inventor of this particular rationalisation which, to my knowledge, first appeared in *The Calculus of Consent*, pp. 192–7.
24. Or unless the United States is conquered and hence the citizenship vanishes.
25. For an elaboration of this argument see 'Information Without Profit' Chapter 4 below.

2 Objectives of Income Redistribution*

The purpose of this chapter, oddly enough, is not so much to inform its readers as to solicit their assistance for the author on what our goals should be when we talk about income distribution in society and, in particular, the distribution of burdens and benefits of government activity. I am not able in this case simply to examine my own ideas in this area, because it would appear that my ideas are rather eccentric. I am not particularly in favour of income redistribution. I feel that some aid should be given to the poor, but clearly my position is not that of the average intellectual.

I am, however, a positive economist and am willing to advise other people on how to achieve their goals. In particular, since a great many people talk about various redistribution objectives, and since the demand-revealing process[1] permits much more precise adjustment of governmental behaviour to desires of the citizenry, it should be possible to achieve whatever goals are desired in the area of income distribution much more precisely with the demand-revealing process than with other methods.

The problem I have encountered, and for which I wish to request your assistance, is that there does not seem to be anything in the literature which indicates what redistribution we should desire, granted this greater precision made possible by the demand-revealing process.

The demand-revealing process makes it possible to make use of a close approximation of Lindahl taxes for public goods. Note that I say a 'close approximation'. There is some doubt as to how close an approximation we would be able to achieve, but it seems to me that it is only sensible to assume that the approximation will be very close indeed. If we assume that it is close and then develop a set of criteria we would use on that assumption, and it later turns out to be somewhat more difficult than we expected, we can easily correct our reasoning for this inaccuracy. If, on the other hand, we assume that the approximation is very rough, and therefore only a very crude set of criteria is necessary, if we later discover that the approximation is very good, we will have to go through the whole process again. I would therefore like to ask that you bear with me and assume that the Lindahl taxes will be very closely approximated—indeed, for ease of explanation, we might assume that they will be reached perfectly.

Note that, although we seldom mention this, the Lindahl taxes can be negative. In Figure 2.1 we show a two-person, A and B, society, in which

---

*First published in *Sociological Economics*, ed. Louis Levy-Garboua (London and Beverly Hills: Sage, 1979), pp. 161–81.

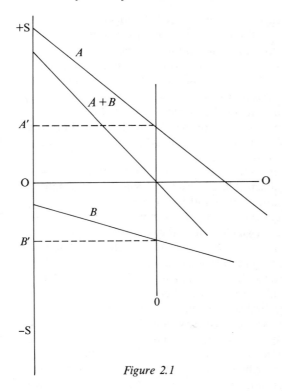

Figure 2.1

there is some public good to be purchased which will benefit A and injure B. The demand curve for B, then, is negative, as shown in Figure 2.1. We sum the two demand curves to A + B and note the point where it crosses the 0 line. This gives us the optimum shown by 0. We then charge A a tax of A' and B a negative tax of B'.

This procedure, although geometrically different, is a mapping of the usual method of computing the optimal amount of pollution. Furthermore, it gives A and B roughly the same consumer surplus on this social improvement. It is, of course, simply the application of the Lindahl tax scheme, except that one of the taxes is negative.

Distribution of costs and benefits of this sort is not what most people mean when they talk about redistribution of income. In a moment I shall turn to the more normal meaning of redistribution, but I should like to raise questions here as to the appropriate distribution of benefits and costs of government action. In a way, I am going to follow the traditional economic distinction between discussion of an efficient change and of deliberate income redistribution; but, in my case, later I am actually going to talk about deliberate income redistribution. I simply want to clear the decks by talking about certain problems of efficient change first.

Note, then, that although public finance specialists (including myself) have always been deeply enamoured with Lindahl taxes, this has been essentially because they are theoretically so nice. Everybody is paying his true marginal evaluation of some particular public good because the different evaluations of the public good by different people lead to their paying different prices for the same quantity. Furthermore, we can, in the demand-revealing process, obtain that quantity of public goods which is optimal, so everything seems fine.

When one begins thinking about it, however, it is not so obvious that the Lindahl tax is a sensible tax. Suppose that we have some public good for which A's demand is high and B's demand is low, as in Figure 2.2. We sum the two demand curves, using the demand-revealing process for the project, find the optimum (which turns out to be 10 units), and charge B $10 (or $1 a unit) which is the value of the marginal tenth unit to him, and we charge A (the high demander) $100 (or $10 a unit) which is the value of the marginal unit to him. For $11 a unit, we can produce the 10 units. B is paying $10 total and A is paying $100, and there is no obvious reason for us to believe that A has a higher consumption surplus than B. Indeed, the first approximation would be to say that they are probably about the same.

This certainly has little or no resemblance to what happens in the private market. Nor is it obvious to me that distributionally this is a good idea, whatever else may be said about it. Thus, my first problem with respect to income distribution under the demand-revealing process is to ask if it is indeed a good idea to use Lindahl prices, granted we can do so. Before trying to answer this question, remember that just at the moment I am only talking about changes in government process and *not* about the kind of redistribution we think of as assistance to the poor. I will turn to that in a moment. We should assume, then, that the income distribution before we contemplate purchasing this public good from A and B was one which had been socially accepted, although up to now I have not explained how we will obtain such an income distribution.

We also have the question of what we would do if we decide against the Lindahl price. But there is an even more difficult problem. In many cases of government action, there is a net social benefit of a unitary nature, i.e. we cannot carry the production of the public good out to the point where the marginal price—summing all individual demand, positive *and* negative—is equal to the cost. For example, suppose it were decided to abolish the Common Agricultural Community. Clearly, the benefit from this action would be much greater than the loss, and it is hard to think of any way to regard this as generation of a continuous type of public good.

This raises very real problems for income distribution. As an example,

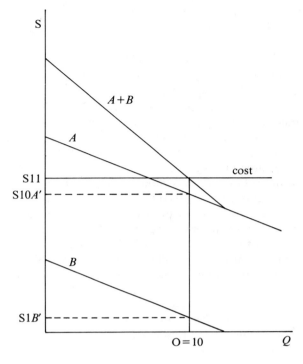

Figure 2.2

suppose that A has an Interstate Commerce Commission-granted monopoly on trucking between two cities in the United States. His income from this government-granted monopoly is $10,000 higher than what we would achieve in a competitive trucking market. B and C, on the other hand, are users of this truck line, and the cost to them of the monopoly is $9,000 and $6,000, respectively. This would, I take it, be roughly the typical situation, although normally there are many more parties involved. If we obtain the actual values the parties would place on the abolition of a monopoly, which is –$10,000 for A and a sum of +$15,000 for B and C, we note that it is clearly a socially desirable act because there is a larger profit than there is cost.

But having decided that it is socially desirable, which is all that traditional economics has done, we now have the problem of determining who should get the $5000 social profit. Indeed, we could ask who is to get the full $15,000, since it is not inevitable that we will compensate the loser. Nevertheless, most economists have argued in such cases that the loser should be compensated and I am going to adopt this assumption. Note that the problems I raise later would not be changed particularly if we decided not to compensate A, but the amount of money to be distributed would be increased.

What, then, do we do with the $5000? The traditional economic explanation is that we would let it remain in the pockets of B and C, with B getting $4000 and C getting $1000, and simply compensate A for his losses. But surely there is no strong argument for this. Why not divide it into three equal parts and give one-third to each of them? Or, if we think that A is a nasty man and should not be compensated, why not arrange that B and C will each get $2500? Note that all of this is perfectly possible with the demand-revealing process.

Even these proposals are fairly modest. Why should any one of these three people have control over this fund? Why not contribute it to the well-being of the untouchables in India? Or why not pay it into a fund which is designed, when many further similar contributions are made, to be divided among all citizens of the world on a so much per head basis? Or we could even concentrate it on the poor—that is, this money will be paid (once again, together with similar funds from the elimination of other uneconomic institutions) to, let us say, the 5 million poorest people in the world.

I can find no signficant discussion of this problem. What is the objective which would be recommended by a person who believes in a great deal of equality or, for that matter, an economist who does not have any particularly strong feelings about equality but who just wants a 'good' outcome. If you happen to be a property right devotee, for example, *who* has the property right in this fund?

There is, by the way, another candidate for the money—a candidate whom I would regard as exceptionally deserving, although administratively hard to locate. Presumably the abolition of the United States Interstate Commerce Commission would be the result of entrepreneurial activity by some group or individual. Giving them the bulk of the social profit, or at least enough social profit to motivate this kind of work, would seem to be highly desirable. This would mean that the present situation in which, in general, it is easy to organise a minority to push for some act which is contrary to the public interest, and very difficult to organise one which benefits the public interest, would be reversed. Granted we are going to compensate the losers, there would be no significant interest group organised to avoid this change in the law; and if we used the profit to compensate the political agency that brought about the change, then we would motivate political entrepreneurs to go into this business and we might end up with a massively more efficient government.

The problem here is essentially administrative. Even with the demand-revealing process, very few people are motivated to become well-informed.

Thus, the reward might well go to the wrong people, and therefore it would not serve its motivating function. Still, I would think some experimentation along these lines would be desirable. Note that if we decide to give half of the social profit to whoever pulls off the political *coup* that makes the social profit possible, we would still have the other half for other distribution, and the questions I have raised above would still be important ones.

Having whetted your interest (I hope) with these subsidiary, but nevertheless intellectually challenging problems, I would now like to turn to what I regard as the major problem in redistribution which is conscious, deliberate redistribution of income for the benefit of the recipients.

I should like to begin by pointing out that there is one great advantage of the demand-revealing process: it does not permit transfers which are motivated *only* by the desire of the recipients to receive money. If we look at modern democratic states (and, also, for that matter, at dictatorships), we observe an immense amount of transfer from party to party which is motivated entirely by the desire of the recipients, with the people who involuntarily make the contribution not having any interest in the matter at all or being opposed. The Common Market agricultural policy is an example; almost all protective tariffs are further examples.

All of these transfers, so far as I know, can be justified only on the grounds that the political process does indeed grind them out because the recipients want them, and under democracy it is hard to organise any opposition to them. It is a case of an intense minority getting transfers from a dispersed and not deeply interested majority. All of these things would vanish if we used the demand-revealing process, because the mild opposition to these various programmes of the average man would, when added up, be greater than the intense desire for them by the minority. This seems to me an immense step forward.

Still, so far as I know, there is absolutely no rational explanation for any of these transfers, except that the recipients want them and the political process happens to be such that they can get them. The change in the political process that eliminated them would, I think, be widely supported. Even some professors of economics would be willing to back a programme which would surely greatly reduce the demand for professors of economics.

We are thus left with transfers to people who, for one reason or another, attract the favourable attention of the donors. Mainly, these are the poor and the ill. There are other groups, of course, but I trust you will not object if I confine myself to these particular groups. It would be one of the advantages of the demand-revealing process, then, that transfers would be concentrated in a group of people who are, at least by some, thought to merit the transfer. Farmers, so far as I know, are not thought to merit transfers by anyone except the farmers themselves nor are the beneficiaries of various protective tariffs thought to merit the money by anyone but themselves. However, that is not true with respect to people who are sick and/or poor.

Here again I have frankly to confess that I am not very much of an egalitarian, and therefore I would probably choose a fairly low level of transfers. It is not obvious that I would choose as low a level of transfers to the poor as we actually observe in most democratic states—where the transfer tends to be of the order of 2 to 3 per cent of GNP—but, in any event, I would not be in favour of a very high transfer rate. My objective, however, is not to present my own preferences but to use this chapter in an effort to solicit the views of people who do believe in considerable transfers, so that, having found out what they have in mind, I can design a political process based on the demand-revealing process, which will tend to generate that outcome.

There is, however, one problem with which I should begin. Suppose that Professor Bleeding Heart tells me that he knows perfectly well what income transfers should be. We should find the world average income and tax everyone who has an income above that amount by 90 per cent of the excess, and then use the funds derived to give to all people who have less than the average income 90 per cent of the difference between their income and the average income. I have not looked at the numbers recently, but I suppose that the average yearly income in the world is something like $500 per family.

There is nothing easier than designing a governmental structure which does this. We simply put the requirement that this be done into the constitution. To say it is easy to design is not to say that it is easy to implement. I doubt very much if such a constitution would be acceptable in any country which has an average income much above the world average, and I also doubt that we could get world acceptance simply because the wealthier countries, such as the US and France, would object very strongly to this large transfer to poverty-stricken countries such as China and India. Thus, although it is easy to design such a procedure, it is very unlikely that we would get beyond the design stage.

Furthermore, I am sure we would find that although Professor Bleeding Heart regards this as a good system, many other people would have different ideas. What we need, then, is a constitution or a method of making decisions on income transfers which has acceptable elements in itself and which succeeds in aggregating in one way or another the preferences for redistribution of many different people. Selecting one dictator for this subject is an easy course. Furthermore, selecting a single first preference is particularly attractive if we are going to use ours. In other words, we could all stand around and each one of us offer his own personal preference for redistribution.

The fact remains, however, that we are not dictators, not even collective dictators, and there is no obvious reason why our decision as to how much redistribution we think should be carried out is the socially binding one. And, in practice, it would not be. We can only hope to get some particular method of redistribution adopted if there is some procedure of aggregating the preferences or at least a large enough or powerful enough group so that there is some possibility that the procedure will be implemented. Since I take it none of us prefers the dictatorial route, that means that we must aim at a policy which a great many people will adopt.

But note here a particular problem with what we might call Rawlsianism. Since *The Calculus of Consent* (Buchanan and Tullock, 1962) also talks about things 'behind the veil of ignorance', I might be regarded as a premature Rawlsian.[2] There is a difference, however. We talk about establishing a constitution in *The Calculus of Consent* to deal with future problems—these problems, of necessity, not being fully known at the moment. As it happens, we argue that there is a particular set of constitutional arrangements which is more efficient than others, and hence the present discounted value of this constitution from the standpoint of a person who is uncertain of the future would be positive. Furthermore, there is a set of side-payments which could be used, granted that we were going to use the optimally efficient constitution, to compensate people who, being able to make calculations about the future, realise that they will not do as well as other people. Thus, in our case we are simply using a sort of variant of Pareto optimality, which we call Pareto optimality in large.

The Rawls proposal, however, does not claim that there is any particularly efficient level of income redistribution; and, indeed, I believe from my personal knowledge of Rawls that he would probably argue that a zero income redistribution would generate the largest total income; hence, in a way—a very special way—it might be regarded as the most efficient. Thus, he is not attempting to solve a problem with a solution which in fact could be to the benefit of almost everyone, but he is suggesting that people act as if they did not know in order to improve their morals. I doubt very much that any practical government is ever going to do this. In a way, Rawls has made a contribution to the way we should think and talk in the event that we decide that we will devote some time to the discussion of what is the optimal income redistribution in some ethical sense. He has not produced a method which we could expect to have any great effect on income distribution in the real world.

From the standpoint of the egalitarians this is fortunate, because the Rawls' method surely would lead to less income redistribution than we now have. The point of the veil of ignorance is to make it impossible for people to make their decisions in full knowledge of their real-world circumstances. We do not have the veil of ignorance, and decisions are therefore made with this forbidden knowledge. Since the median income is below the average income, this would mean that we would anticipate in a democracy that there would be more money transferred than would be transferred behind the veil of ignorance (Wagner, 1974).

We need, then, a method of aggregating people's preferences: one method in general use today is the market, another is democracy. For redistribution of income, there is indeed a market solution—voluntary charity—and, in those cases in which there are not large government transfers, it tends to be quite extensive. However, I am going to ignore the market as an income transfer mechanism and concentrate on government or coerced income transfer.

Traditionalists like Anthony Downs sometimes argue that the amount of income transfer generated by simple majority voting is the optimal amount. Downs, of course, then supplements this argument by arguing that a democracy is desirable because it transfers the optimal amount. The circular nature of this line of reasoning is clear. So far as I know there is absolutely no reason to believe that majority voting or any of the variants of democratic government transfer an 'optimal' amount. Indeed, I would argue that they do very badly, since the bulk of the transfers they generate are transferred back and forth within the middle class; and, so far as I know, there are no arguments that would indicate that these transfers are desirable.

However, there is in democracy a very important problem which is normally ignored, i.e. the weighting of the individual votes. Characteristically, in democracies people's votes are weighted either 1 or 0. I can think of no argument for this except tradition, together with the fact that it might be politically extremely difficult to get any kind of agreement on a particular modification. In a way, this particular voting scheme is a Schelling point.

So far as I know, however, no justification has ever been offered for it other than that. There are occasional justifications for weighting all votes at 1, but the fact that we do weight some votes at 0 and some at 1 is, so far as I know, completely unjustified. Perhaps the reader knows of some discussion of this point. Speaking personally, I would rather prefer that if we are going to weight people at different weights, we have more than two weightings. For example, a person who believed in very large transfers of income might argue that individual votes should be weighted inversely with income $(1/N)$,[3] so that the poor have much higher voting power than the wealthy, and they can use this to extract additional transfers from the wealthy. Another method which is used in most corporations weights people's votes in terms of their economic interest in the matter at hand, with the result that large stockholders have many more votes than small stockholders. If we look around, we can find many other cases of differential weighting of votes which have used continuous variation, but the dominant one in the present-day world of politics is the 0,1 weighting.

With the demand-revealing process, different people's votes are weighted differently, depending on their demand for various government services, including transfers. The 0,1 dichotomy, however, is very easy either to implement in the demand-revealing process or to leave out.

Let us suppose, then, that we are in France where the poorest part of the population are Algerian immigrants. Suppose that the French citizens are interested in benefiting the Algerians who are, after all, very poor and live badly. Let us discuss how this should be done. For simplicity in diagrammatic exposition, I am going to assume that there are only two Frenchmen and one Algerian, but the demand-revealing process usually works much better with large numbers than it does with small numbers, so I trust the reader will accept this as merely a convention.

Consider Figure 2.3 which shows the demand for charitable transfer to the Algerian by two Frenchmen, A and B. The transfer itself is assumed to be done in franc units, and we will assumed that the Algerian's demand for the transfer is simply 1 franc per unit, i.e. the horizontal cost line is his demand curve.[4] In a world of private charity, the situation is fairly simple: B would probably make a contribution to the Algerian, equivalent to the

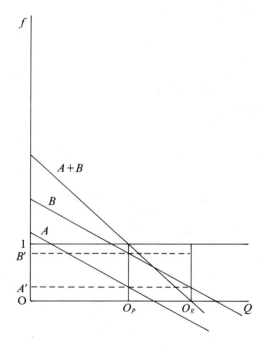

Figure 2.3

point where his demand curve crosses the cost curve; and A, observing that the Algerian has received a transfer larger than he wanted to pay, would pay nothing.

There is, clearly, a Pareto-optimal move from this. We sum the two demand curves to get the line A + B, which is the social optimum. We then charge B a per unit transfer, marked B′, and charge A a per unit transfer, marked A′. If we have presented their demands correctly, the Frenchmen will be better off, and the Algerian, who is now receiving more money, will be better off.[5] This amounts to using Lindahl taxes to pay for the transfer.

The demand-revealing process can very easily achieve this particular result—a result which I believe cannot be achieved by any other method. Note that, of course, there is the problem of approximating the Lindahl taxes, and it might turn out that we are rather bad at doing this with respect to transfers; but, once again, for the purposes of this paper let me assume that we can do it very well. If it turns out that later experimentation indicates that we cannot, our results can be appropriately modified.

It is interesting that in this particular case, we have now generated the result that Milton Friedman uses to justify government coercion in the field of income transfer. He points out that income transfer does have neighbourhood effects, which show up in our diagram by the fact that the line A + B lies above B at the point where it crosses the cost line. Thus, the demand-revealing process in this case achieves a goal which has the interesting characteristic that I cannot think of anyone really being opposed to it. One can argue that there should be more transfer than this, and I shall turn to such arguments in a moment, but surely it is hard to argue against this particular use of coercion which benefits everyone and injures no one.

This is the demand-revealing process equivalent to the way the French democracy currently treats the Algerians, i.e. the Algerians are not permitted to vote on various transfers given to them. It should be noted that the French are not unique in this. The guest-workers, who are the poorest part of the population all over Europe, face the same situation. The United States, as it happens, does not have any guest-workers, but it has illegal immigrants. The exact number is not known, of course, but it is thought to run into millions. They are treated this way, although, interestingly enough, they are frequently able to obtain full services of various government bureaux which deal with income transfers, because the bureaux do not realise that they are illegal immigrants.

The problem is more significant in the world as a whole when it is realised that the nation-state itself is simply an artificial creation. There is, as far as I can see, no justification whatsoever, other than tradition,[6] why the citizens of India are not permitted to vote on transfers of funds from the United

States and/or France to India. I am sure most 'egalitarians' would be horrified at any such proposal, but I have never read any egalitarian explanation as to why we should *not* do so that, quite frankly, does not abandon all egalitarianism. Limited egalitarianism within the group traditionally permitted to vote is what is normally aimed at, together with some modest income transfers to the really poor people who are not permitted to vote. For the modest transfer to the relatively poor people who are not permitted to vote, the demand-revealing process would obviously work very well.

It is notable that the present situation in which recipients of transfers within the society are permitted to vote is not universal and has not been historically universal. Until quite recently people who were on relief or receiving other kinds of public charity were automatically deprived of their vote. Furthermore, in many states government employees were deprived of the vote for the same basic reason.

I am not arguing for deprivation of the right to vote, but I am asking the people who favour income redistribution to explain to me who they think should be permitted to make decisions on income transfers, and I would also prefer that they tell me why. Perhaps they feel that the 'Wogs', 'Wops' and 'Chinks' and other lesser breeds without the law should not be permitted to interfere in the decision processes as to how much will be transferred to them.

In democracy the actual situation we have is that some of the beneficiaries of charity are permitted to vote and some are not, and there is no reason why the demand-revealing process could not be adjusted to permit exactly the same people to vote or to permit all people to vote. Therefore, let us assume that France changes its constitution and permits Algerians to vote in French elections, and thereby to influence the transfers to them.

Turning once again to Figure 2.3, you will note that there is a portion of the diagram which is normally omitted, i.e. the part below the 0 line. Furthermore, the A + B line crosses the B line instead of stopping at B in the traditional way. The explanation for this is simply that the demand, after a while, becomes negative. A regards transfers to the Algerian—even if they come from his own pocket—as worth more than their cost, left of the point where the A demand curve crosses the 1 unit cost line. He regards them as worth something, albeit less than a unit, to the point where his demand curve crosses the 0 line. For example, at O_p he regards the transfer of 1 franc to the Algerian as worth, let us say, 10 centimes.

Eventually, however, he gets to the point where he is positively annoyed by the transfer, and therefore he would be willing to pay something to bring the transfer to a halt. For example, suppose a government programme were inaugurated to take $100 from each reader and use it to make a gift to

Ghadaffi on his next birthday. I suspect that most of the people, if given
their choice, would prefer to put up a sum of $100.01 to avoid making this
particular transfer which would be positively annoying to them. I may be
wrong in this judgement. Perhaps people are nicer than I think they are, but
I do think that there are many people who have positively negative feelings
about some recipients of money drawn from their pockets. It is on the basis
of this feeling that I have drawn Figure 2.3.

Thus, our donors at some point become positively annoyed by the
transfer. If we are going to count the Algerian's preferences, however, his
preference will, to at least some extent, counterbalance this annoyance.
Using the demand-revealing process but including the Algerian's
preferences, the amount transferred will be the amount O_g. Note that this is
a case where the donors as a class cease to get any gain at all from the
transfer, i.e. the annoyance of those who are annoyed by that size of
transfer just exactly counterbalances the gain of B who is in favour, still, of
transfers (although he regards them as worth less than their cost). He has
squeezed out the entire social satisfaction from the transfer because, from
this point on, although the Algerian will continue to gain 1 franc for every
franc paid to him, the cost of A and B is greater than 1 franc.

The allocation of the tax cost between A and B can be carried out in such
a way that they do not pay true Lindahl taxes but in such a way that the cost
to them is equal, i.e. each one will be paying about 50 centimes more than
his personal demand for the transfer, which in this case would mean that
A was paying about 25 centimes and B about 75 centimes. This amounts to
each one paying 50 centimes more than the gain he receives, which in A's
case is negative, which sums to 1 franc, exactly the gain which is being made
by the Algerian.

So far I have simply talked technically about the way of applying the
demand-revealing process to either of the two possible vote-weighting
systems now in use in democracy. The choice between them would, of
necessity, mean that we would have to make up our minds on this issue and,
as far as I can see, most intellectuals simply have not given the matter any
thought. There are various possible reasons for this but, rather than
looking into these issues, I would prefer simply to urge that some thought
be given.

I have read this paper in three Canadian and one American university.
In each case I asked the audience to vote on whether they think that
recipients of transfers should be permitted to vote on the size of the
transfers or whether they think they should not. The question is usually
hard to put over, because most Canadians, let us say, think it perfectly
obvious that all Canadians—whether they are recipients or not—should
vote on income transfers, and that it is perfectly obvious that all non-
Canadian citizens—whether recipients of transfer or even contributors to

the Canadian tax base—should not. This is the traditional *legal* situation; but, so far, in the various discussions on this matter I have never encountered a single argument for it except that this is the way it has been done for some time.

Having got through this barrier, I find that the people voting on the issue do split roughly equally. About one-third are in favour of permitting the recipients to vote on transfers, about one-third are opposed, and about one-third don't know. I take it that this is a reasonable indication that they had not given any great thought to the matter before the question was raised. I also take it that this would be true of the present readership also. However, I believe it is an important question and suggest that it be given thought.

Indeed, it seems to me all three of the questions I have raised in this chapter are important and that all three are cases where people interested in income redistribution *should* have an answer but apparently do not. The Chinese sage, Mencius, argued that before a person takes action, he should first clarify his thoughts. I would suggest that before proposing any income redistribution, its proponents first clarify their thoughts on these issues. Once they have done this, I think the demand-revealing process will reveal its superiority over ordinary voting in achieving whatever goal they have chosen. But in order to use the demand-revealing process, they first have to make up their minds on what will be the basic parameters of the redistribution they favour.

NOTES

1. See, Tideman, T.N. and G. Tullock, 'A New and Superior Process for Making Social Choices', *Journal of Political Economy*, 84 (December 1976), for an explanation of this process.
2. Note, however, that although we wrote before the present surge of Rawlsianism, we were, at the time we wrote the book, familiar with Rawls' ideas from his previous work.
3. David Chapman has in fact so argued in an unpublished paper.
4. This is not a necessary assumption but, without it, things become quite complicated graphically.
5. Note that it is not really certain that A would be better off. If B is already making a gift to the Algerian out to the point where his demand curve crosses the one franc line, then A clearly can gain (as can B) from an agreement under which further payment out to the line O_p is made, with A paying the amount A' and B paying amount B' on the increment. It is possible, however, that movement to the line O_p, if it is accompanied by payment by A of A' for the entire range of payments, would be inferior from A's standpoint to leaving the situation as it was.

6. I realise, of course, that tradition in this case has been built into constitutions and laws.

REFERENCES

J.M. Buchanan and G. Tullock *The Calculus of Consent* (Ann Arbor: University of Michigan Press, 1962).

Mencius. *The Great Learning*.

Public Choice 29–2 (special supplement to Spring 1977).

T.N. Tideman and G. Tullock (1976) 'A New and Superior Process for Making Social Choices', *Journal of Political Economy*, 84 (December).

G. Tullock 'The Charity of the Uncharitable', *Western Economic Journal* 9 (December 1971).

——, 'Revealing the Demand for Transfers', R. Auster and B. Sears (eds), *American Re-evolution: Papers and Proceedings* (Tucson: Department of Economics, University of Arizona, 1977).

R.E. Wagner 'Politics, Bureaucracy, and Budgetary Choice', *Journal of Money, Credit, and Banking,* 8 (August 1974).

3 The Charity of the Uncharitable*

If I understand the common view among modern intellectuals, income redistribution is considered to be a rather simple and almost entirely ethical matter. There are, basically, two theories. The first is that those of us who are well off use the state as a mechanism for making gifts to the poor. This is well represented by James Rodgers and Harold Hochman in their article, 'Pareto Optimal Redistribution'.[1] The second view, which I shall call the 'Downsian', is that in a democracy the poor are able to use their votes to obtain transfers from the rest of society (Downs [2] esp. pp. 198–201). These two views are sometimes combined into the view that the bulk of the population takes money from the rich and gives it to the poor by use of the democratic process.

Although I have presented these two points of view very briefly, I think nevertheless that they sum up the standard justification for redistribution. Unfortunately, these essentially ethical approaches cannot explain the bulk of the redistribution in our society. It is true that they *do* explain a small amount of it, but most of it comes from other motives and achieves other ends. Since these two ideas are probably fairly firmly engrained in the mind of the reader, I should like before I begin formal analysis briefly to discuss the facts of redistribution.

First, the poor vote, and the amount of redistribution that they receive, in part, is a function of the extent to which they vote [5].[2] Thus, to at least some extent, the money received by the poor must represent the use by the poor of their political power, rather than a charitable gift from the rest of society. This would seem to indicate that the first of the explanations given above cannot, at the very least, be the entire explanation.

Secondly, anybody examining the status of the poor in the modern world must realise that democracies do not make very large gifts to them. Webb and Sieve in comparing incomes in England in 1937 with 1959 come to the conclusion '*the estimate of inequality of final incomes remains constant over the period of twenty years which saw the establishment and growth to some stability of the "welfare state"*' [12, p. 109][3]. Granted the massive amounts of income that are transferred back and forth through the population by the British government, it is evident that the major effect and probably the

---

*First published in *Western Economic Journal*, 9 (December 1971), pp. 379–392; and reprinted in *The Economics of Charity*. (London: Institute of Economic Affairs, 1973), pp. 15–32; and *Against Equality. Readings on Economic and Social Policy* (London: Macmillan, 1983), pp. 328–44.

major purpose of this transfer cannot be to help the poor. With well in
excess of 30 per cent of the average individual's received income being
taxed away in one way or another and the defence burden much lower as a
part of GNP than it was in 1937, it is clear there are massive resources
available for aiding the poor if that was indeed the objective of the British
government.

Leaving aside for the moment any further discussion of the empirical
facts about redistribution, let us turn to what has been done in a way of
more formal theory of redistribution in a democracy. The first of these in
point of time is the argument of Anthony Downs that democracy will
always lead to transfer of income from the wealthy to the poor. Indeed, he
regards this as a major justification of democracy. We may contrast this
with Benjamin Ward's view that redistribution in democracy would be
essentially indeterminate.[5] Finally, there is the view expressed in *The
Calculus of Consent* (Buchanan and Tullock [1], pp. 144–5) that the nature
of the voting process in democracy is such that real resources will be
transferred away from the rich, although it is not specified who will receive
them. It will surprise no one that I espouse the Buchanan and Tullock view,
but the Ward model will be used to supplement it by indicating that the
actual output of the political process is not predetermined.[6]

The essence of the difference between the Downs model and the Ward
model is simply that Downs implicitly assumes that redistribution must take
place along a one-dimensional continuum in which people are arranged
from the poorest to the wealthiest. At first glance, there would seem to be
no obvious reason why the bottom 51 per cent of the population, using
their majority to take money from the wealthy, would be more likely than
the top 51 per cent using their majority to take money from the poor.
Indeed, the 2 per cent of the population lying at the middle line would be
the determining factor in such a choice, and hence we might anticipate that
money would come from both ends to the middle.

In practice, of course, the wealthy have more money, and hence can be
subject to heavier taxes. Thus the cost of admitting a wealthy person into a
coalition, which proposes to transfer money away from the 49 per cent of
the population not members, is higher than the cost of permitting the entry
of a poor person. Following William Riker, one would therefore anticipate
that voting coalitions would be made up in such a way as to minimise the
number of wealthy members. This is, indeed, the element of truth in the
Downs model, is part of the Buchanan–Tullock model, and must be
admitted as a modification of the Ward model.

If the dominant coalition is likely to be made up of the bottom 51 per cent
of the population, this tells us nothing very much about how that coalition
will divide the spoils. Further, it is obvious that this coalition must contain
a good many persons who are not poor by any ordinary definition. If we

accept the bottom 10 per cent of the population as poor, then they make up only 20 per cent of this coalition of the bottom 51 per cent. If we are more generous and count 20 per cent of the population as poor, then they make up 40 per cent. Clearly, this minority cannot dominate the coalition. If they received more per head than the other members of the coalition, they would do so because the lower middle class was generous.

Turning to formal bargaining theory, it is obvious that any transfer mechanism must provide at least as much for the top portion of this bottom 51 per cent coalition as for anyone else in the coalition because if it does not, the 49 per cent who are not members can very readily purchase the top 2 per cent for a coalition that transfers a small amount from the top income groups to this small 2 per cent group and to no one else. Indeed, such a coalition might take the entire transfer out of the bottom part of the population instead of out of the top. The reasoning so far would indicate that the people towards the top of the bottom 51 per cent might receive much more than the people at the lower end. The only restriction on a delivery of the bulk of the resources transferred from the wealthy to the upper end of the bottom coalition (other than charitable instincts on the part of the members of the upper end) would seem to be the possibility that the wealthy would attempt a coalition with the very poor.

If we look at the real world, we do see some signs of such coalition attempts. Among those persons who argue that all transfers should be strictly limited to the very poor by way of a stringent means test, it is likely that wealthy persons predominate. This is, of course, sensible from even a selfish standpoint. They could arrange to give to the present-day poor considerably more money than the poor are now receiving, in return for a coalition in which transfers to people in the upper part of the bottom 51 per cent are terminated, and make a neat profit. This particular coalition has so far foundered largely because of miscalculations by the poor. The poor realise that the interests of the wealthy are clearly not congruent with their interests, but they do not realise that the interests of people between the 20th and the 51st percentile of the income distribution are also not identical with theirs. They therefore tend to favour a coalition with the second group rather than the former.

The situation is interesting, and we may pause briefly to examine it by way of a three-person model. Suppose we have wealthy Mr A, middle-class Mr B, and poor Mr C. B and C form a coalition for the purpose of extracting money from A, and let us begin by assuming that the money is to be equally divided between them. Suppose, further, that C's income is $1000 per year before transfer, B's is $2000 per year, and A's is $3000 per year. Clearly, if the amount of transfer were somehow externally fixed at $500 but A were permitted to decide how it was to be allocated, he would give all of it to C.[7] He would reason that not until C's income had risen to

$2000 per year was it sensible to supplement B's income. B receives his payment simply because he wants it, not because there is any charitable motive involved on the part of anyone.

Under the circumstances, it is clear that A would be willing to enter into a coalition with C under which a transfer of $300 was made from A to C and none was made to B. This would be to the advantage of C, and it seems likely that only the generally bad information and low IQ and/or motivation which we observe among the poor prevents such coalitions. Indeed, it is possible the poor would do better if they depended entirely on the charitable motives of the wealthy. It might be that A, if left entirely to himself, would be willing to give C more than $250, although he objects to spending $500 for $250 apiece to B and C. Most persons, after all, are to some extent charitable and it may well be that the very poor would do better than at present if they depended on the charity of the wealthy.

For example, an organisation of society in which all transfers were made by a special electorate composed of persons in the top 10 per cent of the income stream who tax themselves for the purpose of benefiting other persons might lead to larger transfers to the genuinely poor than they now receive. Certainly, if we fixed the total amount of transfer away from the upper income groups at its present level but gave them complete discretion as to how it was to be spent, they would spend far more of it on the very poor.

So far, however, we have unrealistically assumed that transfers must be made between different income groups along a unidimensional continuum. If we look at the real world, we observe that the bulk of the transfers are made to groups not defined by income. Farmers, college students, owners of oil wells, owners of private aircraft, older people regardless of their income, and in all probability, the intellectual class are the major recipients of transfers, even though the bulk of the members of these groups are by no means poor.[8]

If we accept the real-world situation as being one in which transfers are made to organised groups and these organised groups receive their transfers largely in terms of their political power (which seems to be a correct statement about the real world), there is no reason why we should anticipate that the poor would do particularly well. For one thing, they are hard to organise. Thus, the very large transfers that we do observe in the world are essentially demonstrations of the Ward proof, supplemented by the Buchanan–Tullock logrolling process, which only rather accidentally benefit the bottom 10 to 15 per cent of the population. For the reasons given above, we would anticipate that the top income groups would do rather badly from these transfers, and indeed they do. The Lampman study shows a transfer away from the upper income brackets of about 13 per cent of their income. The beneficiaries of these transfers, however, we would anticipate would not be particularly concentrated among the poor and, indeed granted their general political ineptness, one might expect that they would do rather badly, which is what we observe in the real world.

A somewhat cursory examination would seem to indicate that the actual percentage of income derived from wealthy people in democracies is an inverse function of the ease with which they can migrate. In no case, so far as I know, is the actual amount of progression in the taxes collected as high as the progression in the tax tables, but it is nevertheless real in the larger countries.

When we turn to expenditures, a quite different picture emerges. Any individual's vote is worth as much as any other individual's vote in getting expenditures. Indeed the wealthy, well-informed person who is capable of making sizeable campaign expenditures may well be able to receive a considerably larger portion of the total tax collections than is someone without these advantages [3]. If we subtract tax payments from receipts, we would anticipate some negative amount to turn up from a wealthy person and perhaps, although not certainly, a positive amount for the rest of the population. The reason the second sum is not necessarily positive is because of certain intrinsic inefficiencies in the transfer system. It is to be expected that expenditures that actually cost more than the net total benefit will be made [7]. Under the circumstances, it is possible that, although the rich are injured, the rest of the population make very small or negative profits.

Thus, to repeat, we would anticipate that in a democracy there would be some transfer of money away from the wealthy, but there is no obvious reason that this transfer would go to the poor. If we look at the real world, we do find this pattern. This pattern is, however, a relatively minor part of the redistribution of income as seen in the modern state. Economists frequently point out that confiscation of *all* the income of the wealthy in a typical modern state would pay only a tiny part of the routine expenditures of the existing government. On the other hand, there can be no doubt whatsoever that massive redistributions of income do occur by ways of the political process. These redistributions, however, are not in the main transfers of funds from the wealthy to the poor, but transfers of funds among the middle class. The bulk of these transfers come from people who lie between the 20th and the 19th percentile of income, and the bulk of them go to the same income classes. This is, of course, the area with the largest taxable capacity, and also the area where political power is concentrated in a democracy.

These transfers do not meet any egalitarian criteria. Basically they are transfers from groups of people who, for one reason or another, are not politically powerful to people who are. Always and everywhere in democracies, the farmers do very well. As a matter of practical fact, the

United States probably wastes fewer resources in supporting its farm programme than almost any other western country. This may surprise Americans, accustomed to our massively inefficient method of transferring money to some people who are, on the whole, about as well off as the people from whom the transfers come; but examination of what is done in the Common Market will convince them very quickly that Americans are fortunate in this respect.

The farm programme is not the only example; the social security administration transfers money from the young to the old, regardless of income. Indeed, in this particular case, the very poor are badly damaged by the institution. Due to the method in which the taxes to pay for social security are collected, the poor pay a very substantial part of their tiny wages to the social security administration. If, however, they are very poor (i.e. require public assistance when they are old) then the local authorities will subtract their social security payment from the amount they receive. The result from their standpoint is that they pay taxes, but receive no net benefit. This must lead to a significant transfer of resources away from the very poor.

The urban renewal project is another obvious, even scandalous, example of the type of redistribution we observe, and another major example is, of course, the subsidised public education system. The latter is particularly obvious as a redistribution to the well off at the university level. In general students who can get into a university, particularly those who can get scholarships, have enough natural talent so that they enter the university with a lifetime income well above average. At the expense of the taxpayer, they are then given an even higher lifetime expected income. But even if we turn to lower-level schools, a similar problem exists. To begin with, these are clearly transfers from those in society who do not have children to those who do—to say nothing, of course, of the transfer to the children themselves.

Secondly, however, it is fairly certain that the pay-off to education, even at the elementary level, is greatly varying, depending on both the inherited genes and the home environment. Thus, the return in real terms to education is vastly higher to the person who both has the natural talent and the background to have a good income all his life than to the person whose natural talent and background are such that he probably will be poor. We would, if we were interested in relatively egalitarian measures, make direct payments to these two parties which could then be invested in a manner that would be most suitable in each case. By compelling the transfer to be taken in a form that is of maximum benefit to people who are going to be well off anyway and of minimum benefit to people who are going to be poor, we make the average citizen richer and the poor poorer.

These examples are merely a small part of a wide universe. It is clear that in most democracies the poor receive relatively minor transfers, in any realistic sense, from society, although not zero transfers. Although very large amounts of money are redistributed by government action, the bulk of this redistribution is composed of transfers back and forth within the middle-income brackets. It is obvious why these transfers occur. Obtaining such a transfer is a rational investment of resources, and people do put their resources into it. They only thing which is in any sense astonishing about this phenomenon is that it is so little noted. Almost all standard discussions of redistribution imply that it is normally from the rich to the poor. Some such redistribution does indeed go on, but it is a trivial phenomenon compared with the redistribution within the middle class. I find the concentration of discussion of redistribution upon the very minor phenomenon of redistribution from the wealthy to the poor and the general ignoring of the major phenomenon—redistribution back and forth within the middle-income groups in terms of political organisation—most remarkable.

This remarkable concentration on the minor part of this activity and ignoring of the major part requires, I feel, some explanation. Unfortunately, the only explanation I can offer is basically psychological. It will be outlined below, but I should begin by apologising to the reader for introducing a non-rigorous discussion of personal psychology, instead of something more satisfying.

We must begin by talking a little bit about a well-tested psychological phenomenon: 'reduction of cognitive dissonance'. It is well established that individuals' perception of the world is, to some extent, affected by a subconscious desire to reduce internal dissonance. Thus, an individual will, without any dishonesty, believe that certain activities which are in accord with motive A are also in accord with motive B, even if objectively they are not. The reason for this is that he does not wish to admit, even to himself, that he is disregarding motive B. Needless to say, this phenomenon occurs only when motive A and motive B would, in objective terms, lead to different actions and where the individual in fact regards motive A as more important than motive B.

Most of us have been trained in such a way that we are presented with a problem of this nature. All of us from the time we were small have been told that it is our duty to be charitable, to help the poor, and to do various other good acts. On the other hand, most of us have strong selfish drives. Clearly the injunction that if a man takes your coat, you should give him your cloak also, is not descriptive of the ordinary behaviour of most human beings. It is, however, descriptive of what they say. Indeed, if we observe our colleagues in the university, we shall find that their expressed opinions are largely in accord with the ethically-given drive toward 'loving thy neighbour', and 'giving all you own to the poor'. If we look at their actual behaviour on the other hand, it turns out that they make few sacrifices for the poor.

It is clear, then, that they find these two drives—spending your own income yourself and helping the poor—in conflict, and that this should cause some internal tension. I should say, perhaps, that in my classes I commonly tell my students that if they really want to help the poor what they should do is get two jobs, work as hard as they possibly can, and then give all their income except that minimum amount that they need to stay alive to the inhabitants of India. They normally object to this pattern of behaviour, but are normally not willing to admit that the reason they object is simply that they do not *really* feel that charitable.[9]

Indeed, if I ask my students or my faculty colleagues how much they personally give to the poor, it often turns out to be a small amount—in many cases zero. They very commonly explain their attitude by saying that they prefer governmental charitable activity. They seldom give any explanation as to why they should use the government channel for this activity and, in particular, never turn to the perfectly genuine externality arguments that do exist for this purpose. They sometimes allege, however, that it is more efficient for them to vote for charity than to make a charitable contribution themselves because this brings in other people's money, too.

Suppose that it is suggested that I give $100 to the poor. Suppose further that this proposal is in the form of two options. Option 1 is that I take $100 out of my pocket and give it to some charity. Option 2 is that we vote on whether I should be taxed $100 for the purpose of making this charitable payment. The cost to me of making the direct payment is $100. The cost to me of voting for the tax, however, is $100 discounted by my estimate of the influence my vote will have on the outcome. Granted the constituency is 100,000 or more, the discounted cost to me of voting for this special tax on myself is vanishingly small. Thus, if I feel just a little bit charitable, I would not make the $100 payment but I would vote for the tax. I would make this vote in full awareness of the fact that many other persons are also voting on the same issue and that my vote will make very little difference in the outcome. Thus the cost to me of casting my vote is small. Putting it differently, the act that I am called upon to perform in voting is very low-cost, even though it refers to a $100 gift; the private gift is high-cost. Under the circumstances, one would predict that I would be more likely to vote for charitable activity than to undertake it myself.

Here, also, our phenomenon of reduction of cognitive dissonance comes in. If I am possessed both of selfish desires to spend my own money and a feeling that I must be charitable, I am wise to vote charitably and act selfishly. I should also tend, in discussion, to put much greater weight upon the importance of my vote than is actually justified, and to resent people who tell me that the vote makes almost no difference. At this point, the rationale for the ethical rule that private charity is bad and that all redistribution should be public becomes apparent. It provides a rationalisation for 'ethical' behaviour in urging government redistribution while actually making almost no sacrifice. It permits one to have the best of both worlds.

Some further implications can be drawn from this phenomenon. As the size of the constituency in which I am voting increases, the likelihood that my vote will have any effect on the outcome decreases. Consider my paying $100 to charity, voting on a tax of $100 to be levied on me by my local government for charitable purposes, voting on a similar tax for similar purposes for the state government, and finally voting on a similar tax for similar purposes by the national government. Clearly, the cost to me is monotonically decreasing through this set. I would be more likely to vote for the tax by the national government than for the state government, for the tax by the state government than for the local government, and more likely to vote for the tax by the local government than to make the direct payment myself. It is quite possible that this phenomenon explains the tendency to transfer charitable activity from local governments towards the national government. Looked at from the standpoint of the voter, he can obtain the satisfaction of 'behaving charitably' in a national election much more cheaply than he can in the local election.

Note, however, that there is the possibility of a prisoner's dilemma here which might lead to the voting decision being the one which is binding. Suppose a proposal is made to tax everyone in the United States who has more than $6000 a year income $100, for the purpose of distributing it to the poor. Each person might feel that his vote carried practically no weight and that he could gain some pleasure from voting for charitable activity, and hence vote for it. This would mean that the Act could pass and everyone would in fact be charged $100. Note that there is no miscalculation here. As in the usual prisoner's dilemma, the individual would be correct in his assessment of the cost to him of voting for or against this tax. The aggregation of the votes would mean, however, that he would find himself in the lower right instead of the upper left-hand corner of the prisoner's dilemma matrix, and would put out more money for charity than he really wants to. He is attempting to buy at a discount the feeling of satisfaction which comes from a 'charitable act', and finds that he has to pay the full price.

Thus this line of reasoning would indicate that voting on charitable issues might lead to vast over-investment in charity. I doubt that this is so, however. First, the particular pattern of drives that leads to the type of internal cognitive dissonance reduction which I have been describing is limited pretty largely to the upper classes. We intellectuals are the primary holders of these attitudes and we, together with our colleagues among the WASPs and upper-class Jews, make up only a minority of the population. The blue-collar majority are much less prone to this type of thinking, and hence we are free to cast votes in this way without its actually costing us very much.

There is, however, another phenomenon that might conceivably put us in the prisoner's dilemma. Intellectuals, for reasons I shall explain below, may not actually vote for charity, but they certainly talk about it a great deal. In the average university community the individual who said flatly that he is opposed to charity because he likes to spend his money himself would be subject to very large private costs. On the other hand, being in favour of various charitable activities and engaging in political activity on their behalf will normally have a distinct private pay-off. Thus the average intellectual who might or might not be inclined to vote in the way we have described is certainly inclined to engage in political activity in favour of government charity. Over long periods of time this might change the general opinion of society, so that the government would become more charitable, and hence the prisoner's dilemma might exist in the long run by way of the opinion-forming process. I think that it does not, but my reasons for so thinking require a little more elaboration on the structure of our electoral system.

So far the model I have been using has assumed that there are direct votes on charitable transfers. We do not observe this in the real world. The actual situation in our democracy is that we vote only periodically, and that our vote conveys relatively little information in the technical sense to the politician. The politician offers a whole collection of issues and proposals to the electorate, and is elected or not elected in terms of the whole complex. Thus the weight of his stand on any given issue in determining his election is hard to determine. In general, however, it seems fairly clear that most politicians regard transfer of funds by government process as *mainly* a way of purchasing the votes of the people *who receive the funds*, not of those people who might be charitably interested in the well-being of such people.

Thus a politician soliciting the vote of university professors will normally make a number of remarks about how we must help the poor. This is, however, merely an effort to reduce the 'cognitive dissonance' in the professor's mind. What actually counts is his emphasis on how important he thinks it is that research be stimulated, that education receive larger funds, that the income tax law be provided with even more loopholes than it now has for academics, etc. The academic is normally quite capable of rationalising all these things into a charitable activity, particularly if the candidate also makes some remarks about helping the poor. The end product is not that the prisoner's dilemma which I have been describing leads to an over-investment in charity, but that the various pressure groups—including the pressure group of the intellectuals—get very large transfers.

This phenomenon has led me to speculate on whether the poor might not do better if they depended on pure charity, rather than on an attempt to use the weight of their votes to acquire funds. It seems to me conceivable that if *all* persons who receive a significant part of their funds from any government unit were deprived of any vote in electing that government unit, the poor would do better than they do now. However, this is mere speculation.

So far this chapter has been descriptive and not normative. I fear, however, that the bulk of my readers will feel that it is essentially a denunciation of what I have described. They probably expect me now to provide a remedy. In fact I am not at all sure the situation requires a remedy. Individuals who are obtaining a feeling of being charitable without much real cost through their use of the political process are maximising their individual preferences and would be injured, that is, have a lower level of satisfaction, if they were compelled to make a more objectively accurate calculation of the real effects of their behaviour. It is not obvious to me that democratic government should not provide this type of satisfaction to the voters.

For those, however, who are disturbed and wish to 'do something', I can suggest three possible courses of action. The first course of action—and the one which I am sure most persons who are disturbed by the chapter will take—is simply to deny that it is true and go on happily reducing cognitive dissonance by the combination of being selfish in private expenditures and 'generous' in politics. For most, I think, this is the utility-maximising course of action.

For those who find this impossible, there are two remaining possibilities. They can take action to bring reality into accord with what is said, they can try to make people be as charitable in their actions as they are in their language, or conversely, to make people talk as they act, namely, change people's statements so that they are in fact descriptive of what they *do*, rather than mere expressions of loyalty to the prevailing ideals. I myself would prefer the latter and, indeed, I suspect that if we could somehow carry it out, the poor would actually get rather more money than they do now. Granted that transfers to the poor are now muddled up with truly massive transfers to other people, the voter quite rationally tries to restrict the total volume of the transfer. I think if permitted to vote on direct payments to the poor, he would probably choose to give them more. This, of course, is a guess.

Thus, if it is thought that it is desirable to do something about the situation which I describe, I suggest that it is easier to change the way we talk than to change the way we behave. Further, if we do change the way we talk, we shall be better informed about the real world (including the preferences of ourselves and our friends), and hence likely to behave in a more effective manner. The poor, along with the rest of us, would benefit from the change.

NOTES

1. Hochman and Rodgers, of course, are much more sophisticated in their handling of the problem that I have indicated in this single paragraph. Nevertheless, the point of view outlined above is espoused in it. The article has attracted a large number of comments, many of which are markedly less sophisticated than the original work.
2. See also Frey [3] for a discussion of the reasons why the poor exert less political influence than their per capita voting strength would appear to give them.
3. This comment is particularly revealing, since both Webb and Sieve are vigorous advocates of the British welfare state, and the subject-matter of their book is the improvement of statistics on its effects.
4. This paper is entirely concerned with redistribution in democracies because this is the area where our knowledge of politics is best. I should not like to leave the implication that I am convinced that redistribution operates better in despotisms.
5. Note that Ward actually demonstrates that there would be cyclical majority in all cases. Since the process must stop, however, and in observed reality *does* stop at some point, the statement that he proved indeterminancy of the process is not an unjust summary.
6. The two models may be reconciled by use of the apparatus presented by Tullock [10].
7. Such a decision might be made available to taxpayers by allowing them to earmark on their income tax returns a portion of their tax for alternative transfer programmes.
8. The inclusion of intellectuals is essentially a subjective guess, based on general knowledge. It seems to me likely that the principal beneficiaries of those changes in our society that originated with the New Deal have been the intellectuals who, through their control of both the educational process and the media, have been able to divert very large resources into their own pockets. So far as I know, however, there is no statistical evidence for or against this point of view.
9. In general the further to the left the individual student, the more incoherent he becomes in dealing with this particular problem. It is not that the people on the right are willing to admit that they act selfishly, but simply that they are much less embarrassed by the question than the members of the New Left. Being less embarrassed, they are less likely to sputter.

REFERENCES

[1] J.M. Buchanan and G. Tullock, *The Calculus of Consent* (Ann Arbor, Mich., 1962).
[2] A. Downs, *An Economic Theory of Democracy* (New York, 1957).
[3] B. Frey, 'Why Do High Income People Participate More in Politics?', *Public Choice*, 11 (Fall 1971), pp. 101–5.
[4] M. Friedman, *Capitalism and Freedom* (Chicago, 1962).
[5] B.R. Fry and R.F. Winters, 'The Politics of Redistribution', *American Political Science Review*, 64 (June 1970), pp. 508–22.
[6] R.J. Lampman, 'Transfer and Redistribution as Social Process', mimeograph.
[7] W.A. Niskanen, *Bureaucracy and Representative Government* (Chicago, 1971).
[8] W. Riker, *The Theory of Political Coalitions* (New Haven, Conn., 1962).
[9] J. Rodgers and H. Hochman, 'Pareto Optimal Redistribution', *American Economic Review*, 59 (September 1969), pp. 542–57.
[10] G. Tullock, 'A Simple Algebraic Logrolling Method', *American Economic Review*, 60 (June 1970), pp. 419–26.
[11] B. Ward, 'Majority Rule and Allocation', *Journal of Conflict Resolution*, 5 (December 1961), pp. 379–89.
[12] A.L. Webb and J.E.B. Sieve, *Income Distribution and the Welfare State*, Social Administration Research Trust (London, 1971).
[13] US Congress, Senate: Senator A. Ribicoff speaking about Amendments to the President's Welfare Programme—Amendment no. 318, 92nd Congress, 1st session, 22 July 1971: *Congressional Record*, S11783.

Part II
Costs of Giving and Professional Takers

4 Information Without Profit*

Most human beings have charitable feelings, and most make at least some allocation of resources to charitable objects. Sometimes these charitable feelings lead to direct gifts to individuals, but more normally some non-profit organisation is used as an intermediary. This non-profit instrumentality may be the government, in which case the charitable individual votes for or exerts pressure in favour of spending tax revenue in ways that will benefit some person or group whom he wishes to help. In the case of private charities, the individual normally makes a gift to, say, Harvard University or the Cancer Foundation.[1] Although these institutional forms are different, the problems examined here are not much affected by the difference. It will, therefore, mainly deal with gifts to private charities with only occasional references to the use of governmental instrumentalities and tax revenue for charitable purposes.

Economics courses usually will include, somewhere, a statement to the effect that a decision to make a charitable contribution is no more economically irrational than a decision to buy a car. Both are ways of using income to 'purchase' satisfaction; both increase utility. It is not my purpose to contradict this traditional view of the individual rationality of charitable activity, but to suggest that there is, nevertheless, a substantial element of something very like irrationality in the charitable use of resources. The donors of the charitable gift, whether they are private individuals making a contribution to the Heart Fund, or voters disposing of tax funds, are apt to be exceptionally ill-informed about the effects of their gift.[2] As a result of the poor information conditions, charitable activity is likely to be badly designed and ineptly carried out. Once this problem is recognised, it becomes possible to discuss possible improvements.

A recent discussion concluded: 'In a distressing number of cases . . . donors wish simply to discharge their moral obligations by a gift of suitable size, and do not care whether the donation ever bears fruit. In fact, through such devices as the United Fund, they both escape from having to choose carefully among alternative organisations and excuse the recipient organisation from accounting to them for an efficient use of funds.'[3] That

---

*First published in *Papers on Non-Market Decision-Making*, I (1966), pp. 141–59; and reprinted in *Economics of Information and Knowledge*. D.M. Lamberton (London: Penguin Books, 1971), pp. 119–38; and trans. 'Informacion no Lucrativa', in *Economia de la Informacion y del Conocimiento*, ed. D.M. Lamberton (Mexico City: Fondo de Cultura Economica, 1977), pp. 115–133.

this describes much charitable activity, few would doubt. The author, however, offers no explanation for the sharp difference he perceives between the behaviour of people expending resources on charity and on private goods. In this he is typical. The relative lack of interest in the charity itself by its donors has been widely noted,[4] but even attempts at explanation are rare.

As we shall see, the explanation is not difficult when consideration is given to the information costs involved. Before attempting to develop a rigorous model, however, let us consider a parable of vice and virtue: Benefactor organises an enterprise called 'Aid for the Sick and Starving Children of Gwondonaland', and solicits voluntary gifts for its support. This enterprise does not, however, waste any of its money in Gwondonaland. All of the contributions that it receives (except Benefactor's entrepreneurial profit) are devoted solely to raising the utility of the donors. It publishes a newsletter (on what appears to be cheap paper) full of affecting stories of suffering and its alleviation. These stories, produced by the best writers money can hire, are illustrated by touching before-and-after pictures produced by skilled photographers using all the resources of the New York modelling agencies. Any donor who gives more than $10.00 receives a 'personal letter' in a childish scrawl expressing gratitude and suggesting further contributions. Donors of more than $100.00 receive 'native handicraft' allegedly produced by the children of Gwondonaland. Extensive promotional activity with the objective of attracting new contributors is also carried on. As a result of Benefactor's activities, many contributors have the satisfaction of thinking that they are alleviating suffering. As a result of his investment of almost the total value of their gifts into providing 'information' flows to them which indicate that their charity is both needed and successful, they are happier about this charity than the would be if money were put into helping the children and the flow of newsletters, etc. were less well financed.

This project, which is likely to arouse considerable indignation among non-economists, meets the welfare criteria of Pareto economics. It produces a warm glow in the hearts of the donors, provides employment for many writers, models, photographers, printers, etc. in New York, and sizeable profits for Benefactor. Its creation raised the state of satisfaction of many people and reduced the satisfaction of no one. There is no change which can be suggested which would 'benefit at least one person while injuring no one'. In particular it should be noted that the starving children of Gwondonaland are in no way injured by the organisation. They would, of course, be better off if the AFTSASCOG were to divert some of its resources from directly serving its customers, the donors, to help in Gwondonaland, but they would also be better off if US Steel similarly made contributions to their welfare. The fact that the managements of US

Steel and AFTSASCOG are primarily interested in serving their customers, and do not make charitable contributions to the children of Gwondonaland, is no doubt unfortunate, but it does not actually injure the children.

So much for virtue. Now enters vice in the form of Meddler, a man totally untrained in economics who has never even heard of Pareto-optimality. Meddler investigates AFTSASCOG and releases the results of his inquiries to the newspapers. As a result of his failure to give Benefactor an opportunity to make suitable side-payments to prevent publication, the donors lose their warm feeling of righteousness and are made very unhappy. The models, photographers etc. employed by AFTSASCOG are forced to seek other employment, and Benefactor goes to prison which means that the taxpayers must support him for several years. Meddler's uneconomic intervention is almost the exact contrary to a Pareto change. There are some people who get pleasure out of reading sensational news of this sort in the newspaper, and they are benefited by his activities. With the exception of these newspaper readers, no one is made better off by Meddler's action, and a great number of people are injured.

Let us suppose, now, the Benefactor comes out of prison sadder but wiser. He accordingly organises 'Aid for the Sick and Starving Children of Beuchanaland' which is designed to avoid the sad end of AFTSASCOG. It does not spend all of its income on promotional activities, but actually uses some of it to feed starving Beuchanaland children. As a result it is unable to distribute to its donors as much in the way of newsletters, native handicrafts, etc. as had AFTSASCOG. Further, on advice of his lawyers, Benefactor now makes certain that all accounts of suffering and its alleviation in his literature are genuine, and that they are illustrated by pictures of actual Beuchana children taken in Beuchanaland. Since truth is seldom as interesting as fiction, and since the Beuchanas are not as good models as the professionals in New York, nor are there first-class photographers in Beuchanaland, the product is considerably less effective than the pure fakes he has used before. As a result he is able to attract fewer donations and the donors, on the average, are less satisfied than were the donors to AFTSASCOG before the revelation. In a sense, the expenditures in Beuchanaland are insurance against another disease. They protect both Benefactor and his donors against the type of exposure which ended AFTSASCOG.

The situation may be clarified by consideration of a somewhat similar situation which faced manufacturers before the development of fire insurance. The manufacturer in the early nineteenth century, like Benefactor, faced the possibility of a disaster, but in the form of fire rather than exposure.[5] Any resources he put into precautions against fire, for example storing all flammable raw materials at a distance from the factory

with concomitant increases in manufacturing costs, would either increase
the cost he must charge or make it necessary for him to produce a poorer
product. The customers would make their choices solely in terms of the
product and price, and would not be interested in the relative likelihood
that his plant would burn down tomorrow. The manufacturer, on the other
hand, is interested in both selling his product and keeping his factory safe.
Every dollar put into fire precautions reduces his ability to sell his product
profitably, but increases the probability that he will still have a factory next
year. Similarly, every dollar that Benefactor puts into actual aid for the
children reduces the resources he can put into improving the satisfaction of
his customers, the donors.

The analogy is not, of course, perfect. The customers of the
manufacturer are completely indifferent to his future well-being, and
consequently completely uninterested in whether he does have fire
insurance. The donors, on the other hand, will also suffer, by being made to
look like fools, if Benefactor is exposed as a fraud. They therefore have
some interest in information about the likelihood of such exposure, and the
question of whether or not he actually is a fraud would therefore interest
them. Note, however, that this applies only to the possibility that the clarity
is actually fraudulent. If the charity is simply extremely inefficient, or
devotes an undue percentage of its collections to soliciting more gifts, it is
highly unlikely that this will damage the donor. Thus the potential donor
would be interested in information indicating that the charity actually did
carry on charitable activities, but not in the efficiency with which it
operates. This is in fact the pattern of the 'information' that charities put
into their fund solicitations.

The Peace Corps, for example, in its early days put out a very attractive
recruiting poster showing a volunteer doing something in the foreground
and with a large legend 'What in the World Are You Doing?' I wrote in to
inquire what he was doing. This set off a long correspondence in which it
became plain that they did not know or care what he was doing.[6] He was
clearly a very attractive young man, and he surely had only the best of
intentions. This, they implied, should be enough. Inquiries as to what he
was doing or whether, whatever it was, it was a sensible way to help the
inhabitants of the suburb of Bogota in which he was living, were not really
important enough to deserve a careful answer. The issue of efficiency was
too vague to make the likelihood of 'exposure' a real risk.

These results clearly are paradoxical, yet they appear also to be logical.
The problem, of course, is the peculiar nature of the product sold by the
'welfare industry'. If I buy a car I then receive the car, and will necessarily
become aware of any defects that it possesses. Similarly, if I vote for a
candidate for Congress because he promises more money for research in
the social sciences, I will (if enough other special interest groups also vote

for him and the other members of his party) find it easier to get research grants for myself. Both of these activities involve an expenditure of resources to obtain an end which will directly affect me. Since I know that any defect in the product that I am 'buying' will work directly to my disadvantage, I am well advised to invest resources in finding out exactly what I will get before I make any commitment.

With charitable expenditures, on the other hand, I am not inevitably going to have any defects in the product brought to my attention, and defects will in any case, not directly affect me. If I make a contribution to the starving children of Gwondonaland, or vote for a congressman who promises to use public funds for that end, I will not be in any way injured by a *successful* fraud or by inefficiency. As long as I continue to think that the children have been helped by my contribution, the fact that they have not been will not reduce my state of satisfaction. The situation is radically different if I am purchasing some object or service for my own use, since I will automatically find out if the product or service does not come up to expectations.

The basic problem arises from the radically different nature of the satisfactions arising from a charitable expenditure and from the purchase of something to be directly consumed. These different satisfactions lead to a different set of costs and benefits attaching to the investment of resources in obtaining information. Naturally this leads to different attitudes toward information, and a difference in the effort put into getting it. The incentives for becoming well informed are extremely weak in charitable expenditures, and we should accordingly expect that a high degree of information would be rare. Similarly, the managers of charitable organisations, whether private or governmental, will find that they get more funds if they take this fact into account. They are 'selling' a feeling of satisfaction derived from sacrifice, whether the sacrifice does or does not improve the well-being of someone else is not of direct interest to the donor. He is interested not in what actually happens, but in his image of it. The entrepreneurs, accordingly, should polish the image.

In order to consider the matter more carefully, let us use a little simple algebra. To simplify matters we will confine ourselves to private transactions, leaving aside the political mechanism which the individual can use for both private gain and charity. The farmer voting for a candidate who has promised an increase in subsidies is clearly using his vote to purchase a private gain. If, on the other hand, he votes for a man who proposes to cut farm subsidies and let the price of bread fall, he is engaging in charity through the government. But we shall generally ignore this complication and assume that we are talking about the private purchase of private goods or private charitable contributions. In the problems raised here, the basic difference is between private or charitable ends, and the choice of private or public means for reaching those ends will not be of much importance.

Consider, then, a person who has purchased a car or made a contribution to a foreign mission fund. His satisfaction (S) will equal the sum of a number of different factors as shown in equation (4.1).

$$S = P + U + R_p + R_u + P_s - C \qquad (4.1)$$

In this equation P is the actual pleasure he gets from the act of purchase, U the pleasure he gets from consumption of the good or service (if it is a private purchase), R_p is his evaluation of the effect of his reputation of making the purchase, R_u his evaluation of the effect on his reputation of being seen to possess or consume the good or service. P_s is the increase of his satisfaction from the post-sale activities of the seller. Mostly we don't think of this particular source of satisfaction, but most merchants will do at least a little to convince the purchaser of their goods that he has obtained a good bargain. The salesman who tells you that a suit you have just bought looks well on you is perhaps the best example. In private purchases this is a small factor, but in the case of charities it may be a major one. Lastly, there is C, the cost of the purchase or gift the other possible uses of the resources committed to this particular transaction.

Table of Symbols

C=   Cost, price paid.

C_p=   Cost of production, money spent on ostensible object of charity.

I=   Gross receipts, total contributions.

P=   Pleasure derived by individual from making contribution to charity directly or through some collective body such as the state; or the pleasure derived by the individual from the act of purchasing a private good.

P_r=   Profit earned when organisation is, either legally or in fact, profit-oriented.

P_s=   Pleasure derived from post-sale activity of seller.

P_{sc}=   Cost of post-sales activity undertaken to increase satisfaction of contributor or purchaser.

R_p=   Individual evaluation of the effect on his reputation of making a purchase or contribution.

R_u=   Individual's evaluation of the effect on his reputation of possessing good or service.

S=   Total satisfaction from transaction.

S_c=   Sales or promotional costs.

U=   Pleasure from consumption, or use, of good or service.

If we consider the ordinary private purchase of goods or services, it is obvious that the satisfaction derived from P, R_p and P_s are very small and R_u will usually be quite small. Equation 4.2 would be regarded as a satisfactory approximation for most cases.

$$S = U - C \tag{4.2}$$

For a charitable contribution, on the other hand, the individual will not make use of or consume the goods or services which his contribution provides. Equation 4.3 is a correct statement of his situation.

$$S = P + R_p + P_s - C \tag{4.3}$$

But equations 4.2 and 4.3 have quite different effects if it is assumed that information is not free. An individual considering purchasing a private good would be impelled to begin by acquiring information about the good even at the sacrifice of real resources because he is going to get most of his satisfaction out of consuming it, and if it is defective he will be the one who suffers. Given his choice between devoting a certain quantity of resources to the purchase of a car or devoting part of that quantity to investigating the market situation for cars and then purchasing a car with the remainder, he will normally choose the latter. This gives him less money to spend on the car, but also makes it less likely that he will regret his decision. He is purchasing a stream of future services to himself, and will wish to ascertain as accurately as possible the value of that stream before he buys it.

The man contemplating a charitable gift, on the other hand, is essentially purchasing a present good. Both P and R_p depend entirely on his own act in making the gift. He need not make any inquiries about the efficiency of the charity to get the feeling of satisfaction derived from making a sacrifice since he is clearly making the sacrifice. The gain to his reputation, R_p, depends upon the opinion of others, and he should find out what they think, but what he needs to know is what they think now, which means that he need invest no resources in finding out what the charity actually does with its money, only with its reputation.[7] Further, he need not learn its general reputation, but only its reputation with people with whom he normally comes in contact. His gift will improve his reputation with the people who count to him if *they* think the charity is a good one. The existence of a group of sophisticates who disapprove of the Red Cross need not concern the average contributor.

If we return to equation 4.3, however, we will find one factor contributing to the satisfaction of the potential donor which does refer to the future, the P_s, standing for the contribution of his well being by the post-sales activity of the seller. If the charitable organisation conducts itself so that it becomes publicly known as a complete fraud after the donor has made his gift, clearly P_s would assume a substantial negative value. Leaving this matter aside for the moment, however, surely charities devote more resources to post-sales activities than do sellers of private goods and services. The donor to any well-organised charity can expect to be deluged with publications of the charity telling him what a good job it is doing and how great the need for further expenditures. This is rational since this is the only direct service the charity can give to its donors. By raising *their* satisfaction in this way, it makes future gifts more likely.

In most cases the material distributed by the charity itself, or stories planted by its public relations counsel, are the only source of 'information' on its activities available to its donors. This is because most charities are simply not large enough to attract the attention of the mass media with any regularity. Pure fraud by a purported charity might, however, be an exception. The exposure of hypocrites is always popular, and Benefactor of our story no doubt would make the headlines. Simple inefficiency,[8] on the other hand, would seldom rate a newspaper story. In the first place it is hard to judge efficiency of a charity, so accusations of inefficiency might be complex and uninteresting to the casual reader. Secondly, there would be little interest in a story which merely said that a group of well-intentioned people were not meeting some ideal standard. Allegations of wickedness are normally necessary to spice up an exposure.[9]

Thus the donor is unlikely to have his satisfaction in his gift reduced if the charity is simply inefficient. He has, of course, no motive to investigate himself after he has made the gift. Any derogatory information which he might dig up would just reduce his satisfaction. Indeed, at the subconscious level, he probably will avoid information which might hurt his self-esteem by indicating that his gift had been ill-advised. With the newspapers uninterested in inefficiency, and all of the donors having a positive aversion to evidence indicating that they had been duped, it is unlikely that the donor will have any inefficiency of the organisation brought to his notice. Under the circumstances, P_s will consist almost entirely of the flow of 'information' furnished to the donor by the charity itself. There will be a small probability that he will be annoyed by the discovery that it is a fraud, but the likelihood that poor performance on the part of the charity will reduce his satisfaction is small. If there is deception it will probably be successful. Since the donor gets the same satisfaction from contributing to a fraudulent charity which successfully conceals its frauds, as from a contribution to an honest charity,[10] he is not injured by a successful fraud.

But, as we have noted, fraud is not terribly easy to conceal. The newspapers will be interested in it, allegations of fraud are likely to bring on formal investigations by the police, and various employees of the organisation may be motivated to expose direct fraud. The donor, therefore, should be willing to devote at least some resources to making sure that a charity to which he is thinking of making a contribution is not a pure fraud. Inefficiency is another matter. Inefficient operation of a charity is not a crime so the police and other law enforcement agencies will not be interested in it. Rarely would it make a good enough story to interest the newspapers. Under the circumstances it is unlikely that the donor will be embarrassed by an exposure of the inefficiency of the charity to which he makes gifts. He would, therefore, be irrational to invest significant resources in attempting to determine the efficiency of the charity before he makes his gift. His satisfaction from the gift will be little affected if it is actually badly run.

One particular form of inefficiency for a charity would be the investment of 'too much' resources in promotional activity. This would, however, not reduce the satisfaction of the donor, indeed it should increase it unless it is forcefully brought to his attention that too much is being spent on this aspect of the organisation's activities. Since 'too much' is a vague concept, this is unlikely under present circumstances. Most of the remainder of this article will be devoted to this particular kind of inefficiency.

The concentration on over-expenditure on promotional expenditures is not intended to imply that this is the only, or principal type of inefficiency in charitable organisations. Very commonly inefficiency results from the fact that charities hire people to engage in services of various sorts which are intended to help the beneficiaries of the charity. It is easy for the charity to slip into the habit of making administrative decisions in terms of the welfare of the employees of the charity rather than in terms of the well-being of the beneficiaries. Another important source of inefficiency is simply mistake. The federal government's aid to the dependent children programme, for example, pays mothers of dependent children according to a schedule of payments which provides a sizeable incentive for the mother of one or two children to produce more.[11] Since raising the birth rate surely was not the intention of Congress, this is highly inefficient.[12] We will not discuss these types of inefficiency, but only because they would require more advanced tools than the ones used in this article.

But to return to our main subject, an ideal charity would try to maximise its total charitable payments. Putting C_p, the cost of production of its services, on the left, it would try to maximise equation 4.4.

$$C_p = I - S_c - P_{sc} \qquad (4.4)$$

Where I equals total receipts or income, S_c is the cost of sales and P_{sc} is the cost of post-sales activity undertaken to raise the satisfaction of the contributor. Note that this equation would be misleading if used for any other purpose than an analysis of expenditures on promotional activities. Efficiency in the expenditure of funds on the actual charitable output is simply ignored. A profit maximising firm would try to maximise profit, P_r under the conditions of equation 4.5.

$$P_r = I - C_p - S_c - P_{sc} \qquad (4.5)$$

Note that this equation fits a profit-making organisation manufacturing automobiles as well as one engaged in some charitable activity for profit. It is probable that profit-maximising charities exist only in a quasi-fraudulent underworld. There are companies which engage in the business of managing charities, but they normally do not take their return in the form of a residual. Usually they are paid either a fixed fee or their compensation varies with the total size of the organisation which would give them the same maximisation objectives as the bureaucratic organisations to be discussed below. One can readily imagine, however, someone like Benefactor after his stay with the government, who calculates how much he must put into the actual charity as a cost, and takes the remainder for his own use.

Most charities, whether private or governmental, are managed by professional bureaucrats. These people do not draw their compensation as a residual, but as part of the cost of running the charity. In general their prestige, compensation, and power will vary roughly with the total size of the charitable organisation. Like Baumol's sales-maximising executives they are motivated to maximise total receipts, I, as in equation 4.6.

$$I = C_p + S_p + P_{sc} \qquad (4.6)$$

The larger the charity or bureau, the better off they are. Note that this equation is identical to (4.5) if P_r is set equal to zero. The only difference between the entrepreneur and the bureaucrat is that the entrepreneur is permitted to take resources from the organisation for a trip to Jamaica while the bureaucrat can only increase his income by expanding the organisation. Both the bureaucrat and the profit-seeking owner are interested in expansion, but the private owner would stop investing resources in expansion when their return in that use fell below their value to him in his private life. The bureaucrat is prohibited from spending the resources himself, and hence will carry the expansion further. The situation is presented graphically in Figure 4.1.

On the vertical axis is shown the value or cost of each increment of income of expenditure. Each dollar spent on promotion ($S_c - P_{sc}$) costs a dollar, hence promotion costs are a horizontal line. The return on each dollar of promotional expenditure in gifts is shown by the contributions line, which exhibits the usual declining returns. An ideal charity would expand its promotional activity until the marginal return on a dollar of additional promotion was a dollar, or to point a. This would leave·the triangular area bounded by the promotion cost line, the contributions line, and the vertical axis as the amount available for charitable expenditure.

The profit-making entrepreneur, however, would realise that he had to

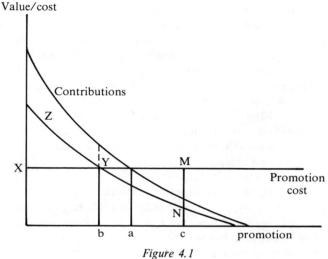

Figure 4.1

put at least something into the charity itself, which means that his profit would be total collections less the promotional cost and the cost of whatever he decided to spend on the charity. It seems reasonable that he would feel that his charitable expenditures should increase when his donations increase, so that there would be at least some charitable expenditure for each additional dollar of income. For simplicity I assume that he feels he must put roughly a third of the contributions he receives into actual charitable activities. Line Z–N shows the amount left over after this necessary 'cost' has been taken care of.[13] The private entrepreneur, thus, will curtail his promotional campaign at point b, and build a small organisation.

The bureaucrat, whose pay and prestige vary with the size of the charity, is interested in using the resources of the organisation for promotional purposes, with the objective of maximising its size. He will be like the profit-seeking businessman, however, in realising that he must put at least some resources into the production of the charity. Once again we assume for simplicity that he puts a constant share of the gifts received into charitable uses, retaining the rest for promotion expenses. He should expand the organisation until the total expenditure on promotion and on the production of charity equals total receipts. In other words, until total cost equal total receipts. On Figure 4.1, triangle XZY will be equal in area to the triangle YMN. Unlike the private owner, the bureaucrat is willing to spend, say $1.20 on soliciting $1.00 because this increases the total size of the organisation and because the $0.20 does not come out of the bureaucrat's pocket while the expansion will improve his position.[14]

From our model we can draw certain simple conclusions about the magnitude of various factors under the three different types of management.[15] The bureaucrat charity will be the largest in overall size with the ideal charity and private entreprise following in that order. The absolute size of the promotional budget of the bureaucratic enterprise will be the largest, with the ideal charity and the private enterprise following in that order. The same will apply to the percentage of receipts spent on promotional activity. In absolute terms the ideal charity will spend the most on the assumed objects of the organisation, and the private enterprise will spend successively less. In percentage terms the ideal charity will put the highest proportion of its funds into the actual charity, but it cannot be said for certain which of the other two would be second in this regard.

From all of this it would appear that the ideal charity is, indeed, the ideal. Unfortunately it is probably rather rare. Small, essentially local, charities may operate in this way, but the larger charities almost always come under the control of their professional employees. Charitable activity by the government is, almost by definition, run by bureaucrats. Granting this, and the inefficiency which results, we now turn to a discussion of possible remedies. The first thing to be admitted is that I have no real cure for the disease, only palliatives. Perhaps the reader may be able to find solutions which have escaped me. If so, I urge that he publish them as soon as possible. Charity is an important part of our economy, and it is desirable that its efficiency be improved.

The basic problem is simply that the man thinking of making a charitable contribution has much less motive for obtaining information about the likely performance of the charity than the man contemplating the purchase of an automobile has for finding out about the car. It is not true, however, that the potential charitable donor has no interest in accurate information, it is just that his motivation is weak. If information were readily available at low cost he might be interested in looking at it. Thus the arguments for compelling the provision of information would seem to be strong. Individuals purchasing consumption goods, stocks, or borrowing money, have strong motives for searching out information on the subject, yet we legally require the purveyors to provide them with a good deal of information. Given the weakness of the motivation for search in the case of charity, making information cheap by requiring the charitable oganisations to provide it would seem much more desirable.

The fact that we have numerous laws requiring private businesses to provide information to potential purchasers by, for example, printing the contents of a can on the label, while there is a complete absence of such legislation with respect to charity[16] probably reflects mainly the fact that people really don't think much about their charitable contributions.

They vaguely think that charities are, by definition, doing good, and hence that they do not need to be supervised like profit-seeking businessmen. This would appear both to reflect and contribute to the poor information that people have about the charitable organisations. Compelling charities to make information readily available to potential donors could hardly help but improve the efficiency of the 'Third Sector'.[17]

Unfortunately governmental action to compel charities to provide information is unlikely to have very much effect on those large and important charities which are operated by the government itself. Still, even here something could be done by requiring that all records be open. Sweden does this on the largest possible scale[18] and a modest beginning has been made in the poverty programme here.[19] Requiring all governmental and private charities to put their records at the disposal of any interested inquirer,[20] would be a sensible first step.

As a second reform, and unfortunately this would apply only to private charities, an equivalent of the labelling laws might be passed. Each piece of literature used by the charity for the direct or indirect solicitation of funds could be required to carry a functional account of how its resources are used.[21] This budget should, in particular, emphasise the size of the administrative and promotional activities of the charity. Since many charities use a great deal of voluntary labour, such labour should also be included. It is hard to evaluate such matters as the time of a housewife soliciting contributions for the Heart Fund, voluntary labour, therefore, could be entered in hours rather than dollar amounts. The additional printing costs for the charity would be as insignificant as the cost of printing details on the label of a can of soup, and granting the difference in information conditions, far more likely to affect the 'consumer's' decision.

The detailed budget, however, could easily be very misleading if simply left to the public relations counsel of the charity. Here we need something like the Securities and Exchange Commission to set standards. It would seem reasonable to require every charity engaging in soliciting sizeable amounts of money to file a statement modelled on the prospectus required for the issue of securities. The governmental commission could set standards for this prospectus, developing criteria which would make it possible for the potential donor to get an accurate idea of the actual functioning of the charity from simply reading this document. The development of criteria for measuring the actual amounts of resources devoted to promotion and administration, as opposed to those directly expended upon the beneficiaries of the charity would be both especially important and especially difficult. These criteria would also apply to the budgets printed on each piece of literature used in soliciting funds, and the commission would also require that these budgets be accurate.

Under the Security and Exchange Act, copies of the prospectus must be given to any potential purchaser of the security. This would put too much of a burden on the charities, and is, in any case, unnecessary.[22] Making such propectuses readily available, both by mail and on display in every office or installation of the charity would be sufficient. All these steps would, by making information very readily available, make it somewhat more likely that potential donors would acquire knowledge about a charity in spite of the extremely weak motives to do so. The purchasers of stocks and books have the strongest possible motives to inform themselves about the securities before purchase. Further, a large part of these securities are purchased by highly expert investment bankers or investors. Under the circumstances, improving the availability of information would be predicted to have only a marginal effect.[23] The 'purchasers' of charity, however, have weak incentives to acquire information about the objects of their self-sacrifices, and few of them are professional experts in the field.[24] Under the circumstances reducing their information cost should have considerably larger effect.

Improving information, however, is merely a palliative, and more drastic institutional changes seem called for. The main aim of this chapter has been not the urging of one particular reform, desirable as I think it would be, but to attracting attention to a generally neglected field. Clearly the charitable sector or our economy should receive much more study than it has so far. We can hope that this further research will lead to further suggestions for reform. Economists normally have made suggestions for institutions which are intended to guide 'as by an invisible hand' selfish men into serving the best interests of others. In charitable activities, the basic motive is a desire to help others, and this has apparently convinced students that the institutional structure is irrelevant. The good intentions of the donors, in a sense, substitute for the careful design of the institutions. The road to hell, of course, is paved with good intentions. Fortunately our present organisation of charity will not lead to disaster, but it does cause serious waste. We must add careful thought and sensible design of institutions to the existing good intentions if we want the 'Third Sector' to be not only 'good', but also efficient.

NOTES

1. The charitable motives may be rather indirect, as in the case of both Harvard and the Cancer Foundation. Instead of directly helping the poor and downtrodden, the donor makes a contribution intended to improve the situation by increasing our knowledge. He may also be interested in improving culture by a gift to a symphony orchestra.
2. A general, and widely noted, information problem in charity turns on the fact

that the donor can hardly have good information on the utility schedule of the beneficiaries. Thus his gift, unless it is a straight money donation, will probably not exactly fit the desires of the beneficiaries. I do not wish to deny the importance of this problem, but the information difficulty discussed in this chapter is a different one.

3. Charles Lindblom, 'Private—But for Profit', *Challenge* (March–April 1966), pp. 20–3, quotation on p. 22. Richard Cornuelle's *Reclaiming the American Dream* (New York: Random House, 1965), is basically a plea for the expansion of the charitable sector, yet it is replete with examples of extreme inefficiency in that area.

4. 'the exhilaration which results from "doing good", that is, from intending to do good, for the average heart does not require assurance of the result.' Lilian Brandy, *How Much Shall I Give?* (New York: The Frontier Press, 1921), p. 20.

5. Also like Benefactor, the disaster might be total or partial. An exposure might effect only a few potential donors just as a fire might destroy only part of a plant.

6. The theories proposed ran the gamut from building a rail fence to constructing some rabbit hutches.

7. During the course of composing this chapter I have been collecting direct mail solicitations for charitable contributions. The sample is small, but it includes such large, well-managed charities as the Heart Fund. They are notable for their lack of figures from which one could deduce how they actually spend their money and their obvious dependence upon emotional appeals. Apparently the advertising agencies who design these campaigns (not infrequently as a 'public service') are trying to increase the satisfaction that comes from giving as an act in itself, not to convince the potential donor that the charity is well-managed and efficient.

8. Note that 'inefficiency' is used as it is by the layman in ordinary speech. If we use the words 'efficiency' and 'inefficiency' to mean what they mean in most economic discussions, then an organisation which maximised the satisfaction of its donors would be efficient, regardless of what happened to the ostensible objects of the charity. In this chapter, then, 'efficiency' will mean 'efficiency in terms of the presumed objectives of the organisation' rather than its technical meaning.

9. The possibility of exposure probably reduces the efficiency of many citizens. The large charities are sizeable enough so that their efficient management would require high-quality personnel. A charity paying its principal executive officer $150,000 would, however, almost certainly face a major scandal. Consequently most charities get by with the less competent management which can be purchased for moderate salaries.

10. Indeed the fraud, as in the case of Benefactor, may give its donors more satisfaction. It can put more resources into giving them favourable information.

11. Note that this chapter was written in the early 1960s. This particular problem has been reduced by amendments to the Act. There are of course other problems.

12. It is possible that this is not the result of miscalculation. The bureaucrats gain by expansion of their funds, when additional children are born into the programme. It would be interesting to look into the advice given Congress by the professional administrators of the bureau.

13. The general conclusions are not affected by the exact shape of this line. As long

as he increases his charitable 'production' when his contributions go up the results follow.

14. The ideal charity would also be unwilling to spend a dollar on soliciting unless prospective returns were above a dollar because it would have to take the difference out of its charitable expenditures which it wishes to maximise.

15. The reasoning here closely resembles that of Armen Alchian's work on the role of profits.

16. Once again, legislation has changed this to some extent. Apparently however, the legislation is neither very honest nor very well enforced. Two of my colleagues who are writing a book on political activities of non-profits discovered that most of the Nader organisations simply leave part of the forms they are required to file blank.

17. Richard Corneulle, *Reclaiming the American Dream* (New York: Random House, 1966).

18. See: Donald C. Rowat, 'How Much Administrative Secrecy?', *Canadian Journal of Economics and Political Science* (November, 1965). A Bill providing much the same set of institutions has died in committee in three successive sessions of the US Congress.

19. 'Local anti-poverty agencies across the nation were ordered today to open all their books for public inspection upon demand. The directive covers all financial records, applications for federal money, minutes of public meetings and details of contracts signed.' *New York Times*, 24 March, 1966, p. 1. Note that the director of the anti-poverty campaign required such publicity only for *local* agencies and did not offer to open up his own records. Even this modest step immediately aroused objections from Senator Javits who apparently feared that full knowledge of the activities of the anti-poverty organisation might retard its growth.

20. A modest fee might be charged to keep frivolous enquiries out.

21. In order to reduce temptation, the expenditure in the past year, rather than plans for the year ahead should be listed. If the charity wished to include a prospective budget also, there would be no objection, but this would be regarded as a binding promise.

22. These prospectuses are in most cases thrown away unread.

23. Recent investigations seem to indicate that the effect was, in fact, either non-existent or small.

24. There are professional experts in the giving of charitable gifts, in the foundations for example, but they tend to put their money into quite diferent organisations than those which solicit public contributions. Perhaps this reflects their expertise.

5 The Cost of Transfers*

Most discussions of transfers have assumed that they are costless. They are movements from one point to another on the same Pareto-optimal production frontier. In utility terms they may naturally move the Pareto-optimal frontier out because, with interdependence of utility functions, everyone may feel better off after they are completed. The point of this chapter is to demonstrate that transfers may well involve significant costs. Further, we shall demonstrate that the mere possibility of transfers imposes certain costs on society. We are thrown into a game which we cannot avoid playing and which is, unfortunately, negative sum. This game, moreover, applies to a number of situations in addition to those that we have traditionally denominated 'transfers'. Specifically, bargaining, voluntary charity, government-sponsored income redistribution, theft and war all produce somewhat the same structural problems. As we shall see, our analysis will fit all of them. It should not be taken, however, as a proof that government income redistribution is theft. It is perfectly possible to be in favour of one and not the other. It will remain possible for those readers who favour income redistribution but who are firm pacifists to keep that pair of beliefs, and those readers who believe we should really hit the communists hard but that government income redistribution is undesirable will be able to retain those beliefs also.

Let us begin with a simple bargaining example. Suppose that we have a two-person society with K and T the citizens. Currently, they are at point 0 on Figure 5.1. Most economists would agree that movement into the area above and to the right of 0 (to such a point as A) is unambiguously desirable because it benefits at least one person and, in most cases, both. Movement to point B, however, is normally regarded as ambiguous. It clearly benefits K, but it also injures T. The Pareto solution is compensation. Since compensation involves simply a transfer of resources from one party to the other without any change in their quantity, it can be represented by a 45 degree angle drawn through B. This line passes to the right and above 0 and, hence, there is some point such as C which could be reached by K and T through agreement, and which would have the same resource input as point B.

---

*First published by *Kyklos* 24 (fasc. 4, 1971), pp. 629–43; and reprinted as 'El Coste de las Transferencias', *Hacienda Publica Espanola*, no. 47, (1977), Instituto de Estudios Fiscales, pp. 231–40; and in *Towards a Theory of the Rent-Seeking Society*. ed. with James M. Buchanan and Robert D. Tollison (Texas: A & M Press, 1981).

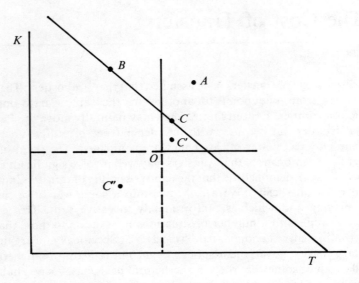

Figure 5.1

This argument as conventionally presented, however, does not fit the real world. If some technological possibility exists which would permit the 'society' to move to point B and T has a veto over the movement, then movement to point C will probably require a good deal of negotiation between K and T. Since this negotiation absorbs resources, the actual point achieved would not be C but some point within the line upon which B lies, such as C'. We can indeed imagine a situation in which the investment of resources in bargaining was so great that the end product was at C" which is below and to the left of the original position. As movement up and to the right is unambiguously desirable, movement down and to the left is unambiguously undesirable. Movement into the dotted rectangle is movement to an area where at least one person is injured and no one is benefited. It is only a movement into the area above and to the left or below and to the right of the starting-point which raise doubts about desirability or undesirability of a change.

Granted that some technological change occurred which made it possible to move to B, it would be expected that the bargaining between the two parties would lead to some point such as C', rather than a point such as C", simply because both of the parties must enter into the bargaining voluntarily, and it is unlikely (although surely not impossible) that they will miscalculate to the point where they actually suffer a loss. If they both make estimates of the likely outcome before beginning bargaining, then each must foresee a positive gain. On the whole, one would anticipate that over time these prebargaining estimates would turn out to be correct and, hence, that voluntary bargaining would not lead to such points as C".

As we shall see, voluntary charity shares this feature with voluntary bargaining, while government income transfers, theft and war are, in this respect, different. Before going on to these issues, however, let us briefly pause and consider some special aspects of the Pareto criteria using Figure 5.2. Suppose once again that we are at point 0. Some technological change occurs which makes it possible for society to move to point A which lies on the 45 degree angle line running through A'. We know from the location of point A that it is possible for society, by compensation, to reach some such point as A'. Further, if T is given a veto on movement from 0 to A unless he is compensated, both T and K will have incentives to reach a bargain which will fall somewhere in the Pareto area. Unfortunately, they each also have an incentive to try to gain the bulk of the profit for themselves, and this means that they will most assuredly use resources in bargaining against each other.

If, however, a proposal is made to move to point C, we know, first, that compensation could not lead to some point above and to the right of 0; there is, in fact, a genuine reduction in the total resources available to society at point C. Further, there is no incentive for both K or T to engage in bargaining since, from the standpoint of at least one of them, any location in the resource area available from point C will be a reduction in welfare. We can, mentally perhaps, say that A is in a location equivalent to something like A', and C equivalent to something like C'; hence, in the first case everyone can conceivably be benefited and in the second, of necessity, there will be injury.

It would be possible to argue that social changes which lie above the 45 degree line running through 0 should be adopted, on the grounds that society in some sense will have its resources enlarged by such a move. The counterpart argument, of course, would be that changes such as C should never be adopted for the same reason. This, as stated, violates the Pareto taboo on the comparison of utilities. It is possible, however, to argue for something like it, on strictly individualistic and Pareto terms. Suppose that we anticipate that in the future there will be a large number of opportunities open, some of which will be like A in that they would lead society to a new point above the 45 degree line running through 0 and some like C in the sense that they would lead to a point below. Assume further that we do not anticipate that these changes, as a whole, will favour one person or one group in society. Under these circumstances, both K and T might agree on a general rule that all changes which lead to movement of the frontier out and to the right will be accepted, regardless of their distributional characteris-

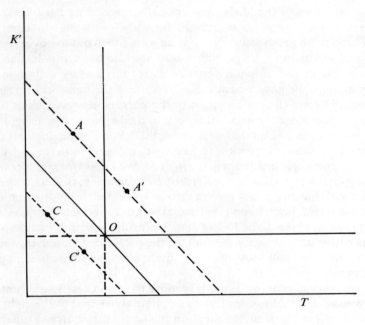

Figure 5.2

tics, simply because the present discounted value of such a rule would, for each one of them, be an improvement in welfare. Note that the production frontier would presumably not have the straight-line characteristic of the the line passing through A on our figure. The line represents the transfer possibilities, not the production frontier.

This, of course, involves the assumption that the progress will be at least evenly enough divided so that each party would anticipate that his particular position would be improved by a large number of such technological improvements, and that no party has too much risk-aversion. By parity of reasoning, and much less controversial, movements to points which move the frontier back (such as point C) would be undesirable. It seems likely that most people would agree that changes which lie above the 45 degree angle line lying through 0 have at least something to be said for them, and changes which lie below it are undesirable, although this rule will offend the Pareto orthodoxy.

The investment of resources in bargaining is always a negative-sum game. As a handy example, suppose that T wishes to purchase a house from K and would be benefited by obtaining the house for any price under $18,000. K, on the other hand, is willing to sell it at any price over $12,000. If

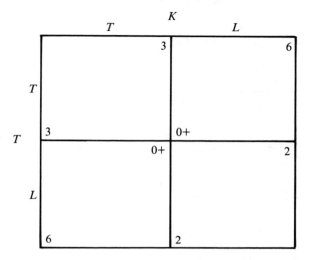

Figure 5.3

both truthfully stated their reservation price, they could split the difference. Each, however, is motivated to attempt to get the entire bargaining cost himself and, therefore, to lie about his own reservation price. Figure 5.3 shows the game matrix. T stands for truthful statement and L for lie. If both speak the truth, the expected outcome is shown in the upper left-hand corner; if T speaks the truth and K lies, then K should be able to get almost the entire bargainning range and T only a tiny part of it; if both lie, the investment in resources involved in sorting out the false statements, together with the cost of the possibility of the bargain being missed, leads to the result in the lower right corner. It can be seen, of course, that this is a prisoner's dilemma game, and that the parties will (as in fact they do in real life) attempt to mislead each other with the result that there is a social loss. If either of the two parties chose to behave in the socially optimum manner, he would suffer considerable loss himself and the other party would make very large gains. Prisoner's dilemma matrices of this general sort will be characteristic of all the situations with which we will deal in this essay.

So much for bargaining; now let us turn to voluntary charity. In order to do this, we must redesign the standard diagram which we have used so far and put not physical values or dollar values, but utility on the two axes.[1] Thus, suppose that once again K and T are a two-man society and society is at 0 on Figure 5.4. If K is oppressed by T's poverty, he may wish voluntarily to make a gift to T and such a gift would increase his utility. If nothing more happened, then the gift from K to T might move the society to point A

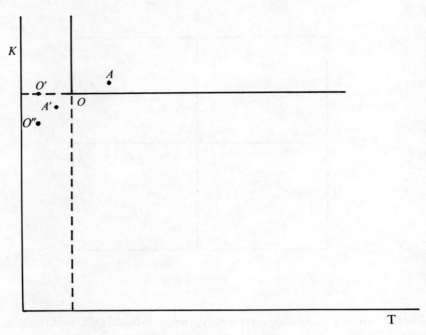

Figure 5.4

which is equivalent to a movement outward into the Pareto optimal region. Thus, a movement which would appear to be simply a movement along the 45 degree line, if we draw Figure 5.4 in terms of physical product, is a Pareto-optimal move in utility terms. The fact that such moves are possible presumably accounts for voluntary charity.

Unfortunately, the situation is not that simple. Suppose that T perceives that K may make a charitable gift. Under these circumstances, he would be well advised to invest resources in becoming a more suitable object of K's charity. This moves the system to O'. Indeed, in the particular cases with which I am most familiar—Chinese beggars—it may move it to a lower level of utility for both T and K. When I was in China, I used occasionally to see beggars who had deliberately and usually quite horribly mutilated themselves in order to increase their charitable appeal, and I always found the mutilations inflicted a considerable negative utility on me.

In the western world, of course, these drastic measures are not normal, but anyone who is at all familiar with people who are objects of charity must realise that they do engage in a certain amount of resource expenditure to improve their receipts. Granted, however, that the potential object of charity may behave in this way, the potential giver is apt to invest resources in attempting to control such activity. This moves the system to O''. Once again turning to a traditional area, the hiring of an almsmonger by medieval princes was an effort to reduce the use of resources in becoming objects of charity by potential beneficiaries of the royal largesse. In modern times, such protection is one of the major objectives of professional administration of charitable programme.

So far, we have moved into the Pareto-dominated area. It should be noted, however, that there is no need for us to remain there. The gift from K to T might still move us to A. It is, of course, possible that it might lead only to A' and, hence, that the society would be worse off, even in utility terms, after the charitable transaction than it would have been had no one thought of the possibility of such charity. Once again, however, the operation is voluntary on both sides, and it thus seems likely that the end-product will be a Pareto improvement rather than Pareto-dominated.

The problem, as was the case in bargaining and as will be the case in the other matters to which we will shortly turn, is that, although the actual operation of charitable giving is profitable to both parties, its mere possibility sets off behaviour on the part of each party which is aimed at improving his own utility and which uses resources. This behaviour is mutually offsetting and, taken in and of itself and ignoring the eventual gift, moves the society into the Pareto-dominated area. The movement from O'' to either A or A' is Pareto-optimal. The movement from O to O'' is Pareto-dominated. If it were possible to see to it that the Pareto-dominated moves never occurred, clearly society would make net gains out of all charitable transactions. There is no way, however, of providing such assurance. Thus, it is almost certain that at least occasionally charitable actions, like bargains, will go wrong, and the net effect will be that society is injured. We may find this unfortunate, but there is no evidence that the world was designed for our convenience.

So far, however, we have been discussing transactions which are voluntary on both sides. There is a sense in which any transaction is voluntary. For example, when the gunman says, 'Your money or your life', you make a deal with him which benefits both of you. The involuntary part of this transaction, from your standpoint, is the arrival of the gunman, not the trade you make with him once he has put in an appearance and threatens your life. Indeed, the minor paradox which is sometimes used in teaching—the question of whether this is or is not a voluntary transaction—is very easily answered. There is a trade of the victim's life provided by the gunman against the victim's money, which makes both parties better off; the only thing the victim can complain about is that the gunman, without his consent, placed him in a situation where he faced a decision on such a trade. The appearance of the gunman very sharply reduced his utility. The trade which he later made with gunman improved both his and the gunman's utility. Thus the transaction can be divided into two acts, the first of which was not Pareto-optimal and the second of which was.

Returning, however, to our main theme, theft, war and governmental income redistribution all involve transfers which are not voluntarily entered into by both parties, in the sense that both parties are satisfied with the entire transaction. Note that with respect to government income redistribution, this is only in part involuntary. Presumably, the taxpayer-citizens are interested in making charitable gifts to other persons, and may choose to use the state as a cooperative instrumentality for that end. In so far as this is true, the redistribution of income is voluntary and should be analysed as such. It seems likely, however, that government income redistribution is carried well beyond the point where those who are paying for the redistribution benefit in utility. The argument which appears below, then, applies only to that component of government income redistribution which is not simply a special way of organising a voluntary gift. As a subjective judgement, I would think that something of the order of 90 per cent of the income transfers by governmental process are of this nature, but I could be very far wrong in this guess. We can, I think, all agree that such major redistributions as the farm subsidy programme, the very extensive facilities provided at the expense of the general taxpayer to make private airplane flying cheap and easy, or the transfers to owners of steel mills through restrictions on the import of steel are not the result of deliberate desires on the part of the 'donors' to make these gifts. They are the result of activities on the part of recipients combined, perhaps, with indifference or, more likely, ignorance and political weakness on the part of the people who actually pay for them.

Let us then consider such redistribution. Note that there is no increase in the total product measured in physical terms or in general utility. Thus, the physical transfer falls on a straightforward 45 degree angle line. No improvement in efficiency in society is expected from such a transfer. The victim will be injured as much as the beneficiary gains.[2] Assume then that we are now at point O on Figure 5.5. Some pressure group—let us say the citizens of Tulsa, who would like their city to be a deep-water habour—invest a certain amount of resources in lobbying in Congress. This moves society to point O'. The amount of resources they would invest would in part be a function of the counter-investment of resources they expect, but let us defer that discussion for the moment.

People who would rather not have their tax dollars spent dredging the river to make Tulsa a deep-water port—K in our diagram—now invest resources in lobbying against the measure, with the result that society moves to O''. Congress then acts. If the measure to dredge the river to Tulsa

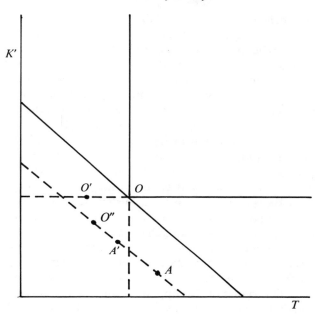

Figure 5.5

is defeated, we would remain at O″. Unfortunately, in the real world, the measure carried. There was, thus, a transfer of resources from K to T. Since the lobbying activity had lowered the total number of resources, this was a 45 degree movement from O″.[3] If the citizens of Tulsa—represented by T in our diagram—had calculated appropriately, the transfer of resources would be such that they would be benefited as a result of the entire transaction, i.e. they would reach some such point as A. If they had calculated inappropriately, the transfer might be less than the loss of resources invested in the effort to obtain the dredging operation; hence, they might end up at A′.

We could, I think, assume—looking at the matter solely from the standpoint of those persons engaged in lobbying to cause such transfers—that when the transfer was successful, it would turn out that they had made a net profit on the operation. When the transfer was unsuccessful, of course they would lose. What the present discounted value of the stream of several such operations would be, we cannot say. It might well be some such point as A′. If we assume, however, that everyone is engaged in attempting to get such transfers and that there is a tendency for them to cancel out among different members of society, then clearly we end up in the Pareto-dominated area. In any event, it is clear that the action as a whole has not benefited 'society', and that if asked whether we would like such transactions to occur in the future, not knowing whether we would be the beneficiary or victims of them, we would be opposed. The *ex ante* value of a stream of such redistributions is negative for the average person.

Let us consider briefly the calculation undertaken by some party who finds himself either interested in obtaining a transfer from someone else by lobbying or interested in avoiding a transfer from himself. Under these circumstances, he invests resources in lobbying as shown in Figure 5.6. Lobbying costs are measured by their costs and the potential benefits from lobbying (assuming that his opponent is undertaking some fixed amount of counter-lobbying) are shown by the curved line, he would choose to invest amount A in lobbying activity and would purchase some particular probability of success. Looked at from this standpoint, this is *ex ante* a sensible investment of his resources. *Ex post*, he may win or he may lose, but over time a policy of always making this kind of calculation and investing an appropriate amount in lobbying would maximise his income stream.

Note, however, that we have assumed that the other party's lobbying activities are fixed. In the real world, each of the two parties would adjust lobbying activities to that of that opponent, and the end-result would be a standard reaction diagram with—assuming everything is normal—the two

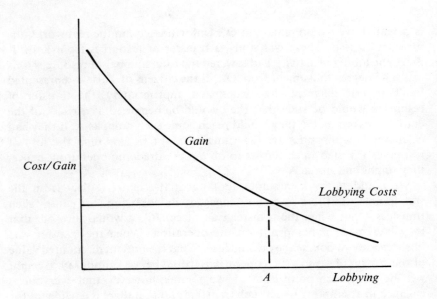

Figure 5.6

curves intersecting at an equilibrium point. Since the resources used in lobbying are self-cancelling—T's resources in part simply offset K's—they represent net social loss. If we could predict the outcome in advance, both parties could benefit by accepting that outcome without the investment of resources. Nevertheless, in the real world the individuals would be irrational *not* to make the investment in lobbying, and we can anticipate that this type of prisoner's dilemma will lead to large-scale investment in lobbying in those situations in which transfers are possible.

This chapter is entitled 'The Cost of Transfers'. As can be seen from the diagram, it could also have been called, 'The Cost of Resistance to Transfers'. The problem is that the possibility of a transfer leads people to invest resources in either obtaining the transfer or preventing it. People who hope to receive the transfer will invest resources until the return in probability of receiving the transfer on the last dollar is worth 1 dollar. Those against whom the transfer would work will invest similarly. One side or the other will win, but from the social standpoint the resources invested in the conflict between the two groups are entirely wasted.

There is, of course, no *a priori* argument for one side or the other being favoured in elimination of this conflict. If we return to the customs of Gladstone's England in which the government engaged in substantially no transfers, and it was known to all parties that the lobbying costs of introducing a change in this custom for their own benefit would almost certainly be much in excess of the benefit received, we would find very little such resource investment. If, on the other hand, the converse situation existed—it was widely believed that any proposal for a transfer would automatically go through and, hence, it was a waste of resources to resist the transfer—once again, few resources would be wasted in conflict. The reason being, of course, that with little resistance to transfers, there would also be very little resources invested in obtaining the transfers.[4] One might choose between these two social situations in terms of a general attitude toward transfers, but this would be outside the scope of this chapter.

So much for government-imposed redistribution of income or wealth. As can readily be seen, war and theft can be analysed by the same apparatus and, indeed, shown on the same diagrams if we change the labelling a little bit.[5] In each case, resources can be invested to obtain transfers, and in each case if the other side invests very little resources, this will be a profitable operation. The Mexicans, for example, are a very poor people living next to the wealthiest nation in the world. Further, as far as I can see, they rather dislike the citizens of the United States. Under the circumstances, conquest of the United States would clearly be highly desirable for Mexico. The reason they do not do it, of course, is that with our present armament, it would be a militarily impossible operation. If, however, we unilaterally disarmed and, hence, made conquest of the United States cheap, they would be fools not to undertake the action. Needless to say, our military forces right now are not aimed against the Mexicans. They are aimed at other enemies who are so powerful that it is necessary to maintain forces that are vastly superior to those maintained by Mexico. Under the circumstances, we are probably suffering nothing from the enmity of Mexico and the Mexicans have nothing to fear from our attack upon them.

If, however, we have two major powers, both of which are heavily armed, it is likely that the conflict between them will cost more than the benefit; hence, one would anticipate that on the whole they would choose not to engage in the conflict—although the competitive armament itself is a form of conflict. It should be noted, however, that this is simply because the armament level is high enough so that the costs of conflict are very great. If the armament level by either or both were permitted to slip back to the point where the costs of conflicts would be low, the probable profits of the war would reappear. Consider, for example, the North Vietnamese government's first attempt to overthrow the government of Cambodia. Granted the military preparations which Cambodia had, it seems to me that the decision to make this attempt was a rational one *ex ante*, regardless of its results *ex post*.

To summarise, it is customary to say that transfers are costless economically, and raise essentially non-economic problems. I do not wish to quarrel with the statement that transfers normally raise non-economic problems; the point of this chapter has been simply to point out that they also do involve purely economic costs. The transfer itself may be costless, but the prospect of the transfer leads individuals and groups to invest resources in either attempting to obtain a transfer or to resist a transfer away from themselves. These resources represent net social waste. Transfers lead to conflict, and conflict is always an example of social waste from the standpoint of society as a whole. Unfortunately, it is very commonly rational for the individual engaged in it.

NOTES

1. More elegant but complex methods would retain the physical value measure on the chart, but design the indifference curves of the two parties appropriately. For an introduction to complexities involved in such voluntary charity,see Thomas R. Ireland and David B. Johnson, *The Economics of Charity*, ed. Gordon Tullock (Blacksburg, Va: Center for Study of Public Choice, 1970).
2. This strictly speaking is not a necessary condition for the analysis which follows. It could be that, although the 'donor' would rather not give this particular amount, he nevertheless acquires some utility from the gift, albeit less than its cost

to him. This would lead to more elaborate analysis, but no fundamental change in our conclusion.

3. This particular transfer might be a movement which, in and of itself, impoverished society. That is, dredging might have been worth much less to the citizens of Tulsa than its cost to other people. Under these circumstances, the movement would be along a line at a steeper angle than 45 degrees. It would be an inefficient transfer. Although in the real world individual transfers may have this type of inefficiency attached to them, it seems sensible to confine our discussion to the simple case where the transfer does not in and of itself involve inefficiency.

4. There might be large investments in attempts to determine which particular transfers were to take place.

5. This also applies to revolution.

6 On the Welfare Cost of Transfers*

Edgar K. Browning

Professor Gordon Tullock has elaborated on the idea that government transfers involve a real resource cost to society even if traditional excess burdens are ignored.[1] The cost reflects the investment of resources in lobbying designed to obtain or prevent the transfers of income: 'The transfer itself may be costless, but the prospect of the transfer leads individuals and groups to invest resources in either attempting to obtain a transfer or to resist a transfer away from themselves. These resources represent net social waste'.[2] Furthermore, Tullock suggests that this waste, or welfare loss, can be quite large. It is possible, for instance, that the recipients of government redistribution of income will invest more resources in lobbying for the transfer than they ultimately receive, so the supposed beneficiaries of the redistribution are actually worse off, on balance. This would truly be a welfare loss with a vengeance.

While correct in arguing that resource investment in lobbying represents a welfare loss, Tullock greatly overstates the likely size of this loss. Indeed, for a great many government transfer policies it can be shown that the 'Tullock welfare loss' will be virtually non-existent. Suppose the transfer policy in question is the degree of progressivity of the income tax structure. Our problem is to determine the quantity of resources devoted to lobbying to affect the policy outcome. Since tax reforms are frequently on the political agenda, let the reader ask himself what resource investment in lobbying he made to influence this policy when it last arose. If my case is at all typical, and I shall argue that it is, the answer is that no voluntary contribution to lobbying was made. As a first approximation, then, it appears that individuals do not commit resources to lobbying in this type of case.

Such behaviour is perfectly rational, despite the fact that lobbying might favourably affect the policy choice. The salient feature of this tax reform, as well as most other government programmes which redistribute income, is that it transfers income from one group of millions of people to another group of similarly large size. Lobbying activity which affects the policy decision then has the attributes of a public good: an increase in the probability of a more progressive tax has indivisible benefits for millions of

*Edgar K. Browning, first published in *Kyklos* (fasc. 2, 1974), pp. 374–7. I would like to thank William Breit and Roland McKean for their comments on an earlier draft.

taxpayers (and indivisible costs for millions more), with it being very difficult to exclude the effects from those who do not contribute to the lobby. Since lobbying is a public good, the freerider problem becomes the central element in the analysis of an individual's decision to invest in lobbying. It is no surprise, then, that individuals would not invest in lobbying since their *individual* contributions would not significantly affect the policy outcome, and they will enjoy the same benefits (or bear the same costs) regardless of whether or not they contribute.

Consider Tullock's explanation of why individuals would lobby: 'In any situation in which transfers are likely, it must be assumed that profit-seeking individuals will invest resources in attempting to get them or prevent them, if the transfer is away from some individual.'[3] But the fact that high-income taxpayers might *collectively* gain from investing in lobbying to reduce progression is no reason to suppose that it is the *individual* interest of even a single one of them to lobby. Tullock has forgotten the freerider phenomenon. (It is worth mentioning that this is an instance where freerider behaviour is a positive advantage in a social system. There are other examples: e.g. the freerider problem is a factor which inhibits collusive agreements among firms trying to establish a cartel.) Therefore, the 'Tullock welfare loss' would be non-existent, or at most negligible, in this situation.

Tullock's argument is thus an incomplete explanation of the existence of lobbies. But lobbying activity is a prevalent feature of the political landscape, and we must now attempt to explain why it does occur. To put the matter most simply: under what conditions can a group overcome the freerider problem and provide a public good? Mancur Olson, Jr has examined this problem in detail, and the following remarks rely on his trenchant analysis.[4]

Olson identifies three circumstances in which a public good such as lobbying can be provided. First, the group may be of sufficiently small size that the freerider problem can be at least partially overcome. Thus, if the government redistributes income in favour of a small group some lobbying may occur. For example, a tariff to protect the firms in a concentrated industry often calls forth lobbying effort. In the small group case, however, the amount of lobbying will tend to be less than the amount which maximises profits for the entire group. In any event, the bulk of government redistribution is probably not of the small-group variety.

Second, an organisation may be able to coerce individuals into supporting a lobby. Coercion presumably accounts for Tullock's example of the citizens of Tulsa lobbying to have the federal government dredge the river to make Tulsa a deep-water port. The citizens of Tulsa, being a large group, would not voluntarily contribute to this effort, but the government of Tulsa may use its power to levy taxes to finance a lobby. Even so, the lobbying effort would be constrained by the existence of a large number of local governments i.e. if the federal government is deciding whether to dredge a hundred rivers, there would be a freerider problem affecting local governments themselves), differences of opinion within the locality, and by the mobility of people among local governments. Nevertheless, some lobbying activity surely does take place by local governments, as well as by other organisation which have coercive power.

A third way lobbies can be supported arises when an organisation is financed by selling an essentially private good to people and using some of the proceeds to finance the lobby. This is Olson's by-product theory of pressure groups, with the lobbying activity a by-product of an organisation which provides some other non-lobbying service. Trade unions and the American Medical Association are good examples of lobbies organised in this way.

The 'Tullock welfare loss' is not a necessary consequence of government redistribution, but results from the possibility of redistribution in conjunction with one, or more, of the factors enumerated above. Granted that some lobbying does occur on redistributive issues, however, can we follow Tullock and conclude that the welfare loss is likely 'vastly larger' than the conventional excess burden of the price-distorting effects of the transfers?[5] There are several reasons for doubting that this is so. First, not all redistribution will call forth lobbying effort, as we have seen. Second, even when the conditions enumerated above do result in lobbying there is no reason to suppose that it will be the amount of lobbying that maximises profit for the relevant group. In all likelihood it will be a much smaller amount.[6] Third, it may be that the cost of lobbying is greater than the expected increase in transfers to the group, in which case it would be irrational, even collectively, for the group to lobby. The fact that some lobbies do exist does not prove that possible benefits are *generally* greater than costs. Fourth, some lobbying may be desirable to convey information to legislators, just as some advertising may be a good thing. Fifth, we should not be misled into thinking that all special interest legislation which redistributes in favour of some group results from a lobbying effort.[7] As Wagner emphasises in his review of Olson's book, politicians may enact special interest legislation to gain votes without any lobbying being involved.[8] Sixth, and finally, the traditional excess burdens are quite large themselves. A conservative estimate of redistribution by the federal government in the US (including budgetary items and rough guesses of the distributive impact of its promotion of business and labour monopoly) is $150 billion annually. The excess burden of this redistribution is probably at least 10 per cent of the amount transferred, or $15 billion, and may be considerably more.[9] For these reasons it is far from obvious that the 'Tullock welfare loss' from lobbying for and against government redistribution will dwarf conventional excess burdens, but this issue must ultimately be resolved by empirical research.

These critical remarks should not obscure the genuine contribution Tullock makes. Tullock suggests that more is at stake with government redistribution than simply the price distorting effects of the taxes and subsidies. In this he is clearly correct, although we may differ as to how important we think 'Tullock welfare losses' are quantitatively. Tullock's analysis also suggests the importance of analysing redistributive schemes within an explicit public choice framework. Further analysis of this sort may well disclose other 'hidden' welfare losses (and perhaps welfare gains as well) which are not apparent in the conventional emphasis on price distortions. For example, I conjecture that a major impact of legislators spending so much time designing a multitude of redistributive programmes is that they are less well informed about other government programmes. If this is so, perhaps the place to look for the hidden welfare losses of government redistribution as presently carried out is in the inefficient performance of other government policies.

NOTES

1. Gordon Tullock, 'The Cost of Transfers', *Kyklos*, vol. 24 (1971), 4, pp. 629–43. Tullock makes the same argument in *Private Wants, Public Means* (New York: Basic Books, 1970), pp. 250–1, and in 'The Welfare Costs of Tariffs, Monopolies, and Theft', *Western Economic Journal* (June, 1967), pp. 224–32. Some closely related matters are discussed in 'The Charity of the Uncharitable', see Chapter 3, this volume.
2. Tullock, 'The Cost of Transfers', p. 642.
3. Ibid., p. 642. The quoted passage is in the 'Summary' not reproduced here.
4. Mancur Olson, Jr, *The Logic of Collective Action* (New York: Schocken Books, 1968).
5. Tullock makes this claim explicitly in *Private Wants, Public Means*, pp. 250–1.
6. The difficulties faced by a lobby attempting to maximise the 'profit' of its members are closely analogous to those facing a cartel. See George Stigler, *The Theory of Price*, 3rd edn. (London: Macmillan, 1966), Chapter 13.
7. Tullock, to be sure, does not claim this explicitly.
8. Richard Wagner, 'Pressure Groups and Political Entrepreneurs', *Papers on Non-Market Decision-Making*, 1966 (first issue of journal now called *Public Choice*).
9. It should be recalled that transfers have a double excess burden since there is a distortion introduced by the tax as well as the benefit payment. If the excess burden per dollar of revenue (ideally including administrative and compliance costs) is 5 per cent and the excess burden per dollar of expenditure is also 5 per cent, we would then have the 10 per cent figure given in the text. (I have made a very rough estimate of the excess burden for a specific negative income tax,

considering only labour supply distortions and ignoring administrative and compliance costs, and the result was an excess burden equal to 15 per cent of the amount transferred. See Edgar K. Browning, *Income Redistribution and the Negative Income Tax: A Theoretical Analysis* (unpublished doctoral dissertation, Princeton, 1971), Appendix B, Chapter 4.

7 More on the Welfare Cost of Transfers*

That lobbying for income transfers in many cases generates public goods or bads cannot, I think, be denied. If this is so, then the investment in obtaining such a transfer would be less than the total present discounted in value of the transfer. As I shall argue below, this offers an explanation for the fact that in democracies we see a very large amount of self-cancelling transfers of income back and forth within the middle income groups.

Before turning to this matter, however, I should like to discuss the political costs of transfer mechanisms. Browning is, of course, quite correct in his final remark about cost of 'legislators spending so much time designing a multitude of redistributive programmes' with the result 'that they are less well informed about other government programs.'[1] What we actually have for many of these programmes is what we might call Wagner-type lobbying.[2] The congressmen consider that the voters in their district are more interested in getting projects in the district than in almost anything else, and hence spend much of their time in attempting to get transfers to their districts. Some congressmen also specialise in obtaining transfers to special groups in society who are represented in their district but are also of wider scope—the elderly, farmers, etc.[3] Surely this cost in terms of that very scarce resource, legislator's time, must be immense. Further, it must have exactly the offsetting characteristics which I discussed in the original article.

We can go further, however. Another group of people who engage in active lobbying are the bureaucrats in each government bureau. These bureaucrats are essentially interested in transfers to themselves by way of expanding their particular bureau, but the social costs must be immenses.[4] Once again, competition between the bureaux would set off the kind of phenomena that I described in my original article.

Note that in both of these cases, however, the actual effect of this kind of lobbying is much greater than the direct resource cost because a great many people who are not involved in lobbying find themselves affected by the outcome. A dispute between the Department of Interior and the Army Corps of Engineers for appropriations would lead to an investment of resources by those two bureaux which probably fairly well discounted the value to the two bureaux of the switch in appropriations between them which they are fighting for. The effect of that appropriation on the economy as a whole

*First published in *Kyklos* (fasc. 2, 1974), pp. 378–81.

may be vastly greater. But since these are the only people involved in the actual conflict for or against the appropriation, we would anticipate that the effect on the economy as a whole would tend to be relatively random. If so, we would expect that the transfer effect of the outcome of this dispute on the economy as a whole would only by coincidence fit some idea of social policy. Basically, it would simply be a random transfer.

In my original article, I talked mainly about transfers of this sort, i.e. decisions on appropriations or programmes which had a fairly concrete and narrow direct effect for some limited group of people. Browning refers to 'tax reform' as a typical example and says, 'The salient feature . . . as [of] most other government programs which redistribute income, is that it transfers income from one group of millions of people to another group of similarly large size.' His example is 'the degree of progressivity of the income tax structure'. He argues that 'no voluntary contribution to lobbying' was made on this issue.[5]

Clearly we are talking about different types of programmes and I am willing to argue that the type Browning describes is relatively rare. First, turning to facts, the Musgrave and Musgrave text summarises the situation fairly well.[6] The total tax burden on Americans is approximately proportional to their income for a long range from about $5700 a year to about $35,000 a year.[7] Taxes below $5700 are lower and they rise above $35,000, although not very steeply. If one turns to the net result of government action,[8] somewhat the same picture emerges. In other words, the net effect of our tax and government activity is not particularly progressive.[9]

In practice it seems to be necessary for most governments to have a nominally progressive tax system and the fact that it must be nominally progressive no doubt does indeed have some real effects. In the United States, for example, all basic changes in the tax structure apparently require some increase in the normal degree of progressivity. (Written in 1974.) However, in practice this progressivity is more illusion than reality. Thus, on this matter for which Browning says there is very little lobbying, it is also true that it is not obvious that the government has any particular policy. The actual 'degree of progressivity of the income tax structure' is, however, the result of very intense lobbying on a myriad of detailed provisions.

If one looks at the American income tax in detail, one finds an immense body of law and regulation. Buried in this mass of literature is a gigantic number of special provisions which benefit various small special groups. I believe, and I do not expect that Browning will contest it, that these provisions have all been put in by active lobbying by those particular groups. In many cases the lobbying is, of course, a congressman rather than a professional, but private lobbyists make major contributions also.

Since such provisions are normally public goods (or bads), albeit for normally quite a small group of people—perhaps 10,000—the theoretical objection raised by Browning would appear to apply here also. Indeed, I think it does. However, we do observe these lobbies; let us consider how that happens.

If we consider some action of the government that will affect a number of people, it is normally true that it will affect different people differently. There may be some for whom the effect is quite large and a number of whom the effect is small. If there are some for whom the effect is quite large, it may be wise for them to invest resources in attempting to get a change in government policy.

In general, the desirability of such an investment from their standpoint will depend on how much the return to them would be from the change in government policy, and secondly, the likelihood that there will be opposition. If there is going to be no opposition—i.e. there are no people on the other side for whom there would be a concentrated harm imposed—then the cost of generating the change will be much lower; indeed, it will simply be the cost of overcoming the inertia of the government system. On the other hand, there may be similar concentrated interests on the other side, and hence we may have a conflict. In any event, there surely are very many cases in which it is sensible for at least some people to invest at least some resources in lobbying for or against the change.

In so far as these people do invest resources in attempting to make such a change, then the argument that I offered in my original article would tend to be true, although of course its strength is diluted. For those people who are affected by the redistributional change but for whom the effect is small enough so that it is not worth their time to invest any resources in it, the outcome is apt to be random. For some of these changes they will benefit, for some they will lose. We would anticipate that, over the population as a whole, individuals who are not involved in active lobbying would tend to gain about as much as they lose. Browning gives $150 billion as the total of transfers in the United States. I see no reason to doubt this, but it should be pointed out that the transfer from the wealthy and to the poor is only a very small part of that amount.[10]

The bulk of transfers, however, are back and forth within that massive group of people who make up the bulk of society and pay the bulk of the taxes. Although individual members of this group may suffer very pronounced negative transfers or receive very pronounced positive benefits as a result of what amounts to participating in a lottery, surely most of them end up with about the same income that they would have to begin with except, of course, in so far as the excess burden reduces their total income. The people who are interested in obtaining or preventing transfers on the other hand do invest resources and have a cost which is related to whatever transfer they receive or prevent. Thus, the population either invests resources in lobbying or participates in a lottery. For the first group, which is probably small, my original description is more or less correct. For the second, and much larger group, there is an excess burden but on the average, no net transfer.

NOTES

1. Edgar K. Browning, 'On the Welfare Cost of Transfers', *Kyklos*, (Fasc. 2, 1974), p. 377.
2. Richard E. Wagner, 'Pressure Groups and Political Entrepreneurs: A Review Article', *Papers on New Market Decision-Making*, I (1966), pp. 161–70.
3. Although this article and Browning's article are based primarily on American data, as far as I can see these phenomena are universal in democracies. Since one of the editors of this journal once explained to me the method by which the Swiss government decides where to place *Nationalstrassen*, I would gather that any view is not particularly controversial, at least in *Kyklos*.
4. See David L. Shapiro, 'Can Public Investment Have a Positive Rate of Return?', *Journal of Political Economics*, vol. 81 (1973), March/April, pp. 401–13.
5. Browning, op. cit., p. 374.
6. Richard A. Musgrave and Peggy B. Musgrave, *Public Finance and Theory in Practice* (New York: McGraw-Hill, 1973).
7. Ibid., p. 369.
8. Ibid., p. 376.
9. Indeed, in my opinion it may be sharply regressive. The services which are given by the government are normally evaluated on their resource cost. It seems likely that many of these services, such as elementary education, in fact are of considerably less value to the poor than to the well off. If this is so and the value of benefits given by the various governments was adjusted accordingly, we might find in the middle ranges, which, after all, include most the entire population, the net effect of the government is to make the income distribution markedly less equal than it would be without government activity. Once again, although I am using American data, I regard this as characteristic of most democracies. See, Adrian L. Webb and Jack E.B. Sceve, *Income Redistribution and the Welfare State* (London: Social Administration Research Trust, 1971) for data on the situation in England.
10. There are allegations occasionally found in the literature that the wealthy do not in fact suffer any negative transfers from the tax system. With careful reading, it will usually be found that the author's actual feeling is that the wealthy should have larger transfers of income away from them than they now have, not that they now have no loss through the transfer system.

Part III
How to Redistribute

8 Local Redistribution

As a rule of thumb, economists normally justify government intervention in any part of the economy by the existence of externalities there. The desirable scope of the government agency which then deals with the externality is normally calculated from the geographic scope of the externality. Thus, fire departments are normally local, because the direct externality of an uncontrolled fire is only a few hundred yards, and the somewhat indirect externality of having a large enough fire department to be efficient, normally can be obtained in quite a restricted area. Air pollution on the other hand, in general, could not be controlled locally and hence is rationally allocated to higher government agencies.

There is however, an exception to this rule which is aid to the poor. The normal arguments against having income redistribution allocated to local governments are not that the externalities are broad, but simply that migration would make it impossible for local governments to accomplish much income redistribution. If one particular local government had a higher relief payment than others, the poor would migrate into it. Upper-income people would conversely migrate away from areas where the taxes to help the poor were higher. As a consequence there would be a continuous competition to lower payments.

The theme of this chapter will be that this last position is a mistake. It is a mistake which is made by many economists including myself, but is nevertheless, a mistake. This mistake was, in fact, noticed some time ago by Pauly,[1] and further commented on by Buchanan,[2] but both their articles seem to have been largely forgotten. Further, they mainly dealt with the theoretical possibility. The point of this chapter is both to recall their basic idea and to examine the practical problems and possibilities of actually applying them.

Before dealing with this matter, however, I should briefly discuss the true externalities that do exist in connection with aid to the poor. These externalities first discussed by Milton Friedman in *Capitalism and Freedom*,[3] and elaborated on by myself in, *The Economics of Income Redistribution*,[4] are essentially production externalities rather than consumption externalities. To take an example from purely private charity, my university is currently soliciting funds from all of its alumni. It has made arrangements with one particular wealthy donor to match all funds produced by the alumni on a one for one basis. Thus, they tell the alumni that each dollar they put up will in fact increase the income of the university by 2 dollars. They no doubt told the wealthy donor the same thing.

Superficially, this looks like fraud, but as a matter of fact, it is perfectly correct. If my gift to some person or institution is to be matched by 1 or 10 million other gifts of the same size, then in deciding, either voluntarily as in this case of the university, or through voting on a level of aid which will be compulsory on all donors, I should in fact take into account the cost to me and the total benefit. Thus, for example, if I am voting on the level of aid to the poor, and do not feel that most of my upper-income neighbours would lose greatly by transferring some of their income to the poor, then I should select that total transfer in which that transfer and my tax payment which is a small fraction of the transfer, are in marginal adjustment by my preference function. Characteristically, I will give more by this method than I would by making an independent gift.

Note that there is another externality, but one which does not require any particular centralisation of charity. Currently, there is drought in much of Africa and the Ethiopian government has succeeded in making the drought much more deadly in Ethiopia than in the other parts of the African continent, and at the same time getting a great deal of publicity about the bad conditions of its citizens.[5] International relief agencies are trying, not very successfully, to feed the perfectly genuine starving citizens while not assisting the Ethiopian government in its political objectives.

It is clear that many American citizens feel an externality here in the sense that they are affected by the suffering of the Ethiopian citizens. This however, does not require from the American standpoint that a government agency be set up, whose jurisdiction involves both the United States and Ethiopia. The American citizens can, both through private charity and through government programmes, transfer whatever amount of funds they wish to Ethiopia. The production externality mentioned above is, as far as the American citizens are concerned, internalised by the use of the American government.

In any event, it would appear that the externality generated on people by the suffering of others considerable distances from them, is much lower than that which they suffer from people close in. The amount that the United States is willing to contribute, both through private charity and through government aid, to save the genuinely starving people in Ethiopia, is a trifle compared to the amounts which are transfered domestically. Further, even domestically, there are large difference between the actual level of relief from state to state. Although there are complaints about this, they are not strongly enough felt so that the majority of the American citizens choose to do something about it.

Traditionally, in the United States, this latter kind of externality that is the domestic externality, was dealt with not by a central government programme, but by allocating responsibility for the poor in each community to that community. Before the 1930s the states sometimes did, and sometimes did not, enact standards for the local communities.

Sometimes these standards were actually expenditure standards, but more normally they simply indicated which community had to take care of which person.

The system apparently worked reasonably well, because the feeling of sympathy for the poor, although perfectly genuine and worldwide, in fact falls off as you move away from the sympathising person. The amount that he will give to the poor in his own county is greater than the amount that he would give, on a per capita basis, to the people in the next county. In general, with everyone feeling this way, the citizens of each county give to their poor enough so that the residents of neighbouring counties do not feel it necessary to supplement it. There is, of course, no reason why they could not do so if they wished and historically, through private charity, they have occasionally done so. There is no legal restriction here.

I read in Washington newspapers denunciations of southern states, such as Mississippi, for having very low relief payments. There is absolutely no feeling that the citizens of Washington and its environments, have any responsibility to do anything more about it. They could, of course, tax themselves and send the money to Mississippi. Indeed, since the Washington area has the highest income in the United States and Mississippi a much lower one, if they were genuinely charitably concerned I suppose they would do this. I feel confident that their actual attitude on this matter, however, is that they wish the payments to the Mississippi citizens were higher than they are, but the benefit they would see from having a dollar added to the Mississippi budget is less than the cost of 1 dollar to them.

The production externality listed above, however, would appear to fit here also. Relief to Ethiopia is currently being given by a large number of governments. In each case, the government of the donor country, let us say Sweden, itself makes up its mind as to how much it is to give. If we were to establish some kind of collective organisations in which the citizens of all of these states jointly voted on how much they would transfer to Ethiopia, the production externality argument indicates that they would choose to transfer more than they do now. The Swedes would do more under matching conditions. Nevertheless, once one gets up to numbers of 100 or so, further gains in increasing the total number of donors who are making the collective decision are relatively minor. The gain comes in the early part of the process when you move from 1 to 10 to 100 and to 1000 donors voting on their decision as a block.

But all of this is theoretical. Let us turn a little bit to empirical data, and here I am going to survey briefly what empirical data we have on decentralisation of aid to the poor. The first, and in some ways most astonishing is the English system just before the welfare reform associated with Bentham. The statute of Elizabeth second,[6] provided that the poor would be taken care of by the local parishes in England who had a Board of Commissioners for this purpose. The problem that disturbed Bentham, and apparently all the other people at that time, was that under the so-called Speenhamland system, the amount going to the poor was excessive and was causing severe financial problems.[7] The point of the reform was to prevent the parishes from wasting the taxpayers' substance. Surely, this does not look as if production externalities argument that I gave above was an important factor here. The new system was, in fact, considerably less generous to the poor than the old one had been. It is, of course, true that this change was in part total reorganisation rather than centralisation, but the change was a matter of an Act of Parliament and not of the parishes deciding to take action on their own.

As a second example of the same kind of thing, Lebergott[8] has collected data on the relative payment to the poor from 1850 well into the era of the modern welfare state. The data come from the census and are organised by state, but in many states the actual payments and organisation of the whole programme was a local government rather than a state responsibility. The amount which was, in essence, the minimum income which a poor person could receive under these circumstances, fluctuated, but Lebergott's general conclusion is that relatively the poor did about as well in the 1850s as in the 1950s—or, for that, matter the 1980s. Centralisation of aid to the poor has not greatly benefited them.

As a last item, I am a citizen of the Washington area and read *The Washington Post*, a typical bleeding-heart journal. I find a steady scattering of articles about the very poor in Washington, they used to be called the grating people, and are now referred to as the homeless. These people are far worse off than anyone else in the area and, interestingly enough, are primarily being taken care of privately. I don't want to oversimiplify. Many of the people concerned in aiding these poor are themselves civil servants, or for that matter politicians, and they're quite expert at, rather indirectly, getting federal government money. Further, just before the last presidential election, one of the leaders of this poor movement started a fast, wanting further federal government money. Fearing that bad publicity would come if he died[9] before the election, the Reagan government made a sizeable grant to the particular private organisation with which he was associated. Nevertheless, basically, the welfare state is not helping these very poor people particularly.

This is not a unique characteristic of Washington, or the United States. One of the results of the severe winter in Europe in 1984/85 was the discovery that there were about 5000 people in Paris quite literally sleeping under bridges. The police rounded up most of them before the cold killed them, but some died. They were also found in London, and elsewhere.

I don't read the newspapers of Paris or Rome, but I do read *The*

Washington Post. It is notable that the *Post* is very disturbed about these poor people, and some of its reporters, if their stories are to be believed, regularly make small cash contributions, but they do not suggest that the welfare state be discommoded by being rearranged so that these people are taken care of by regularly appointed civil servants.

Currently, their basic problem is that they have great difficulty dealing with civil servants, forms, etc., and the welfare bureaucracy doesn't want to inconvenience itself for them. The actual private charity made available in Washington for these very poor, in spite of the existence of the welfare state, is a rather strong indication of what I might call the normal state. In the nineteenth century, in addition to the governmental programme whose data were collected by Lebergott, there was a great deal of private charity.

Today, once again, there is a great deal of private charity, but the private charity today almost uniformly takes the form of gifts to research, universities, etc. One of the results of the development of welfare state was that most citizens came to the conclusion that the poor were being taken care of, and hence that their charitable instincts should be directed elsewhere. With the development of various specialised bureaucracies to take care of this money made available by charitably-inclined citizens, all of which are devoted to something other than helping the poor, it is quite hard to get the money back to helping those poor whom the welfare state does not help. I should say, however, that in Washington, private agencies now exist for the purpose of collecting money and using it for the benefit of these grating people. Such agencies are in fact developing rapidly, so one can predict that they will be better off in the future. For the reasons given above, however, it would be far better if the government took up their care, and there are some movements in that direction.

How then, do we have what appears to be a radical difference between theory and practice? Further, if theory has influenced practice, a great many programmes have been shifted to the central government on the grounds that they're impractical at the local level. This was the rationalisation for making social security a national instead of a local programme, and, in that particular case, this was probably sensible. It would not have been feasible to deal with it in a dissagregated way because it involved an intergenerational transfer rather than a transfer to the poor. Transfer to the poor, on the other hand, I believe could be dealt with locally.

This automatically raises the general problem of what can and cannot be done in the way of local government transfers. One can use the above history as a sort of a guide for the future. Apparently, local governments can indeed take care of the poor as well as they're taken care of now. In general, they cannot engage in the very large transfers which are so characteristic of modern welfare states, back and forth within the middle class. It is probable that they can operate minor transfers away from the wealthy to the rest of the society but they cannot organise very large transfers of this sort. Since there is some doubt as to whether democracies in general have, in practice, made large transfers from the wealthy to the rest of us, it is not obvious whether this is a disadvantage of local government as opposed to national government. There are, of course, many people who would say that if it could not make as large transfers of this sort, this would be an advantage.

These are general conclusions. Let us go through my reasoning, and let me begin with the transfers away from the wealthy then the transfers back and forth in the middle class, and end up with the transfers to the poor.

If we look at traditional American society, we observe that the wealthy, one way or another, normally made more or less voluntary transfers to the citizens of the area where they operated. In a way, these transfers were not transfers, but the purchase of respect and admiration from their fellow citizens. When it was completely voluntary, there were, of course, individuals who did not participate in this activity, but most wealthy people did. If we return to the Washington environment, the Wolf Trap auditorium was originally a private gift and, when it burned down, various wealthy people, mainly Mrs Filene, paid to have it rebuilt. Needless to say, the opening of the new Wolf Trap auditorium, consisted of a large, 'We like Mrs Filene' ceremony.

In general, upper-income people who are willing to make gifts of this sort have no particular objection to having these gifts collected by way of a progressive tax, provided progression is not too severe. Those particular upper-income people who don't want to make gifts object; but they're probably outnumbered by their colleagues.

It should be said, however, that all of this permits only relatively modest transfers from the wealthy. Since it is not obvious whether we make large or small transfers now, whether this indicates that local governments could do more, or could do less, is not clear. With a local government, individuals obviously can simply move out, and wealthy people might do so. It should be pointed out however, that if the wealthy people earn their living in one particular city or are wealthy because they own property in it, then they cannot move. One would anticipate that any given level of tax would lead to some equilibrium with presumably at least some people who needed to give immediate direct supervision to the sources of their wealth, feeling that paying the graduated income tax was less of a sacrifice than living somewhere else. The higher the tax, the fewer such people.

There is an interesting example of this in Switzerland where graduated income taxes are in fact collected by the extremely small Swiss cantons. There are limits to the amounts that can be extracted this way without encouraging migration as the Stadt of Basel discovered. In general, they are able to charge a graduated income tax with the wealthy citizens who pay these taxes apparently regarding it something of a matter of pride and getting a great deal of local respect because they do pay them.

Somewhat of the same effect will be found in the United States where many states charge income taxes in addition to the federal tax.[10]

There is no doubt that Connecticut has a good many people who otherwise would live in other parts of the watershed of New York city because it has no income tax. You do find wealthy people, however, living in New York city itself, upstate New York, or New Jersey, in all of which cases they pay taxes which are somewhat higher. Apparently, as long as the degree of progression is moderate, wealthy people do not object too loudly

All of this would indicate that upper-income people have some charitable impulses like the rest of us. The problem with graduated taxation is that you can't collect from them more than a rather modest amount before they begin seriously thinking of moving. Whether this modest amount is greater or less than is in fact collected by the big centralised governments is an open question, but, in my opinion, it is considerably less.

Those people who feel that we should transfer as much or more away from the wealthy as we now do would object to this aspect of redistribution being transferred to local governments. Note once again, however, that it is not immediately obvious how much is transferred away from the wealthy. A great many income redistribution schemes which fall heavily on the wealthy lead not to transfers away from them, but to them losing considerable sums of money because they invest their funds in areas where the return is low before taxes, but after taxes higher than it would be had they chosen more productive investments. This is a net social waste which does have the effect of making the wealthy poorer, but does not involve any transfer to the rest of us. Indeed, the rest of us are worse off because these investments are less productive than the alternatives which would be adopted were the taxes lower. In fact, many scholars think that the actual taxes collected from the wealthy would be higher if we lowered the nominal rate, with the result that they switched out of such tax-saving or tax-sheltered investments.

Nevertheless, I think we have to concede that local governments would have difficulty extracting large sums of money from the wealthy. They could no doubt extract some money; in other words, their tax system could be progressive to some extent, but not to an extreme degree. Perhaps, in this case I am simply reflecting my initial training in economics because Henry Simons was firmly in favour of centralising a graduated income tax on exactly these grounds. He was, of course, thinking of a tax, the upper brackets of which were very very much lower than the upper brackets are now.

The second category is the very extensive transfers that now go on in the modern welfare state back and forth within the middle class. Subsidies for farmers, paid for usually by the poorer parts of the population who eat the lower quality foods: transfers from the economically active to the retired, regardless of whether the retired are poor or not: transfers to workers in the car industry, and owners of stock in American car firms by way of restrictions on imports: all of these and innumerable other activities by modern governments, in net, are simply transfers back and forth in the middle class.[11] Some of these programmes, of course, do indeed benefit the poor as well as other people. Elderly poor people collect their social security pensions[12] as well as elderly wealthy people.

In general, however, most modern welfare states have certain special programmes that deal with the poor. In the United States this is supplementary security income. A poor person who is old will receive a pension from the social security system, but if that person has been poor all his life and hence the accumulated taxes he paid in were not enough to give him an adequate pension, he will be given supplementary security income. Since he will receive the same sum total of a social security payment and supplementary security income, regardless of the size of his social security pension (provided, of course, it is not greater than the supplementary security income) in essence from his standpoint, all the taxes he has paid are wasted. He receives two cheques instead of one, but they total to the same amount;[13] that is, he receives the same as he would have received if he paid no social security taxes at any time in his life. The basic transfer component of the social security is simply from the young to the old, rather from the well-off to the poor.

Anyone who knows anything at all about American local governments realises that local governments also engage in middle-class transfers, but on a very small scale. If permitted by the higher level governments, particular ly the federal courts, they will establish local monopolies for such craftsmen as electricians and barbers. They use their zoning regulations to change the value of land in various parts of the city and in most places there are continuous rumours—true or false, I do not know—that this is a relatively corrupt activity. They also relatively rarely pay their own employees the marginal value of their services. To take one particularly obvious case, the Washington bus drivers are clearly paid more than the marginal value of their services. We find a number of cases in other cities where this kind of thing is done. On the other hand, where the city or local or state government has significant monopsony power and its employees are not well-organised, there may be underpayment.[14] All of this involves transfers back and forth within the local middle class.

But although these transfers are clearly possible and do exist in local governments, they are completely trivial compared to the transfers made by the national government. One of the original arguments for having the social security administration national rather than local was the people would move. I don't think it occurred to most of the people who offered this argument that it implied that really, over their lifetime, most people preferred not to have such a programme. They may, however, not have realised that it was possible to vest the pension right.

The last may not be intelligible to non-Americans, but a great many private pensions, and for that matter government pensions, for their employees are 'vested'. This means simply that if you move or change your job, you retain the appropriate actuarial value of your pension rights, with the pension being paid at retirement. To explain how this could have worked locally, suppose that I am born, brought up in Rockford, and employed by Woodward Governor, as in fact I was, and then left Rockford and, indeed, Illinois. I would have acquired certain rather restricted pension rights and they would remain with me. If I die, they would be extinguished, but if I did retire at the age of 65 living in Hawaii, I would receive pension from the state of Illinois, or from the city of Rockford, depending on how this had been organised.

Clearly, the structure that I've just described would have been quite possible if the pension rights were actuarially accurate. Indeed, at the moment, such vested pensions are regularly offered as an additional employment incentive by private companies all over the United States. There is no reason to believe that local governments could not have done so also.

The problem with the social security is that it is not actuarially sound. Almost everybody in the United States who is under the age of 45 would be better off if they could somehow get out of the programme. On the other hand, if they do get out of the programme, there wouldn't be enough money left to pay the pensions of the people who are now drawing them, and the people over the age of 45 who still gain from the programme, and hence would stay in. The basic problem, of course, is that although a private pension scheme invests the money that you pay into the pension fund, so that when you retire you get the initial amount plus the interest on it, the social security system doesn't. It is true that as the total size of American labour payment increases, partly through increasing productivity and partly, in the past, due to rising population, the pension can be increased. But it can't be increased enough to compensate for the lack of the interest payments.[15] Thus, the young have a very substantial incentive to move out and, if they do, either the old will not be paid, or the tax will have to be raised on the young which would give them a stronger incentive to move out. The problem is, of course, particularly severe because younger people are highly migratory anyway. Further, none of them would tend to feel there was some prestige in being marked out as wealthy members of the society as the payers of moderately graduated income tax might. Thus the system simply could not be implemented.

The same, of course, would be true with respect to the farm subsidies which are such an important part of the governmental distortion of the income distribution in most modern welfare states. Local governments simply couldn't do them. Indeed, most of this back and forth in the middle-class income transfer would be impossible if redistribution was made a local government activity.

In my opinion and, I think, in the opinion of most economists who thought about the matter, this is an argument, although not necessarily a decisive argument, for moving these functions to local government, in so far as these activities can be regarded as simply government-sponsored insurance. For example, the old age pensions, if they are actuarily sound, or medical insurance, there is no reason why the local governments cannot carry them out. Vesting provisions equivalent to those now used for people who move from one employer to another could be developed for people who moved from one area to another without any great technical difficulty. These, of course, are not true transfers, unlike such government programmes as the present American social security system. Once again, I think most economists who thought about the matter would prefer the actuarily-sound schemes, which local governments would be forced to adopt to the kind of tax on the young for the benefit of the old which seems generally attractive to politicians. It is not obvious what the average citizen would think about this. One of the reasons it is not obvious, of course, is that, at the moment, he doesn't understand the issue and hence has no fixed opinion.

Let us now turn to our final area: aid to the poor. The first thing to be said here is that most people are in favour of aiding the poor and that there are perfectly good reasons for collectivising this aid. Collectivisation, however, does not need to go very much beyond the local area in order to obtain most of its advantages. There is no reason to believe that this would cause any great difficulty if the various local government units were of roughly the same wealth and charitable deposition. It is, on the whole, unlikely that this will turn out to be true in most modern states, unfortunately.

Let us then consider a nation composed of two local communities, one of which we will call New York, and one of which we will call Mississippi. Average per capita incomes in New York we will assume are $10,000 per year and in Mississippi, $5000 per year. New Yorkers establish a welfare programme which guarantees that the income of individuals who are unemployed, etc. will not fall below $2500 per capita and the citizens of Mississippi, who have relatively exactly the same charitable instincts, set up a programme where the income will not fall below $1250 per capita.

The first thing to note is that it is clear that the citizens of New York are more charitable towards other citizens of New York than they are towards citizens of Mississippi. There is no legal or constitutional barrier preventing them from supplementing the Mississippi payments to the Mississippi poor by adding on their payments. Let us suppose that for the same budgetary cost they're now using for their $2500 payments they could pay enough to the people in Mississippi so that the poor in both states received $2000 per year per capita. There is no reason why this is not feasible, but we do not observe it.

Why not? The answer, I think, is simple and straightforward. Charitable impulses fall off rather rapidly as you move away from your current location. Those New Yorkers who think about the poor of Mississippi are apt either to feel that the other citizens of Mississippi should tax themselves more vigorously in order to subsidise them, or that other states than New York should be taxed to help the people in Mississippi.

I had, rather by accident, a rather striking example of this while interviewing a candidate for an assistant professor's job in my department. He was from New York and doing a doctoral dissertation on welfare payments to the poor. The theme of the doctoral dissertation was that we should have a national system rather than a set of state systems. The reason that he gave for this—obviously a rationalisation—was that we didn't want people migrating from state to state in terms of the size of their welfare payments. We want them migrating in terms of opportunities for jobs. Thus, a national system would eliminate one possible reason for people moving to places where they are not really needed.

I suggested that his native New York could deal with the problem by simply reducing their payments and he indignantly rejected this. I then pointed out that almost certainly a national system would pay everybody including the poor in New York less than New York was now paying them, and it was clear that he didn't want to talk about the matter further. Note that he was seeking a job and hence trying to make a good impression on me, but he was not capable of saying directly that he thought New York's payments were too high, granted the current institutional system.

In any event, the expectation with this kind of a system would be that a large number of the poor would move to New York. Indeed, people who could obtain jobs in Mississippi and who would prefer a Mississippi job to the Mississippi welfare payment might decide to go to New York because they prefer the New York welfare payment to the Mississippi job.

The solution to this problem, traditionally, has been simply to return the citizen of Mississippi who becomes unemployed in New York to Mississippi. In New England, in the 1820s and 1830s, for example, a recent immigrant into a local town who in the opinion of the supervisors was in danger of becoming a candidate for public charity would be told that he should return to his native town. If he chose not to, he would not be eligible for relief if he later needed it.[16] With this system, a wealthy community could offer higher payments to its poor than a poor community could without there being any tendency of people to migrate to the wealthy community in order to collect the payments.

In more recent years, the standard situation has been a little more humane. We are now wealthier and can now afford to give better treatment. Thus, a person who came from Mississippi and who shortly[17] after applied for relief would simply be given a one-way bus ticket back to Mississippi.

Interestingly enough, this system is today still maintained at international levels. The United States spends a good deal of time and effort trying to prevent non-Americans from benefiting from the American welfare scheme. They are either prohibited entry or physically deported.

This scheme permitted different communities to pay different amounts of support to their poor depending on local preferences. Presumably the wealthier communities paid more and the poorer communities paid less than would a national scheme.

The Supreme Court, not very long ago, in one of its more muddle-headed decisions ruled this unconstitutional. They said that all Americans have a constitutional right (nowhere specified in the constitution but nevertheless something we would on the whole like to have) to travel, and that denying them relief payments violated that right. I refer to this as muddle-headed. One of my reasons for this is that states are still permitted to prevent outsiders (i.e. immigrants) from earning a living. Suppose, for example, that I am an electrician living in Mississippi and New York has organised a licensing scheme for electricians controlled by the existing electricians who quite naturally don't like competition. The Supreme Court takes the view that I do not have a constitutional right to move to New York and practise my trade as an electrician, but I do have a constitutional right to go there and go on relief.

But regardless of the muddled nature of the Supreme Court's views, the current situation in the United States is that local governments cannot pay a higher than average benefit to the poor and confine that to people who have resided in the local area for some time. This does not mean that such aid cannot be given by the local governments and indeed it is a local function in the United States today. It does mean, however, that there are considerable difficulties for various local governments, particularly those that wish to be generous to their own citizens.

A return to the earlier system in which they returned the unemployed to their place of origin, would, in my opinion, be an improvement, but we now live in the computer age and a more sophisticated system is possible. The right to unemployment payments could, in a sense, be vested just like pensions. Suppose, for example, that I have been a citizen in Mississippi for 25 years and then move to New York where I am employed for one year before I become needful of government aid. I could be given 25/26th of my Mississippi payment and 1/26th of my New York payment either partly by the Mississippi government and partly by the New York government, or entirely by the New York government. This would be treating the charitable provisions as rather like an insurance policy supported by the taxpayer on the analogy of vested pension rights. We could call it vested unemployment insurance rights.

It might be argued that the base for such a scheme should be only years after the age of 18 or only years employed. It is also not necessary that the actuarial accounting be as simple as in the example above. Any good economist or actuary could work out several thousand variants on the basic idea, but there is no need to go through them now.

Thus, it seems to me that there is no obvious reason that aid to the poor should not be made locally, as indeed it was during most of the history of the United States. This requires, of course, that the upper-income citizens of the locality are not likely to move out because of the taxes to aid the poor. Granted what a small portion of the budget that aid to the poor is everywhere, however, that seems fairly secure. Further, as I have said before, helping the poor is something most of us want to do, and most of us do not have any great objection to paying moderate amounts of money to that end.

The centralisation of aid to the poor in the United States is a hangover from the Great Depression. The immense increase is the number of people to be helped put a severe strain on both private charity and local relief organisations. That they would like to be helped is obvious, but it's not obvious why the federal government stepped in. Probably that had something to do with the political mystique of the period.[18] As a general rule, emergencies frequently lead simply to reorganisation without much thought as to what that reorganisation is. We may be observing an example here.

The general theme of this chapter has been that it is not obviously impossible to get a good deal of income redistribution with local government organisation rather than national. It is true that transfers of large amounts of money away from the wealthy are difficult locally, but modest amounts can be transferred away. It is not obvious that our present system actually does transfer more than the modest amounts which could be obtained by state and local governments. Transfers back and forth within the middle class would be much harder, although not impossible, if carried out by state and local governments, but most economists would regard that as a decided advantage. Aid to the poor would work as well locally as at a national level; in fact it could be argued that it would work better. The amount of aid paid would vary from community to community in terms of local preferences and resources. Those who believe that all Americans should receive a particular minimum income which is higher than that which some of our communities would choose to pay,[19] may find this offensive. We should keep in mind, however, that a national system will not only raise the amount paid in the poorer communities, it will lower the amount paid in the wealthier communities.

All in all, it seems to me that the very simple straightforward line of reasoning which is so common among economists in this area is wrong. I say that even though I am one of the economists who has frequently used it. Most of our income redistribution could be done locally. The fact that transfers back and forth within the middle class would be harder locally than nationally is obviously an advantage. Those who feel that the upper-income group should be despoiled of more money than local government could undertake would be in favour of a national tax on the upper-income brackets. Granted how little we transfer away from these people now, however, such a tax would be quite an inconspicuous feature of our national revenue accounts.

It would appear that the United States had a better system on these grounds before 1930, when there was a graduated income tax on the upper brackets, than it has had since. The change was a by-product of the Great Depression, and, like many other things that came out of the Great Depression, it was a mistake.

NOTES

1. Mark Pauly, 'Income Distribution as a Local Public Good', *Journal of Public Economics*, vol. 2 (February 1973), pp. 35–58.
2. James M. Buchanan, 'Who Should Distribute What in a Federal System?', in *Redistribution Through Public Choice*, ed. H. Hochman and G. Peterson (New York: Columbia, 1974).
3. Chicago: University of Chicago Press, 1962.
4. Boston, The Hague, London: Kluwer-Nijhoff, 1983.
5. There is no doubt that the citizens are in a very bad condition and there's no doubt that the Ethiopian government is taking advantage of this opportunity to maximise a number of its domestic goals such as suppressing guerrilla warfare by its domestic opponents.
6. i.e. the second year of Elizabeth I, not Elizabeth II.
7. 'One-sixth of the population was in receipt of parish relief of one kind or another'. Gertrude Himmelfarb, *Manhattan Report*, vol. V, no. 1, p.3.
8. Stanley Lebergott, *Wealth and Want*, (Princeton, N.J.: University Press, 1975), the data below are drawn from his chapter 'A Century of Guaranteed Income in the US', 53–68.

9. I do not think that he was running a complete and total fast, however, since he seemed to have lived too long for that.
10. This is a little misleading for foreigners. The federal government permits the local government tax to be subtracted from the income upon which the federal government tax is calculated. Thus, the real effect of that state tax is less than its normal effect. It is nevertheless real.
11. There may be a certain small part of this which is financed by the taxes on the wealthy.
12. And in fact, on a proportional basis, do better.
13. This is an administrative matter, he could have the two payments given in one cheque.
14. This leads to underqualified personnel.
15. See my *Economics of Income Redistribution*, op. cit., chapters 7 and 8.
16. Samuel Colt, as a young man, came very close to receiving such a warning. Indeed, he would have had he not on the evening of the relevant meeting of the city council saved the life of the daughter of a prominent local man. He later married the girl and of course became one of the wealthiest men in New England. We can see, that the local government's judgement as to who was likely to become poor was decidedly defective.
17. I emphasise shortly.
18. In another fiscal crisis, the civil war, the federal government, by way of providing the states with quotas of enlistments that had to be met either by volunteers or by conscription, led the states to enact gigantic enlistment bonuses programmes. Thus, the fiscal difficulty of the federal government was in part taken care of by hiving off a large part of the payments to the soldiers in the federal army onto the states.
19. And who of course also believe that other human beings, non-Americans, should be given only trivial payments.

9 Aid in Kind

In many cases, instead of simply giving the poor money to spend as they wish, aid has taken the form of providing gifts in kind, usually with some provision by which the recipient may not resell. It is obvious that such provisions are not maximising from the standpoint of the recipient who would prefer cash. After all, if he wants whatever is provided in kind, he can purchase it on the open market.[1] Analysis of redistribution in kind by economists has, to an overwhelming extent, simply taken the form of pointing out that it is less beneficial to the recipient than direct cash payments. I will not quarrel with this point, but I nevertheless feel that redistribution in kind deserves more analysis. What analysis has been done on redistribution in kind normally begins by assuming that there is an altruist and a poor beneficiary and that the altruist is interested in the consumption by the beneficiary of only one good. The utility function of the altruist takes the form:

$$V_B = V(X_B, Y_B, Y_A)$$

while the utility function of the recipient takes the form:

$$V_A = V(X_A, Y_A)$$

As can be seen, the recipient is uninterested in the consumption of the altruist, and the altruist's interest with respect to the recipient concerns only one good of a two-good universe.

This is an incorrect representation of the situation. In practice, altruists are not simply interested in the consumption of one good by whomever they are attempting to benefit. The person who is strongly concerned about the housing of the poor would be most unhappy if they starved to death in mansions. What he is objecting to is the mix of goods which they consume. He thinks they consume the goods in improper proportions, but he does not concern himself solely with the consumption of one good.

Look at Figure 9.1. We show there a two-good X and Y, universe, and start with a budget constraint for the potential recipient of charity, I-I. Granted the indifference curves for the potential recipient, $IA_{1,2}$ he chooses to consume at 0. There is also in this world another person, Mr B, who is concerned about the well-being of Mr A. He feels A is both too poor and is expending his income improperly. His indifference curves for consumption of X and Y by A are shown by $IB_{1,2,3,4}$. He feels that given the income restraint I-I, A should be consuming the bundle Z instead of bundle 0. He could, of course, in some societies, simply order A to consume the

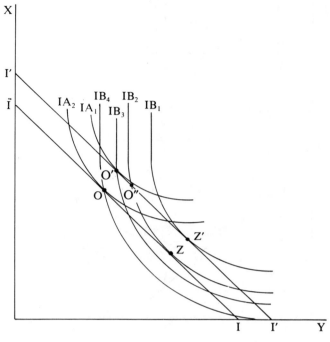

Figure 9.1

appropriate bundle and we will indeed discuss that situation below. For the moment, however, we will talk about circumstances in which he cannot simply order A to change his consumption.

Suppose then that a transfer is made to I so his new income constraint is I'-I'. Left to himself, I would choose 0', which from the standpoint of the altruist is better, but still not very good. The altruist would much prefer that he choose 0". Further, if the gift is made conditional upon his changing his consumption bundle to 0", A will indeed regard that as better than 0. In essence, he has been bribed but the bribe is conditional on his changing his consumption pattern.

The indifference curves in Figure 9.1 for B are his preferences for expenditures of A. They do not include any element of cost to him. Suppose, however, that we introduce a possibility of B making a gift to A. The gift is, of course, a cost to him. Under these circumstances, we can draw a new set of indifference curves for him as we do in Figure 9.2.[2] We show his preferences for various consumption bundles by A, granted that if A consumes more than I-I, the difference will have to be paid by B. Under these circumstances we would expect that the indifference curves would be

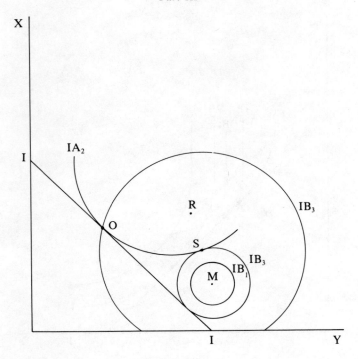

Figure 9.2

closed in the way that they are shown by $I_{1,2,3}$, on Figure 9.2. There would be an optimum for B which is shown by M. Reaching M, however, can only be by direct orders and not by bribery. The best that our altruist can do is to choose that point where his highest feasible indifference curve is tangent to the indifference curve of A at the *status quo* or S. Note that S is Pareto-optimal, and under the circumstances there is no change which will benefit both parties.

It is, of course, not necessary for us to seek this kind of tangency. It might be that the optimum of B for A's consumption, together with B's subsidy, would be a point which lies within the indifference curve for A which passed through the *status quo*, a point like R. In this circumstance he would simply provide the gift in kind at R without concerning himself about other parts of his indifference surface. Once again, this outcome is Pareto-optimal.

This assumes, of course, that it is possible for the altruist to provide the gift in a form which prevents A from retrading it and reaching some other location. For many governmental subsidies in kind this is fairly easy. For

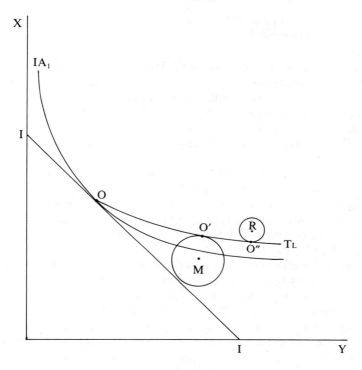

Figure 9.3

example, subsidised housing where housing is actually literally provided by
the government. In others, for example, food stamps, it is probably
possible but not quite so easy. In fact, the government has not made any
very serious effort to achieve that goal. Reselling raises quite complicated
issues which will be discussed below.

Meanwhile, let us turn to another form of subsidy which occurs when the
altruist, instead of providing a mixed bundle which is to him optimum,
subsidises the consumption of whatever good he thinks is ranked too low in
A's preference function.[3] The situation can be analysed by Figure
9.3. In this case the then poor person is consuming at 0 where his
indifference curve IA_1 is tangent to the budget constraint. If the altruist
begins to subsidise consumption of Y then the budget constraint will swing
out, pivoting on the point where I-I intersects the X axis. This will increase
A's consumption of good I as he adjusts to his continuing changing budget
constraint, and the line labelled T_L shows the locus of his consumption
bundle as the subsidy grows.

We have drawn in two different sets of indifference curves for the donor.

In one case the optimal is at M and he would try to select that subsidy which puts his highest possible indifference curve tangent to the purchase curve of I, ie. at 0'.

This is, of course, perfectly standard. The second possibility shown by R and the indifference curve drawn around it is somewhat more surprising. It is possible, but not likely, for the altruist in this case to have this kind of indifference curve and optimal relation to the performance curve because there is no way of guaranteeing by subsidy that the performance curve passes through the optimum. In any event, this would lead to 0'' as the outcome.

It should be noted that neither of these points is Pareto-optimal. This is simply because the donor has restricted himself to an inappropriate way of making his gift. If we assumed that this restriction is somehow a fact of nature or, alternatively, that the individual values this particular method so highly that he is willing to take inefficiency in other areas then 0' and 0'' would indeed be Pareto-optimal.

It may be sensible here to pause briefly and make a few remarks about Pareto-optimality in charitable transfers. In general, bargaining between the two parties is impossible except in so far as pure transfers of information may be helpful. The problem is that any sacrifice made by the donee in order to make the donor better off is equivalent to simply a different gift from the donor than the one he has chosen. Thus, if there is a point which is superior to the current donor choice of policy and gift, and which is favoured by the donee, the donor can always move to it without the donee's permission. Hence, bargaining cannot reach Pareto-optimal locations.

When the donor makes his gift in kind in order to change the consumption of the donee, it is sometimes possible for the donee to resell the goods and use the money obtained to purchase other goods. This situation is analysed with the aid of Figure 9.4.

As is customary, we show the initial income constraint, I-I, and two indifference curves for the recipient. We assume that the donee makes a gift to G which together with a cost he charges puts the donee initially at G. Since this is superior to 0 where he started, he will agree to go along with it. He can now, however, sell the product Y to whatever extent he wishes. He will not, however, when selling it, receive the same price that he would have paid if he were buying it because the market functions like most markets do. Thus, he faces the line G-0' as his sale line and sells enough of product Y to move to 0' which in his view is superior to both 0 and G.

It would be possible to draw a set of such reactions to various gifts from the donor and then the donor could choose which reaction was highest on his indifference curve and make the gift which led to that. Note the complexity of this problem, however. The donor has to make guesses as to

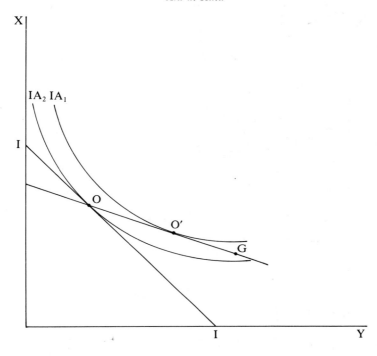

Figure 9.4

how much it will cost him in gift at G to get the recipient to 0'. This involves not only a knowledge of how much of the stuff 0' will sell, but also a rather complex geometry. I have not chosen to attempt to present this on the diagram, but I suspect that this difficulty may be one of the reasons why there are fairly extensive efforts to prevent donees from reselling various gifts in kind which they receive. In the case of food stamps, these efforts have not been either very heavily enforced or very successful, but in the case of subsidised housing they are usually applied pretty strictly. The difference may reflect the differential difficulties of policing the two areas. Note that if we were capable of preventing the individual from reselling, then the donor could achieve a Pareto-optimal point. If he cannot prevent resale then the outcome will not be Pareto-optimal.

So far I have talked solely about direct charitable payments in which the charitably-inclined person has no power to compel the recipient of his charity to do anything, he must bribe him. It is true that in the real world we observe that there is a good deal of use of the police power to change other people's consumption patterns. For example, altruistically-inclined Mr B may think it is bad for Mr A to consume cocaine, copies of *Penthouse*, or the

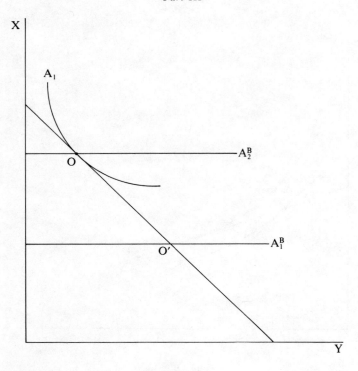

Figure 9.5

services of a gambling casino. One way of dealing with this is simply to make it illegal. Further, in general, desires of this sort are not directly connected with efforts to benefit A by other means, although as we shall see in a moment, sometimes they are.

This situation is shown very simply on Figure 9.5. Assume that commodity X is a commodity which the individual is not supposed to consume, and that he is currently consuming it at level 0. Our altruist or meddler, depending on what the readers of this paper prefer, would like to have him consume less and is willing to use police power to do so. He has a set of indifference 'curves' such as $A_1^B A_2^B$. Once again pushing A downward on this table consumes resources and hence his optimal situation is not the horizontal axis but some point slightly off the horizontal axis where the expenditure on police force resources exactly balances his disutility from observing A consuming X on Figure 9.5 this is 0′ and, once again, this is a Pareto-optimal point because no bargain between the two parties is possible as long as B controls the police force and has preferences we have specified.

Strictly speaking, this analysis has little to do with charitable provision, but as a matter of practical fact a great many people seem to think that if we are making charitable provisions for someone or other, we should have further control over his expenditures. We don't want him to drink it up, gamble it away, or use it entirely to consume drugs. Thus, a libertarian who would be totally unwilling to enforce laws against drug consumption on the population in general may nevertheless feel that an object of charity can reasonably be required not to consume drugs as a condition of receiving his charity. Granted that the recipient of the charity can always turn down the charitable offer, however, it would not be possible to push A down below the indifference curve I_1 at which he can attain the monies through his own efforts. All that really can be done in this case is that the police power can be augmented with respect to people on charity so that they have less possibility of cheating than does the ordinary citizen.

NOTES

1. It might be that the government is capable of providing the gift in kind at a lower cost than its market provision. Under these circumstances, a gift in kind could be argued for as benefiting the recipient. So far as I know there are no examples of this in current redistribution programmes.
2. In essence we have moved to a three-dimensional diagram in which expenditure by the altruist is the third dimension. Figure 9.1 is the base plane of this diagram and Figure 9.2 a plane cutting the figure at an angle so that the altruist's expenditure rises to the right.
3. He could, of course, tax the other good, the one in which he wishes to have the volume reduced, but we are assuming that he is attempting to raise A's total consumption. The mix of a tax on one good consumed by the aided person and a subsidy on the other which ends with A better off is, as far as we know, not used in the real world and is rather complicated and hence we shall not discuss it here.

10 Demand Revealing, Transfers, and Rent Seeking[1]

Several new and radical methods of aggregating preferences, i.e, voting, have been proposed essentially by mathematically inclined economists in recent years. One of these, 'Demand Revealing' is in my opinion, far superior to the others or for that matter for our current methods.[2] This system involves the 'Clarke Tax', a (usually miniscule) tax on the voter which has the bizarre characteristic of improving the quality of the vote.

Let us begin with a simple situation, one group of people, let us say the farmers, wish, via the government, to obtain transfers from another group, let us say all taxpayers. This is, of course, characteristic of substantially every modern democratic country.[3] Figure 10.1 shows the net social cost of the transfer (per dollar transferred) by the line CC, and the benefit the farmers receive by the line BB. It is assumed that the demand by the farmers for their transfer is literally its dollar value. This seems reasonable.

Line BB, or the social benefit of retransfer, must of necessity lie below line CC if there is any administrative cost of making the transfer at all. Since there always is, the demand-revealing process which would sum the demand of the farmers, together with a zero demand of the non-farmers for this particular procedure, would show its appropriate size as zero.[4]

The Clarke tax here is probably non-existent. The reason for this is that it seems likely in any realistic case that the costs of administering a transfer and hence the distance between line CC and BB would be greater than the taxes paid by any individual taxpayer. Under these circumstances the removal of any individual, for the purpose of computing the Clarke tax, would make no change in the outcome, and hence there would be no Clarke tax. If this were not true, that is some individuals' tax burden were larger than the entire cost of administering the transfer, then the outcome is indeed strange. No transfer would be made to the farmers, but every taxpayer whose potential tax burden exceeded the administrative cost would pay a Clarke tax equivalent to the amount that he would have paid had the transfer proposed by the farmers gone through. In theory, although not probably in any realistic case, the sum of these Clarke taxes paid by the various objecting taxpayers could be equal to the total transfer which would otherwise have been made. The farmers would not receive any benefit from this, however, and it seems very dubious that they would even propose the transfer unless we were in a society with a really ferocious class struggle.

Farm aid programmes frequently, however, take the form of administra-

Figure 10.1

tive rules which implicitly transfer resources from the general citizenry to the farmers. The American system, for example, consists both of a tax subsidy and a price support programme.[5] There is, in so far as it is a simple administrative rule, no direct tax cost.

Such administrative regulations can be dealt with by the expedients shown on Figure 10.2. The individuals are permitted to indicate the loss that they receive through the administrative rules. Thus, line BB is the benefit the farmers receive, line 0 is of course zero, and the victims suffer the cost shown by line CC. When we add these lines together, we get the dashed line marked NN which is below zero and hence, once again, there is no programme. This figure could be made a little more complicated by drawing another line which shows the administrative cost slightly above the zero line. Here again, rent seeking is eliminated.

Once again, there is at least a theoretical chance of significant Clarke taxes falling on the potential victims, but there would be no transfer.

The general policy of permitting people to cast such negative votes through the demand-revealing process seems to be a desirable one. After all we can be damaged by things other than taxes. The alternative, of course, would be to compute the implicit tax involved, but that would require a government bureaucracy making decisions as to how much things cost

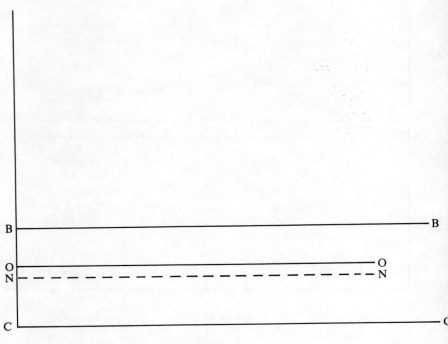

Figure 10.2

people, and it's better to let the people make the decisions themselves.

There would, however, be a small problem of education here. One can readily understand an individual who objects to a particular government policy solely because it will cost him some tax money, mistakenly feeling that he should cast a negative vote instead of a zero vote. This would be unwise because it increases his chances of paying a Clarke tax. There is, of course, no reason why the demand-revealing system could not be converted so that the tax always showed itself as a negative amount below zero, but the system would be less elegant.

So far we have been dealing with pure transfers in which the victim is injured and the beneficiaries gain less than the injury. Most economists do not like such transfers, but there are some cases in which at least some economists would be in favour of such a transfer. If the majority of the voters wish to tax a particular minority—millionaires or Jews, to take two groups of which this apparently was true in certain countries in recent times—then the result of the demand-revealing process would be radically different from that of majority voting. There is, of course, no reason why, if we have two different ways of making decisions, one of them majority voting, and the other the demand-revealing process,[6] they should lead to the same conclusion always. The decision between them must be made on extrinsic grounds.

Let us now turn to cases in which there is a genuine public good involved. In Figure 10.3, we show the situation which would arise if it were proposed to put a bridge across part of the Puget Sound, with A and B being people who would benefit from that bridge, and C being a resident in New York who never intends to visit the Far West. I assume that A and B have exactly identical demands for the bridge, for simplicity. Their demands are then shown by the line A and B. The man living in New York, C, has a zero demand, and this is shown by the horizontal axis. The sum of the three is shown by A+B+C and is, of course, identical to the line which could be shown A+B. A socially-optimum amount of bridge building is 0. If we use Lindahl pricing, and one of the advantages of the demand-revealing process is that it permits close approximation of Lindahl pricing,[7] the cost of the bridge would be evenly split between A and B: C would pay nothing. Indeed, with Lindahl pricing, simple majority voting, which in this case

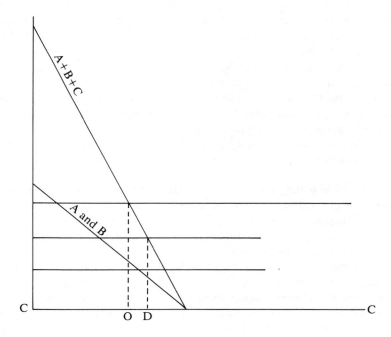

Figure 10.3

might well be unanimous, would show as much bridge purchased as the demand-revealing process.

If we assume that A and B, making up the majority, would like to exploit C a bit, and hence decide that the cost of the bridge should be evenly divided between the three of them, then they would choose to purchase D bridge. If they decided to use their majority to exploit him even further, and put the entire cost of the bridge on him, they would of course buy out to the point where their two demand curves reached the horizontal axis.

Here again, majority voting, with the majority also permitted to vote on the tax, leads to an outcome which is different from the demand-revealing process. I have difficulty believing that there will be many economists who, in this particular case, prefer the majority voting outcome.

I have not drawn in the mechanism for determining the Clarke tax, because in real-world situations there are many more voters. The total size of the Clarke tax shrinks as the number of voters rises, and in fact becomes very small eventually. It will always be larger than it would be, however, if C's interests were not strictly opposed to A's and B's.

There is another case in which the interests of the two parties are opposed, but where there is at least some desire to produce the good on the part of all of them. Suppose A and B are well off, and C is poor. A and B have a demand for aid to C as shown by the line A and B in Figure 10.4. C's demand is, of course, the line CC showing what he will receive. Adding the two well-off demands, we get the line A + B, and 0 shows what could be argued was the social optimum. C, however, has a demand for the transfer which is exactly the same as the transfer itself. If we add C to A + B, we get the line A + B + C, which I have shown falling below the cost line at 0' on the theory once again that there is at least some administrative cost. It can easily be argued 0' is the social optimum.

Note that, in this case, a simple majority vote with A and B splitting the cost of the transfer between them, which is of course the Lindahl tax price, would generate 0. This is, however, merely an artefact of this particular example. With a larger number of voters, and the poor making up a minority of the voters, the demand-revealing process would normally lead to more redistribution than simple majority voting. The exact amount would, of course, depend upon whether the poor did or did not vote.

The problem here, as can be seen, is one of the franchise. If we look at the real world, we find that sometimes beneficiaries of charitable activities are permitted to vote and sometimes not. At the moment, the ones who are not permitted to vote are mainly those foreigners to whom we give aid, but historically it has not been particularly uncommon for domestic recipients of charity being automatically deprived of their vote. Dicey, in fact, was quite upset when England, breaking a precedent, provided that certain old age pensioners should retain the vote while receiving their pensions.[8] If you

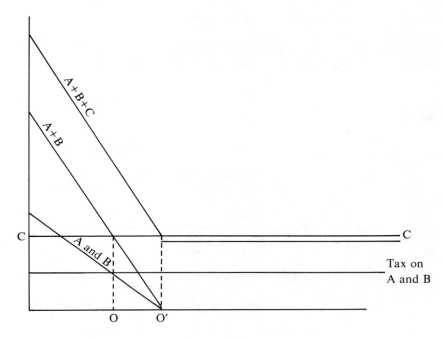

Figure 10.4

look at the real world, it is not obvious that it makes much difference whether the poor are permitted to vote or not. *A priori*, one would assume that the poor would do better when they vote on the amount they will receive. What little empirical evidence we have, however, seems to indicate it makes little difference.[9] In any event, if the recipients of charity are not permitted to contribute their vote, the demand-revealing process should transfer to them somewhat more than they would obtain under simple majority vote. If they are permitted to cast their vote, it should transfer more.

In sum, my initial feeling that the demand-revealing process would not work very well in transfer cases turns out to be largely misplaced. The Clarke tax prevents a number of transfers where the transfer itself is not welfare-enhancing, and in other cases where it doesn't actually prevent such transfers, it as least reduces them. In those cases where the transfers are welfare-enhancing—that is, charitable transfers where the donors obtain at least some benefit from the charity—the demand-revealing process will lead to somewhat more transfers than simple majority vote, and quite possibly considerably more. It depends on franchise.

Thus, what I think has been the most important argument against demand revealing, is, in actuality, a result of comparing the demand revealing with perfection. When you compare it with other realistic voting methods, it works better in transfers as well as in other areas.

NOTES

1. The author benefited from very helpful comments by T. Nicholas Tideman and Ed Clarke.
2. For a simple explanation see, 'A New and Superior Process for Making Social Decisions', T. Nicholas Tideman and Gordon Tullock, *Journal of Political Economy 84*, (October 1976) pp. 225–73.
3. In this example, and in all others in this chapter, we will assume that the amount is a continuous variable. Adjustment of the models to deal with discontinuous outcomes is simple.
4. This same result can be obtained by two other ways. We could assume that the transfer is intrinsically inefficient as all farm transfer programmes in fact are, with the result that line BB lies much further below CC than it does in Figure 8.1. Secondly, we could assume (probably correctly) that the donors of this gift not only do not want to pay their taxes at the value of those taxes, but actually were somewhat annoyed by the whole procedure. Under these circumstances their demand curve, instead of lying along the horizontal axis, would lie somewhat below it and when we summed the demand curves, line BB would be once again moved down.
5. The system is even more complicated than that. The bulk of the tax subsidy is used to fund the price support programme.
6. Or any other way which insures that only Pareto-optimal decisions are made.
7. See T. Nicholas Tideman and Gordon Tullock, 'A New and Superior Process for Making Social Decisions', *Journal of Political Economy 84* (October 1976) pp. 225–73.
8. A.V. Dicey, *Law and Public Opinion in England* (London: Macmillan, 1962), p. xxxv.
9. This subject is discussed at great length in my, *The Economics of Income Redistribution* (Boston: Kluwer-Nijhoff, 1983).

Part IV
What to Redistribute

11 Giving Justice*

In recent years, the practice of providing 'free' defence lawyers at government expense has steadily grown. It is obvious that resources are not unlimited, and hence the defendant cannot have as many lawyers, or as good lawyers, or as many appeals as he wishes provided by the government. There is no real pretence that the public defender system gives the defendant a free hand in the government kitty to hire legal advice. There must be some rationing device. In one way or another, the public defender must decide how much of his energy will be devoted to each of his cases. If the public defender's office is large, some senior official will decide which defendant gets which lawyer, a decision which may have a very great effect on the outcome. Once assigned, the lawyers must decide whether they are going to accept the prosecution's plea-bargaining offer or go to trial, which is a major resource decision.

I have been unable to find any serious discussion of the way these decisions are made.[1] The literature more or less implies that the public defender behaves like a private lawyer, but this is absurd. The private lawyer's decision as to the size of the resource commitment is not his own; it is made by his client. He merely makes the decision as to how a given bundle of resources will be allocated during the trial. Presumably, he is willing to ask for as many appeals, rehearings, etc. as his client will pay for. If legal services are free, as they are for a person with a public defender, obviously the beneficiary of those services will want an infinite quantity; and, equally obviously, this cannot be provided. In this case, there then must be a decision as to how much resources will be given to an individual defendant. Equation (11.1) shows the decision process undertaken by the man making his decision.

$$R_D = F(E, R_G) \qquad (11.1)$$

He should take into account the evidence (E) and his estimate of the resources which will be invested by the prosecution (R_G). He will probably have good information on the latter variable. The public defender and his prosecutors are very commonly housed in the same building, and they have fairly continuous contact. It should be noted that the decision as to the resources which will be assigned to the defence of a given person will no doubt affect the resources assigned by the prosecuting attorney, and vice

*First published in *Trials on Trial* (New York: Columbia University Press, 1980), pp. 139–41, 144–7, 112–18.

145

versa. If, for example, the public defender decides to assign his best man to a given case, the prosecuting lawyer may well do the same. Further, if the case is subject to a fairly large resource commitment in the form of careful preparation by one of the two sides, the other is apt to increase resources also.

In the case of the public defender, there are some special issues that do not arise with the private lawyer. First, suppose the public defender feels that the prosecution's offer of a plea bargain is in the best interest of his client, but his client rejects it.[2] Let us further assume (which might well be true) that he is convinced that the reason his client rejects it is simple stupidity. Suppose, for example, that the public defender feels that he has about a one in four chance of winning the case if it goes to trial, and that the sentence normally administered in such cases is five years. The prosecutor, however, has expressed willingness to accept a guilty plea under circumstances in which the defendant will get only six months. Actually defending the case in court will not only consume government resources but may make the defendant worse off.

Under current law, the defendant's government-paid lawyer cannot force his client not to go to trial.[3] Suppose, however, that the prosecutor comes to him with a proposal: if the public defender will agree not to push his case very hard, with the result that the prosecution's success is certain, the prosecutor will see to it that the sentence is not more than nine months. It clearly would be in the best interests of the client for the government-appointed defence lawyer to accept this deal, but it is not obvious to me that this is what our present rules say should happen.[4]

In practice, I imagine the matter is not of much significance, because I presume that when the government-appointed defence lawyer goes to his client with a bargain he thinks is advantageous,[5] the client really has no choice. For example, the public defender may subtly make it clear to the client that he is going to get a very poor defence if he chooses to go to trial. I have no evidence that this is so; it simply seems to me a reasonable outcome. In any event, I have been unable to find any clear discussion of the way in which public defenders are supposed to allocate their resources.

The second special problem with respect to the public defender concerns the guilty defendant. The lawyer is supposed to defend a client even if he thinks he is guilty. This is indeed the reason why defence lawyers are prohibited from making statements in court as to their personal beliefs regarding their client's innocence.[6] But should a public defender vigorously defend a man whom he knows to be guilty?

Suppose, for example, that A robbed a bank and is now on trial for the robbery. He has a public defender. There is an eyewitness prepared to identify A as a participant in the robbery; but A, after all, was also there, had a better vantage point of the robbery than the eyewitness, and since he was engaged in his normal profession was not as excited as the eyewitness. In consequence, he knows that the eyewitness has made several mistakes on some details of his testimony. It is obvious that if his lawyer concentrates on these mistakes in his cross-examination, he may be able to reduce gravely the credibility of the witness.

But can the bank robber tell his lawyer that he was in fact guilty and, therefore, has this special information which will be of use in his trial? In the case of a privately-hired lawyer, there is no problem. The defendant informs the lawyer, who makes use of the information.[7] In the case of a public defender, however, it would seem that this government official should have an interest in a correct outcome. The prosecuting attorney, after all, is supposed to refrain from bringing cases if he believes the defendant is innocent, no matter what the evidence is; and, on parallel grounds, it would seem that the public defender should be unwilling to defend if he believes the defendant is guilty.

This is clearly *not* the law, but there is still the issue of the situation which arises when the defence is certain the defendant is guilty because the defendant has told him so in the course of assisting in the preparation of his defence. Even more significant in this case, private lawyers sometimes will devote a good deal of time to the preparation of their client for his own testimony. Can a public defender assist his client, whom he knows to be guilty, in preparing perjured testimony? The only suggestion I have heard about this particular problem is an oral one: an attorney told me that a public defender should not participate in perjury, and therefore he would not put the defendant on the stand if he knew the defendant was going to perjure himself. Since the defendant can get on the stand by himself if he wishes, this is not very helpful.

Note that the problem here is the mystique of adversary proceedings, not anything of greater importance. Presumably, we wish to have guilty people convicted. A legal rule which makes it necessary for guilty people to conceal their crimes—not only from the court but also from their own lawyer—would surely increase the likelihood of guilty people being convicted without injuring innocent people. However, this is *not* the Anglo-Saxon rule. Unfortunately, I am unable to find out what the Anglo-Saxon rule is. I find that if I discuss the subject with lawyers, most of them begin by giving me a very definite statement on one side or the other side. Some of them, the more clever ones, change the subject quickly.

Leaving this mystery aside, the decision that the government will provide a defence lawyer for some defendants seems to be based on the assumption that the provision of a prosecuting lawyer is somehow a fact of nature. In fact it is not, and there is no reason why a court has to have either a prosecutor or a defence lawyer present. Even if we do not want completely to abolish the lawyers on both sides, it would still be possible to reduce their influence.

Suppose that we have a court system in which the government is in the habit of providing prosecuting lawyers. Some of the defendants appearing before this court cannot afford defence lawyers. It is now suggested that the government provide defence lawyers for these defendants. There is another possibility, which is to do away with the prosecuting lawyer or, in any event, to reduce sharply his allotment. Indeed, for example, one could take whatever resources were previously used for the prosecuting lawyer in the case and divide them evenly between a prosecuting and a defence lawyer.

So far as I know, this has never been seriously suggested. I believe the reason is simply that almost all of the advice we ever receive on such issues comes from lawyers, and they have much to gain by increasing the demand for their own services.[8] Since judges, members of the bar, and most commentators on legal matters are all lawyers, as are mainly legislators, their strong material motives for expansion of the demand for legal services is obvious. Unfortunately, it has not been obvious to most people making policy decisions in this area, in so far as these people are not themselves lawyers.

Even the general counsel of General Motors would be in favour of government provision of free lawyers for anyone who wishes to sue General Motors. It is in his interest to have such counsel provided, although it might not be in his interest to say so openly within the hearing of his employers. If there are more suits brought against General Motors, the legal division will be expanded, and its head will probably find himself with a higher salary, larger office, etc. As a general rule, in making decisions as to the governmental allocation of resources for hiring lawyers, the one group that is most influential are the lawyers themselves. It is not surprising that we find an increasing share of our resources being spent in litigation.

So far as I know, the only argument against the kind of reduction of legal resources I have recommended above is one of accuracy. It is alleged that as resources are increased on both sides of a case, the probable accuracy of the outcome increases. I believe that this is true, although no doubt the increase is very slow. A doubling of the fees to the lawyers on both sides surely does not double accuracy.

Granted, however, that accuracy can be increased by increasing the resources on both sides, this is only certain if the resources are increased proportionately. If the resources on one side are increased more than those on the other, then the increase might contribute to inaccuracy. Suppose, for example, that there is some trial procedure to which the prosecution would contribute resources equivalent to, let us say, $1000 if there is no public defender. If a public defender is appointed, the public defender would normally contribute resources worth $1500, and the prosecution, raising its bid because of the existence of a public defender, goes to $2000. Assume that this is the allocation of resources which—granted the fact that we do not purchase infinite accuracy because accuracy costs resources—is optimal for this society. Lowering the resources to $1000 for the prosecution and $750 for the public defender could leave the same conditional probability but decrease accuracy.

Leaving the conditional probability unchanged while decreasing accuracy seems paradoxical, but this is, I think, the best way to describe a rather odd situation. In order to explain it, I have made up a set of probability matrices. Note that the specific numbers on these matrices were selected for the purpose of making a mathematical point with the minimum complication. A more realistic matrix would not have the neat straight-line characteristics of the ones shown here, but it would still be possible to make the same point. Figure 11.1 shows the situation in which we have a person accused of a crime. As outsiders, we think there is an even chance that he is guilty or innocent, and we happen to know that this court is a very simple court in which all decisions are made by flipping a coin. There are four possibilities: the court can convict a guilty man, acquit a guilty man, convict an innocent man, or acquit an innocent man. Granted there is a 50:50 chance of the defendant being innocent or guilty, and the court flips coins, there is a one in four chance for each of these possibilities, as shown in Figure 11.1a. Note, however, the 50:50 break between convictions and acquittals.

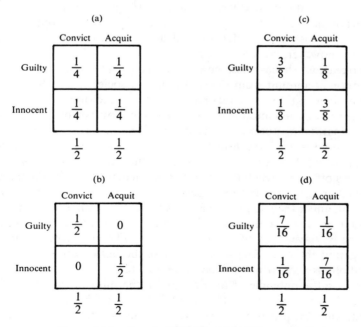

Figure 11.1 Equal probability with different accuracy.

In Figure 11.1b, we show the situation in a court which has divine guidance and therefore never makes mistakes. All of the decisions are either to convict the guilty (one-half of the decisions with a 50:50 probability of guilty), or to acquit the innocent (the other half). Note that the probability of conviction or acquittal, however, remains one-half on either side. From the standpoint of the person on trial, however, these situations are radically different. He is, of course, the only person in the courtroom who knows for certain whether he is guilty or innocent, and hence from his standpoint the probability of conviction in Figure 11.1b is either 1 or 0. For the outsider, however, it is one-half/one-half. Figure 11.1c and Figure 11.1d show more realistic situations, in which the court is either accurate three times out of four, as in 11.1c, or seven times out of eight, as in 11.1d. Both provide conditional probabilities of one-half from the standpoint of the outsider. But the conditional probabilities are three-fourths/one-fourth and seven-eighths/one-eighth for the defendant, who starts with knowledge of his innocence or guilt. The more resources we invest in a court, the more accurate it will become; and hence with increased resources, we move from 11.1a through 11.1c and 11.1d, and perhaps to some approximation of 11.1b.

Since accuracy is not infinitely desirable we will not make any serious effort to proceed to 11.1b. Indeed, in the type of adversary procedure we are now talking about, we will reach an equilibrium between the two parties far short of that which would prevail if the parties were investing their own funds. If we wish to consider a social decision on one or both parties' resources, however, the matter is much more difficult. Indeed, there seems to be no reason to believe that the amount that private parties would put up is the optimal amount from the standpoint of society as a whole.

The problem is that optimality requires that the decision on resources for both the prosecution and the defence be made simultaneously, instead of by two separate institutions. Currently, we have the prosecution deciding whether to go to trial and how many resources will be committed to the trial. There is, then, another decision on the same facts by the public defender's office, in which they decide not whether they will take the case, but whether they will try to impose a negotiated settlement upon the defendant, and if they do go to trial, how large the resource investment will be. There is, then, a third investigation—i.e. the formal trial process itself—so we have three different government officials involved, each one investigating the case. The first two make the basic decisions as to the amount of resources which will be committed to the case, which surely has an effect on the outcome of the decision in the third process.[9]

Granted that we have two different officials making the decisions, one on each side, then the prospect of error is great. Suppose, for example, that the prosecution has decided to invest $2000, but the public defender's office decides that $1250 would be adquate for the defence. This not only lowers the accuracy, but it also moves the centre of distribution—it makes the likelihood of conviction of the defendant greater than it would have been under the $1000–$750 allocation for resources.

So far as I know, my suggestion that we lower the resources given to the prosecuting attorney instead of providing a public defender has never been canvassed before. There does not seem to have been very much careful thought given to the problem of providing public defenders, etc. I incline to the view that the reason for this is simply that it is contrary to the best interests of the attorneys, as a class, to consider such matters. They also normally, as a result of their education, are not trained to consider it, and the decisions are, in our society, heavily influenced by them. Thus, they are in a position where they can use public funds for the purpose *both* of increasing their incomes and increasing the respect accorded them in the community, because these cartel-like activities are thought to be highly moral. There is no reason to believe that our actual system is optimal or that it even aims at optimality. It seems to be based instead on the idea of 'fairness', with 'fairness' always obtained by an increase in resource allocation rather than by a reduction.

The only argument for this kind of increase in resources would appear to be increasing accuracy: we should have enough resources present to provide the optimal balance between cost and error. In order to have this trade-off, it is necessary not only that the total resources be optimal but that their division between the two parties (indeed, between the two parties and the decision-maker) be optimal. It seems hard to believe that our present institutions even make any effort to attain this optimality.

However, there are no doubt people who argue that our present criminal justice system does seek, and does achieve, optimality. If it is optimal, and I gravely doubt it, then it most certainly would be true that those suits in which the parties themselves provide the resources for both sides would not be optimal. Thus, arguments for either subsidising or taxing the provision of legal services in private litigation would also appear to be sound. Basically, however, the problem is that there has been little scientific investigation. Vague ideas of 'fairness', together with the self-interest of lawyers in expanding the resources involved in litigation, seem to have been the main drives. It should be possible to do better.

CIVIL LITIGATION

Sometimes one or the other party to a potential private law suit is too poor to be able to afford a lawyer. In recent times, there has been a movement to provide legal assistance to such people. In general, we do not want the taxpayers to take a partisan role.[10] We would like to have the judicial system, as a whole, reach relatively impartial conclusions. Thus, if we decide to subsidise someone's legal fees, we would prefer that this only be done where it is more likely to lead to a just conclusion than not. It is not at all obvious that any of the existing set of institutions under which the government pays one side's legal fees have this characteristic; but let me take them up one at a time.

Suppose someone comes to one of the new government-financed neighbourhood law centres in a poor district and asks for legal aid in getting a divorce. If the divorce is contested, the other party might also want legal aid, but let us (for the time being) confine ourselves to cases in which only one side is to be given legal assistance.

Success in this particular litigation will, once again, be partially determined by the resources put up by the plaintiff and by the government lawyer, on the one hand, and by the defendant on the other. Since I am assuming that the government helps only one side, this means that the defence must pay his entire cost himself.[11]

Once again, the plaintiff is going to use very few of his own resources in court; the bulk of the costs will be borne by the government. The government, however, presumably does not wish to allocate infinite resources to helping people win cases. In practice, these neighbourhood law centres have resources which are distinctly limited, considering the demand, and they must decide which cases they will take, and how much energy they will put into them, in terms of inability to take other cases or the necessity of skimping on cases.

Obviously the government attorney must undertake some kind of an investigation to determine whether or not to undertake this particular case. The possibility of simply taking cases as they come in and then putting maximum resources behind the first few is too foolish to give any serious consideration. Another possibility is that of appropriating enough money so that all cases anyone wishes to be brought *can* be brought, and maximum resources can be applied to each one. But this is politically implausible.

Thus, there is a restriction on the resources, and some decision must be made as to how these resources are to be used. One hopes that the lawyers look into the matter and select the 'best' cases. Since they are using the taxpayers' money, one would indeed hope that they only accept cases in which they feel their client is 'in the right'. In these cases where they feel doubtful about the rightness of their client's case, their investment of resources may lower accuracy. Thus, in general, they should aid only those cases which they think are right.

This is particulary important, since on my present set of assumptions, the government is not going to pay the other side's lawyer's fee, and hence the other side must either face a trial without legal advice (which is costly) or acquire an lawyer on his own. Thus, the lawyer, in deciding to take a contested divorce case, is not only deciding how some government resources should be allocated,[12] he is also—even before any court proceedings have begun—inflicting heavy costs on a third party. One hopes that he only does this in those cases in which he is confident that he is correct. Indeed, many people accuse the legal aid lawyers of selecting cases not in terms of the convenience of the client but in an effort to establish precedents for future cases. This policy is particularly hard on the potential defendants, who are compelled to invest resources not so much to defend themselves as to defend a category of other people—people in their same situation—from the establishment of an unfavourable precedent.

Let us now consider the situation that would occur if the government is asked to subsidise *both* sides. For simplicity, let me return to the case in which someone approaches the legal aid office for a divorce, and assume that the other partner to the marriage also approaches the legal aid office seeking assistance in defending the case. If legal assistance is given, then the outcome will be determined by the set of equations below (11.2).

$$P_v = \frac{P+G_1}{P+G_1+G_2+D} \, M - P$$

$$G_1v = \frac{P+G_1}{P+G_1+G_2+D} \, M - G_1$$

$$G_2v = \frac{D+G_2}{P+G_1+G_2+D} \, M - G_2$$

$$D_v = \frac{D+G_2}{P+G_1+G_2+D} \, M - D \tag{11.2}$$

P_v indicates pay-off of the plaintiff winning and D_v of the defendant winning. G_1v is the pay-off of the particular government lawyer on the side of the plaintiff winning and G_2v is the pay-off of the lawyer on the side of the defendant winning. P and D are respectively the resources invested in the trial by the plaintiff and defendant, and since they are poor these will be small numbers. G_1 and G_2 represent the amount invested by the government in preparing the plaintiff's and defendant's case. M is whatever is the issue in the case.

The lawyers on the two sides, both employees of the legal aid office, would each obtain satisfaction from having his side win, but in other respects their situations are identical. The bulk of the resources would come from the legal aid office and not from the two parties; hence, G_1 and G_2 would be fairly large and P and D would be small.

Of course, this assumes that the case is actually litigated. If I were in charge of the legal aid office, or if the people who were in charge of it considered my well-being as a taxpayer, the result of this visit to the office by both parties would be an investigation of the issue, a decision as to the merits of the case, and a suggestion to the two parties that they accept that decision. If either of them refused, then legal assistance should be provided only to the other party. I am not at all convinced, however, that this particular prescription will be that of the reader. In any event, I have never seen it proposed before, so let us look at the alternatives.

To make matters simple, let us assume that the divorce itself is not contested but the custody of a child is at issue. The husband first approaches the legal aid office and requests assistance in obtaining the divorce and custody of the child. Without legal assistance, he would have only a 10 per cent chance of getting custody; if the legal aid office decides to assist him, he has a 40 per cent chance of getting custody of the child. Now his wife approaches the legal aid office and asks them to represent her. Let us assume here that as a result of their dual representation, the odds for the wife getting custody of the child are 85 per cent and for the husband 15 per cent.[13]

Under these circumstances, should the legal aid office undertake the representation of the wife also? The first thing to be said the moment one begins dealing with these problems is that representation is not of zero value. In this case, since the parties are investing no resources to speak of, and indeed are unable to invest any resources to speak of, the government must invest the resources for both sides, and clearly each party would like to have an infinite amount of resources on his side. This cannot be provided, and hence the government must make a decision as to how much it should invest on each side. I can see no way to do this without a considerable degree of arbitrariness; but, in any event, let us assume that some kind of decision is made.

If the government decides to provide legal assistance to the wife as well as to the husband, they should increase their legal assistance to the husband. The amount of legal assistance which is appropriate in dealing with someone who will have to handle their own case is considerably less than the amount appropriate in dealing with someone who will be represented by a lawyer. Thus, the decision to represent the wife not only involves a direct expenditure, but it also involves an increase in the amount of money spent representing the husband.

So far as I know, there is no way to determine the optimal amount of resources to be introduced into the litigation process under these circumstances. An inquiry into what private parties would do under the same circumstances is not helpful, because the income of private parties is one of the variables in their determination of how much resources they will invest in a divorce action: hence, one would have to decide what income one is going to allot to these impecunious customers of the legal aid office in making one's calculation.

Let us suppose that it is decided to invest $500 in representing the wife and $750 in representing the husband; this will, as we said before, provide an 85 per cent chance that the wife will obtain custody of the child and a 15 per cent chance for the husband. It is immediately obvious that we could obtain this 15 per cent chance for the husband and the 85 per cent chance for the wife in a much more economical way. Assume that if we were supporting the husband only, not the wife, it would only cost $100 to improve his chances from 10 per cent to 40 per cent. Instead of giving that $100, we could give him, let us say, $25 in legal assistance, thus moving his probability not from 10 to 40 per cent but only from 10 to 15 per cent. The wife would receive no assistance under this plan. Thus, we would have a net expenditure of $25 to purchase the same present discounted value of the outcome for the two parties as can be obtained with $1250. Clearly, this is the dominating solution.

Although this is clearly the dominating solution, so far as I know it has never been discussed in the literature before. Indeed, it took a very long period of thought before it came to me. It is always possible that an idea which has never been discussed has just not been thought of before. It is also possible, however, that there are very good reasons why the idea should not be applied, and the lack of discussion stems from the fact that everyone realises that there are such good reasons. The only suggestions that I have been able to unearth as to why we might prefer to have the government paying lawyers on both sides to having them get the same probability of outcome by helping only one side are, in my opinion, unconvincing.

First, there is the possibility that we just have some primitive ethical idea involved here. For example, perhaps it is thought that adversary procedure is right in some metaphysical way, regardless of the outcome attained. If this is the explanation, then people who do not happen to have that particular moral set would not agree. People who do not have that moral set should at least be willing to consider the costs.

There are two other possible explanations. In a way, they are closely related but not identical. The first is that we might feel that the adversary process, with good representation on both sides,[14] is an efficient way to reach the truth. It might be argued that the more resources we invest on *both* sides, the more likely we are to achieve an accurate outcome. Not everyone seems to argue this way. When discussing matters in which the accuracy was important, I have sometimes been corrected by lawyers who tell me that improving the quality of the legal representation does not increase accuracy. I am somewhat puzzled by this, partly because it seems to me that it should, and partly because it would seem to me that it would be

156 *Part IV*

in the interest of the lawyers, or at least the best lawyers, to argue that it does.

It seems likely that we are indeed improving the accuracy of the court procedure when we increase the resources put into the adversary proceeding. Unfortunately, the increase is a very slow one. Doubling the resources of both the man who represents the truth, and the man who represents falsehood, may make it more likely that the court will recognise the truth from the falsehood, but it surely does not double the probability. Indeed, I would anticipate only small improvements in accuracy from quite large increases in resource investment.

The second reason is, in a way, a derivative of the first. We could always, by reducing the resources being invested on one side of the case, obtain the same probability we can obtain by increasing the resources on the other; hence, it is always possible to obtain the same probability of a correct outcome by a cheap method as by an expensive one. It might be difficult, however, for us to predict accurately the result of changing the resources on both sides. In our simple divorce case, if there are no legal representatives, the odds are nine to one in favour of the wife obtaining custody. If both sides are represented, the odds are 85 to 15. Without running the case 100 or so times, it might be difficult to determine what those odds are; hence, it might be difficult to duplicate them by reducing resources for one side only.

I am not at all sure that this is true; what little experimental work has been done seems to indicate that lawyers are quite good at estimating the odds. But if the odds are indeterminate, it is not at all obvious why we would regard one resource investment as better than another unless we had an implicit belief that the adversary proceeding does increase accuracy as the resources invested in it are increased. To repeat what I said before, I am inclined to go along with this assumption, but I think that the accuracy is purchased very expensively.

NOTES

1. There is some descriptive material mainly by sociologists. For example, see James Eisenstein and Herbert Jacob, *Felony Justice* (Boston: Little Brown, 1977).
2. Note that plea bargaining, although it is talked about more in connection with American legal procedure than with any other, is in fact a rather uniform characteristic of criminal law. In general, the accused criminal who cooperates with the accusers will be given a lower penalty than the one who does not. For example, in Communist China:

[t]he principle in dealing with the criminal is to integrate a policy of suppression with a policy of leniency—leniency to those who confess and severity to those who resist. The criminal can lessen the gravity of the crime by making a contribution to the settlement of the case. If the criminal makes a big contribution he can be treated leniently, or even be

rewarded. (Gerd Ruge, 'An Interview with Chinese Legal Officials', *China Quarterly* (March 1975), 61:122)

3. The Charles Manson case, and a couple of other cases similar to it, seem to indicate that a public defender *does* have the right to prevent his client from pleading guilty even if the client wants to.

4. A reader of the manuscript pointed out that the client might be a risk-lover, and hence wish to take the chance of the court proceeding even though the odds were against him. This is, of course, conceivable, but I do not see any reason why government funds should be used to finance gambles, merely because the gambler likes to gamble.

5. It could be to the advantage of the client simply because the public defender's office is hard pressed at the moment and will not have time to give him a really good defence.

6. They are extraordinarily good at implying their beliefs without actually stating them.

7. I may be oversimplifying here. I am sure that his is the correct practice, but it is not necessarily the correct ethical theory. See Monroe H. Freedman 'Professional Responsibility of the Criminal Defence Lawyer: The Three Hardest Questions', *Michigan Law Review* (June 1966), 64 (1469): 1485–92; and David G. Bress, 'Professional Ethics in Criminal Trials: A View of Defence Counsel's Responsibility', *Michigan Law Review* (June 1966), 64 (1469): 1493–98, for a discussion which presents rather neatly how badly muddled lawyers can get when they try to talk about these matters in formal context.

8. 'The First Law of Expert Advice states: Don't ask the barber whether you need a haircut'—Daniel S. Greenberg, 'When Quackery Dons a Starched White Coat', *Washington Post*, 2 August, 1977, p. A19.

9. If it does not, obviously we should drop the public defenders because if their resource commitment to defence is not of much significance to the outcome, we can save money without having much effect on the outcome.

10. In some cases, politicians or bureaucrats may indeed want the government to take one side for strictly partisan reasons. In general, however, this is undesirable.

11. Note, I am assuming that the government is helping the plaintiff. It might well be helping the defendant. This makes no difference in the basic principles we are going to discuss.

12. Normally the contest concerns alimony, custody of children, etc. and not whether or not the divorce will be granted.

13. In order to keep things symmetrical, assuming that they chose to represent the wife only and not the husband, the odds would be 95 per cent for the wife getting custody and only 5 per cent for the husband, I omit the prospect of the legal aid office providing a third lawyer to look after the interests of the child.

14. This is apparently the view of Arthur Okun:

> In some important noneconomic areas, we do regard whatever results emerge as untouchable, because they are generated by an explicitly accepted ideal process. I do not believe that the winner of an election is always the best candidate, but I believe that it would be wrong to overturn the results. Similarly, I do not care whether a jury finds a particular defendant guilty or not; I care only that justice be done. And I am prepared to respect the jury's verdict, unless I learn that the intended process was violated by tampering or the like. 'Further Thoughts on Equality and Efficiency', in Colin Campbell (ed.), *Income Redistribution* (Washington, D.C.: American Enterprise Institute for Public Policy Research, 1977), p. 25.

12 Giving Life*

Some time ago an acquaintance of mine was told by his doctors that he would die within four months unless he had open-heart surgery. They further told him that he had about a one in three chance of dying under the knife if he chose to have the operation. He chose the operation and died in the intensive care unit a few hours after being removed from the operating table. Most people would refer to this as a tragic choice. It is not exactly the kind of tragic choice examined by Guido Calabresi and Philip Bobbitt in their book of the same name, but some analysis of my acquaintance's situation will serve as an introduction to the issues that they raise.

First, the choice itself depended on the state of medical technology. One hundred years ago the doctor could have done nothing for him and probably could not even have diagnosed his condition properly. It is likely that in another 100 years medicine will have advanced to the point where he could be easily cured. The nature of the problem is in this way determined by the historical time in which it is posed. Most of the cases discussed by Calabresi and Bobbitt share this characteristic with my acquaintance's difficult choice.

Another aspect of the problem was that merely making the choice would itself be painful. Careful thought about whether one wished to live for four months or take a gamble in which one had a two in three chance of having a fairly long life[1] and a one in three chance of dying immediately would surely make anyone unhappy. People in such situations sometimes refuse to think about the problem, remarking that doctors are all incompetent, or something similar. This means, of course, that they have indirectly chosen death in four months, with the decision modified a bit by the possibility that the doctors may be wrong.

The person who, when faced with a problem of this sort, refuses to give it any consideration may be maximising his utility. The pain and suffering he would inflict on himself by careful thought about the problem might be greater than the cost of not thinking, which in his case would be death in four months. Note, however, that it is not possible for the person consciously to choose *not* to decide the basic problem because the cost of such a conscious choice would be too great. Yet conscious thought about the problem whether to think about the problem could be as painful as

*This article first appeared as 'Avoiding Difficult Decisions', review article of Guido Calabresi and Philip Bobbitt, *Tragic Choices* (New York: W.W. Norton/Toronto: George J. McLeod, 1978), in *New York University Law Review*, vol. 54, no. 1 (April 1979), pp. 267–79.

conscious thought about the final problem.

If we were to find people who regularly avoided decisions in such matters, an investigation of their thought processes would be an interesting one. We would probably begin by thinking that it was a study of abnormal psychology, assuming that in such a situation one should think the problem through and reach the best solution. Some reflection, however, indicates that the assumption is not necessarily valid. If persons faced with a tragic choice can quietly and without much thought bypass the problem they will, perhaps, be happier than if they did not. Certainly, my friend would have been better off, since he would have had four additional months of life and would not have struggled with the tortuous choice that faced him.

Calabresi and Bobbitt's study is an essay on avoidance. It is devoted not to the way tragic choices are made, and how they could be better made, but rather to the way in which people avoid thinking about them. This is not the description that they themselves would use, but I think it is an accurate one. To make this observation is not to criticise the book. Their subject is important and they analyse it with great care.

The particular tragic choices the authors discuss involve social decisions about providing aid to individuals rather than, as in the example of my acquaintance above, choices made by individuals for themselves. The tragic nature of the choice arises from the fact that society is not willing to save everyone and hence must decide who will be saved. The decision process, the authors note, has two stages. The first stage, called the first-order determination, is the decision about the amount of resources society will allocate to aiding people in some tragic situation. The second stage, the second-order determination, is the choice of who will receive these particular resources.[2]

Let us examine the specific type of tragic choice in which Calabresi and Bobbitt are interested. As an example, consider the kidney dialysis machine, which can, at very great cost, allow people suffering from an otherwise fatal disease to go on living. Let us temporarily put aside the actual history of these machines and consider a hypothetical case that will help in the further analysis of the book. Suppose that a wealthy man, knowing that dialysis machines existed and that there were many people in the community who could not afford them, decided to buy some of the machines and give their services away free.

He would have two problems, the first of which is the first-order choice of the number of machines he will purchase. Of course, in an alternative not specifically named by Calabresi and Bobbitt but nevertheless directly involved in much of their analysis, he could, instead of buying kidney machines, invest the same amount of money in some other way of reducing pain and suffering. This, however, is simply a special sub-category of first-order decision, because putting money into something other than kidney machines reduces the number of kidney machines available free of charge.

The individual wealthy man must then decide who should receive the use of the machines he has purchased. This second-order decision is of necessity a difficult one, and is indeed the 'tragic choice' that Calabresi and Bobbitt analyse: whoever must make this decision decides who should live and who should die in just as direct and straightforward a way as if he were sitting on a bench and wearing a black robe. It should not surprise us that a wealthy philanthropist, in much the same way as my terminally-ill friend, might wish to avoid making the final choice.

In the case of the philanthropist, unlike that of the heart patient, the decision affects not the decision-maker but other people. The motives for careful thought about a painful problem are hence much weaker than they would be were the conclusion to affect the wealthy man himself. We could therefore expect that he would in general try to avoid the decision but might occasionally interfere to aid some particular client who had attracted his attention. This phenomenon of interest in a few particular cases occurs in social decisions as well. Immense resources are committed to attempts to rescue pilots ditched at sea, miners trapped in pit-falls, and others in situations in which the plight of the individual attracts public attention.

When the social choice is less visible, however, the usual decision-avoidance techniques come into play. For instance, when I was in the foreign service, the areas that I served always had a large number of people who wanted American visas. But the number of such visas was restricted. The officers charged with allocating them (fortunately I was never one of them) had a number of ways of avoiding the choice process.[3] There were a number of papers to be filled out; applicants were required to sit on hard chairs for long periods of time; and in general there was a lengthy delay while the applications were being taken. All this imposed a cost on the applicant, not in straightforward monetary terms (although there were some direct fees), but in terms of inconvenience.[4] In addition, the actual rules that governed the granting of visas involved a certain number of non-discretionary criteria that once again reduced the difficulty of making a decision. Leaving all these factors aside, however, the ultimate decision was made as a result of correspondence between the consuls in the field and the officials in Washington. I discovered rather early that no one was willing to admit responsibility for the ultimate decision. The people in the consulate always maintained that the choices were made in Washington, and the people in Washington always maintained that they were made in the consulates. The decision was a painful one and responsibility for making it had been successfully avoided. Again, the avoidance of tragic choices is not confined to private decisions.

Further examination of the problems associated with tragic choices can be made if we return to our wealthy man. The decision as to who shall get the treatment is a difficult one in two respects. First, he must make the terrible choice of who will live and who will die. Second, merely making this decision reminds him that he has not spent as much money as he could have buying the machines. To use Calabresi and Bobbitt's terms, the second-order decision draws attention to the first-order decision. Our philanthropist is apt to feel guilty about the size of his gift every time he decides that someone will have to die because there are not enough machines available, unless he has exhausted all of his resources on the machines. We should not be surprised to discover that the wealthy man was concealing this problem from himself.

II

We are finally in a position to examine directly the Calabresi and Bobbitt analysis of tragic choices. The situation is identical to that of our wealthy man except that the giver is the average citizen by way of the government. This average citizen has all the problems we have canvassed above in our two simpler cases plus two more. First, in political matters the individual voter is normally poorly informed. This statement is empirical in character[5] but the rationality of the average voter's ignorance may also be theoretically derived from careful analysis of the functioning of a democracy.[6]

The second additional problem is that the cost to the individual voter of any increase in the amount of resources allocated to a particular problem is generally trivial. Of course, the voter cannot afford to help everyone everywhere with a serious problem. A concerted effort, for example, on the part of Americans to raise the living standard of the average citizen of India to one-half of what we regard as the poverty level would require our diverting something like 45 per cent of the average voter's after-tax income.[7] Nevertheless, in any particular case, the cost spread over a very large number of voters is minimal. Thus, whenever the individual voter hears of someone denied the use of a kidney machine he is apt to feel that he service should be extended because the cost to himself is small. And the decision eventually made, to provide kidney machines for anyone who needed them,[8] probably does cost the average voter only a trifling amount. Difficulties arise only if we try to generalise our attitude toward renal failure to all diseases. A willingness to spend as much to save people suffering from other diseases as we now spend for kidney problems would be very expensive for most voters.

One of the virtues of *Tragic Choices* is that it makes the dilemma, or as I shall shortly point out, trilemma, clear. Resources are scarce and we cannot help everyone who is suffering. The point is well made by the cases that draw public attention—when a person trapped in a mine disaster, or perhaps a lost explorer, is saved with the expenditure of several million dollars. We cannot possibly expend that large a sum for every person in danger.

We therefore ration the total amount of funds we make available to people in severe difficulties. Once we have decided how much we will spend—the first-order problem—we must then make the second-order decision about how this rationed quantity will be allocated. Making it, however, imposes upon us the same kind of cost to which we referred above in the case of our wealthy individual philanthropist. A combination of the poor information that we expect in democratic politics, together with the fact that any individual expansion of total resources will have its cost spread over the entire electorate, means that the decision will be inherently suspect. Furthermore, in facing the second-order decisions, we may come across questions about the first-order decisions that eventually lead us to change the first-order allocation.

Indeed, it seems like that the decision to universalise the availability of the kidney machines described in *Tragic Choices*[9] was reached because of questions about the way the second-order decisions were being made. But that solution cannot itself be generalised. Providing relief to everyone is possible for any particular limited class of tragic choices but not for all. Moreover, the decision to aid people in one particular tragic situation is at the same time a decision not to aid people in others.[10] We have a kind of lottery in which the government stands ready to spend a large amount of money to assist those with, for example, serious kidney diseases. But the government will then be very much more niggardly toward people who need heart shunts, even though they may be in equal danger and the cost of a shunt may be less than that of dialysis.

There is, in addition to the first- and second-order problems, a third-order problem. This third problem is the intellectual attitude we will take toward the first two. Shall we frankly admit that resources are limited and that we are going to let a certain number of people die of curable medical conditions?[11] This decision to let some people die is not, of course, inconsistent with making considerable contributions to helping people in trouble. It does, however, mean that we will have to make definite choices about who gets the aid, and that we cannot pretend it goes to everyone. The third-order decision could involve, as one alternative, simply accepting the situation. As a second alternative, we could adopt one of a large number of ways of concealing from ourselves the dilemma between the first- and second-order decisions. It is to this aspect of the tragic choice that the Calabresi and Bobbitt book is largely devoted. They analyse, frequently with much acuteness, the advantages and disadvantages of various mechanisms for making decisions about who will receive the aid. These decisions, however, are uniformly analysed in terms of their efficiency in relieving social tension among the general citizenry and not in terms of their efficiency in reaching an optimal distribution of the aid.

Here a paradox at the heart of the authors' approach becomes evident. Efforts to solve the third-order problem, which is what this book is about, are as likely to cause social distress and unhappiness on the part of the people who must make them as is the decision about the amount of resources to be devoted. Third-order problems thus cannot be faced openly by people who want to take advantage of avoidance techniques to conceal the actual dilemma. Calabresi and Bobbitt can talk about the techniques and their readers can think about them only so long as they take a cold-blooded scientific attitude inconsistent with the use of methods of concealing the decisions.

Their analysis can, of course, be thought of as an élite analysis. We, who understand these things, are considering the methods used by the general citizenry who do not, and can advise them on the methods that will maximise their utility. Utility in this case derives from a mixture of decisions on first- and second-order problems together with some mechanism for concealing the actual, tragic nature of the decision. If we consider ourselves part of the group making the allocation decision, however, then the third-order tragic decision is just as tragic as the first- and second-order choices.

There is apparently no way out of the paradox. If we engage in rational thought about the choice, we will not be deceived. But avoiding deception means that we suffer a loss of utility because of the nature of the choice made. Of course, if we attempt rational thought and do it clumsily, we may be able to conceal the painful nature of the situation from ourselves. We may feel happy about our self-sacrifice (which may be genuine) in providing facilities for the poor without noticing that this means that certain other poor people, whom we could have helped with a little additional sacrifice, will die.

In tragic choice situations, rational thought in and of itself may lower overall utility even if it increases the real physical output. The poor and unfortunate would benefit if the members of our donor group behaved in a highly rational manner, because the funds chosen in the first-order choice would be distributed in a most efficient way. The donors would suffer, however, because they would be compelled to think about unpleasant problems. The other alternative, to use some method that conceals from the donors the full tragedy of the dilemma, will certainly lead to a less than optimal allocation of resources. Hence, the poor and unfortunate would be worse off although the donor group would be better off.

So far, what I have been saying has been more inspired by than directly drawn from Calabresi and Bobbitt. Yet all the elements I have discussed above are in the book—they simply are not given the same emphases of organisation or structure. In a way the authors have failed to make what we may call a fourth-order choice, namely, to discuss the tragic implications of third-order choices. Instead, they have devoted the bulk of their book to a careful and insightful discussion of the techniques actually used to conceal the problem of the first- and second-order decisions. In this discussion they assume that, in what I have called the third-order area, an implicit decision has been made that we will not directly face up to the shortage of resources and to the consequent necessity of choosing who shall live and who shall die. The book is empirical and not normative in its discussion of third-order choices. This aspect would appear to be the result of a fourth-order choice to be 'cold-bloodedly scientific' in avoiding the third-order choice.

The authors ably survey the various allocation techniques that can be used. But assisting a conscious, rational choice among these techniques, which is the only practical use the book would have, would involve making a third-order decision as painful as the decisions Calabresi and Bobbitt are attempting to avoid. They do not make such a third-order decision and the reader should note that I also have not done so. The problem is indeed a painful one.

These third-order decisions in general, unless they are a decision to face the whole matter directly in a scientific manner, have to be made subconsciously. As in the case of my acquaintance with the heart ailment, there is no gain if one chooses to conceal with open eyes; nothing then is concealed. We would thus expect general ineptness in methods of successful concealment simply because the choice cannot depend on careful thought.

The authors do not make a choice about whether to conceal, and, as I said before, I myself have nothing to recommend. As it is difficult to see what should be done in these cases let us turn to the actual content of the book, the exhaustive catalogue of methods. (Note that I have just made my own fourth-order decision not to deal with the third-order problem, and that my editors have made a fifth-order decision not to deal with my decision.)

The first method the authors discuss for dealing with the problem is one included more as a strawman than for any other purpose. It is a 'pure market' mechanism, which simply permits people to buy kidney machines or other costly items if they have the money and to die if they do not.[12] The obvious advantage of this method is that it solves the first- and second-order problems in one fell swoop. The decision as to who will get the machines also determines how many of them will be built. The reasons for not using this system are not absolutely clear, because it is hard to explain why we do sometimes decide to help our fellow man. But for whatever reason, the pure market solution does not appeal to many people and certainly not to Calabresi and Bobbitt.[13]

A modification of this pure market mechanism is apt to appeal to those economists willing to apply their training cold-bloodedly. Assuming that the basic problem here is one of income disparity, we could redistribute the income in society to reach some distribution that we think is optimal and let individuals spend that money as they wish. If they wish to purchase kidney machines, or more probably purchase medical insurance that would provide a kidney machine if the policyholder needed one,[14] we would permit them to do so. If they choose to spend their money on something else and the need for a kidney machine arises, we would let them die.

Under this system the poor are given the right to make decisions about how any aid given to them will be spent. If they value something else more highly than insurance against the contingency that they will need a kidney machine in the future, we would permit them to buy it. This would surely be better for them than a kind of warden relationship in which we would force them to accept that part of the aid in kind by, for instance, lowering their income and using the difference to buy kidney machine insurance for them.

This solution, as I say, is apt to attract economists who permit their science to guide them. The objections to the system seem limited to three. One is that the poor just are not very bright and will spend their money badly, usually capsulised in the phrase that they would 'drink up anything you would give them', this point of view is rarely expressed openly, but is certainly held by many. I shall leave this one aside; I do not believe it is worth discussing.

The second objection is that as a matter of fact public charitable agencies are likely to come to the aid of a person in dire need even if he gets into the situation by failing to buy proper insurance beforehand. We as taxpayers will often find ourselves paying for emergency treatment because we will face at that point a second-order decision whether to let the man die. Knowing that *we* will behave this way, people will be less likely to buy the appropriate insurance than they would have been if we were more cold-blooded in making the ultimate decision. The donor group may thus be forced to require that persons purchase the insurance. This argument was important in the original advocacy of the social security programme and I notice it turns up occasionally today in arguments in that field. There is no doubt, however, that it has much wider applicability.

The objection perhaps most relevant to the tragic choice analysis as set out above is that from the point of view of the donor group, the loss in utility may be greater than the gain from the betterment in the condition of the recipients. As Calabresi and Bobbitt point out, it is possible that the external costs to the donors of 'the wrenching spectacle of a rich man and a poor man bidding against each other for life' may be eliminated only by a degree of wealth redistribution we would find prohibitively high;[15] the donor group might balk at the costs, both fiscal and psychological, of establishing a market-based allocation system, even when coupled with some form of wealth equalisation.

Another variation of the modified market scheme is to permit the poor person who has received some government service, let us say the right to the use of a kidney machine, to sell the right to someone else if he feels the money is more important to him that the service. This scheme is characteristically banned, and Calabresi and Bobbitt suggest that the reason is that it puts a strain on the conscience of the donors. That the poor person would be willing to undergo great risk as a result of this type of sale indicates that his basic situation is bad indeed. This 'unquiet indictment of society's distribution of wealth'[16] may cause pain to the people who have not given him more money. The donors therefore prohibit the recipient from undertaking a Pareto-superior transaction.[17] I do not know if this is the actual explanation for restrictions of this sort, but they are fairly uniformly applied by the government in the area of in-kind provision.

Another variation on the modified market method that might be used would be to permit the scarce resource, such as kidney machines, to be bought or rented, but to charge different people different prices in accordance with their wealth.[18] As a simple example (not used by Calabresi and Bobbitt), individuals might bid not dollars but hours of their income stream. Thus, if a millionaire bids 200 hours (which would cost him, let us suppose, $1 million) and a poor person bids 201 hours (the actual cash value of which is $402), the poor person wins. This method permits the use of the market while neutralising differences in wealth. It has some of the efficiency characteristics of market transactions but not all of them. And it is, of course, also non-Pareto-optimal if one prohibits resale. As far as I know, this method is not used anywhere. Calabresi and Bobbitt offer a number of administrative reasons why such 'wealth distribution-neutral' markets would be extremely difficult to use in practice. Chief among these are the problems associated with assessing both the value of the benefit to the individuals concerned and the other elements of the distribution scheme, such as, in our example above, the value of an hour of a millionaire's time,[19] and with the attempt to separate price-conscious preferences from other non-price elements such as cultural preferences.[20]

A third and final 'coherent' solution to allocating the scarce resource might be to distribute it by lot.[21] As Calabresi and Bobbitt point out, first come, first served is simply a special, and a rather inferior, form of lottery.[22] The lottery has not been much used for distributing positive gifts, but it has on occasion been used for conscription into the army, a situation that bears a certain resemblance to the tragic choice problem. The method first come, first served is sometimes used not as a result of conscious choice but because the people responsible can think of nothing else.

These three approaches to decision-making are all intellectually coherent, in that they attempt to apply some consistent set of values to the making of tragic choices. The remaining procedures discussed in *Tragic Choices* are less coherent. In these cases the effort to avoid thought in the area of tragic choice leads to the use of various mechanisms that conceal the actual procedures from outsiders and, in some instances, from the people making the decisions. I do not propose to elaborate the procedures they discuss, but would like merely to list some of them. One is the representative political body.[23] Another is the 'aresponsible agency', such as the trial jury. Such bodies generally are decentralised and representative of society at large, and need not give reasons for their decisions.[25] A variation on this theme is called the 'para-aresponsible agency', which has technical experts among its members.[26] Para-aresponsible agencies reduce inconsistencies of decision by the continuity of their membership, but the presence of the technical experts reduces the agency's representativeness.[27] A third method is the use of a bureaucracy that may obscure the decisional criteria.[28] Finally, various devices may be used to allocate tragically scarce resources in light of the perceived worthiness of the recipients, as measured by criteria that may be either expressed or tacit.[29] All these methods are complex and may be combined with each other in various ways. Calabresi and Bobbitt's discussion of these techniques is insightful, but the authors offer no recommendation regarding them and no general principle by which to select among them.

These discussions of less coherent methods are worthwhile reading not only for people interested in tragic choices but for people interested in government decision-making procedures in general. Many of Calabresi and Bobbitt's observations apply also to other bodies making choices that they would not classify as tragic. Government commissions appointed to deal with general policy and regulatory problems, for example, would appear to function, at least until the recent trend toward the adoption of 'sunshine laws' and administrative procedure codes, in much the same way as the 'God Committee' that for a while allocated the use of the dialysis machine in Seattle. The God Committee, essentially an aresponsible parajury composed of both professionals and lay persons, 'chose those who . . . were most deserving to live'[30] on the basis of loose, internally promulgated guidelines. It worked anonymously and gave no reasons for its decisions.[31] There seems to be little difference between the decision-making machinations of the God Committee and those of agencies charged with regulation in accordance with 'public convenience and necessity.'

It is no criticism of *Tragic Choices* to say that the discussion in this area is 'wisdom' rather than 'science'. The authors have been unable to produce a coherent, integrated theory of the area. Since I cannot do so either, I cannot criticise them for their failure. And there is no doubt that their discussion of the pros and cons of the various decision-making schemes will leave the reader considerably better informed than he was when he began.

Altogether, the book deals with an area where government does not perform well. The reason for its poor performance in the case of tragic choices is that the task given it is impossible. Voters want to economise on expenditures in the 'tragic' area. They then want these insufficient resources allocated in such a way as not to call their attention too vigorously to the fact that by economising they have caused deaths. The voters' desire to abdicate active or even visible decision-making is not necessarily irrational from the standpoint of maximising their utility. The result, however, is that rational thought is almost of necessity banned. Our wealthy philanthropist similarly desired to avoid the emotional and psychological costs of making life and death decisions. Incoherence in the actual allocative decision is, therefore, more or less called for. The value of *Tragic Choices* lies in its success in demonstrating that such incoherence is provided.

NOTES

1. My acquaintance was in his twenties.
2. p. 19.
3. Calabresi and Bobbitt cite Menotti's opera *The Consul* on more or less the same point. See p. 98.
4. The authors discuss such non-monetary allocational mechanisms and their problems as a variant on the pure market. See pp. 92–8.
5. See A. Campbell, P. Converse, W. Miller and D. Stokes, *The American Voter* (abridged ed. 1964), pp. 99–102.
6. For a simple explanation, see G. Tullock, *Toward a Mathematics of Politics* (1967), pp. 100–14.
7. The figure was calculated from the UN *Monthly Bulletin of Statistics*. It is only approximate, because I did not have readily at hand any figures on family size distribution in India and hence used a four-person family as a proxy. For the reader interested in experimenting with other values, here is a simple rule of thumb. Per capita income in India is about 5 per cent of our poverty level. Every increase in Indian per capita income equivalent to 10 per cent of our poverty level would cost the average US citizen about 10 per cent of his after-tax income.
8. See p. 189.
9. See pp. 186–9.
10. See p. 189.
11. Or, for that matter, will we admit to letting millions starve to death in The Sahel.
12. pp. 31–4.
13. See p. 31.
14. This would be very expensive but certainly not impossible.
15. p. 33.

16. Ibid.
17. Ibid.
18. pp. 98–103.
19. See pp. 110–14. The difficulties associated with gauging the strength of such preferences may sometimes lead society to abandon the market in favour of other devices, such as aresponsible agencies or even 'simple, muddled, collective determination[s] (p. 109); see pp. 106–10; and text accompanying notes 24–7 below.
20. See pp. 102–3, 104–5.
21. p. 41.
22. pp. 43–4.
23. pp. 34–41.
24. pp. 57–64.
25. p. 57.
26. pp. 64–72.
27. p. 65. Calabresi and Bobbitt 'suspect that while it is need for continuity which limits the degree of true representativeness possible, this lack of representativeness can be justified or explained away by invoking the need for experts' (ibid.).
28. pp. 95–7.
29. pp. 72–8. The major advantage of a worthiness approach is that it obscures the tragedy inherent in the choice. 'Society announces that *it* will not choose to sacrifice lives or fundamental rights, that *it* will not violate conceptions of equality, that the sacrifices which do occur are due not to a societal unwillingness to forgo other goods but to individual failings'. (pp. 76–7) (emphasis in original).
30. p. 187.
31. pp. 188, 233, n.111. The committee had a few formal rules, such as state residency, but made its decisions primarily in an 'unstructured' manner, considering such criteria as the recipient's age, sex, marital status, number of dependants, income, net worth, psychological stability, past performance, and future potential (p. 233 n.111).

13 Inheritance Justified*

Although the early economists were interested in investigating the desirability of inheritance, this issue has been subject to relatively little economic discussion in recent years. I have not been able to turn up any serious effort to apply welfare economics to the problem. Nevertheless, the problem of justifying inheritance of wealth is still very much with us. A great many people who do not object to other aspects of the capitalist system take exception to the inheritance of wealth. It seems likely that the relative neglect of this subject in recent years has been because those who favoured private property regarded inheritance as necessarily entailed in the concept and those who objected to private property felt that inheritance was obviously wrong. As we shall see below, neither of these two positions is apodictically certain.

There have been some of what we may call traditional arguments for inheritance. The principal one, of course, is the conservation of capital. This argument, however, as far as I know, has never been worked out in any detail, nor have modern welfare economics techniques been used to discuss it.[1] There are two other arguments which are occasionally encountered. Some have argued that the heirs of great wealth are free from social pressures. Most of them presumably use this freedom from the burden which the rest of us carry in consumption of leisure time activities. A few, however, like Robert Boyle, use their opportunities to undertake activities which are of great benefit to mankind. It is conceivable that the pay-off from this small group of people might be very great. So far as I know, no one has ever examined this matter in any detail.

A final argument, which in a way is related to the argument which will be presented later in this chapter, is that we permit people to leave their money to whom they wish, not because of interest in the legatee, but because we are interested in the testator. We are, in this view, compelled by the mere logic of private property to permit a man not only to give it away while he is alive, but also to give it away on his death. In these forms, the argument is essentially metaphysical, but as we will see, it is possible to put something very similar to this in strict welfare economics terms.

It seems likely that this lack of much rigorous discussion of what is clearly an important policy issue turns, to a considerable extent, on the fact that decisions with respect to inheritance have become mixed up with

*First published in *Journal of Law and Economics*, 14 (October 1971), pp. 465–74. There were two comments on this paper and I responded with 'Inheritance Rejustified'.

certain other problems. First, a great many people favour income equalisation as a government policy. Secondly, there are a great many people who favour a planned, centrally-run economy as opposed to a market economy; thirdly, many people feel that the government should have, at the very least, a policy as to the amount of capital invested in the economy. Normally, people in this category favour more capital investment, but there is no logical reason why one could not favour less capital investment.[2] These issues are, in fact, independent of the desirability or undesirability of permitting inheritance, as I shall shortly demonstrate. I believe, however, that they have been mixed up with the inheritance issue by most people who thought about it. This makes the issue appear to be an extraordinarily complex issue and has resulted in restricting discussion.

Before turning to demonstrating that these issues are not necessarily involved in the decision as to whether or not inheritance should be permitted, I should like to digress briefly to explain what I mean by permitting or not permitting inheritance. In essence, we will discuss whether inheritance should be permitted, that is, whether 100 per cent tax on inheritance of wealth is desirable. We will not discuss whether such a 100 per cent tax would be administratively feasible in the sense that it might be possible for people wishing to leave money to evade it, nor will we discuss the taxation of inheritance for revenue purposes only. As will be demonstrated, however, the arguments offered in favour of inheritance are also arguments in favour of keeping the tax on inheritance at or below that tax which brings in the largest net revenue. If, as seems likely, a 30 per cent tax level on inheritances would bring in more revenue than a 90 per cent tax, than the argument offered in this article would indicate that the 30 per cent tax should be chosen.

Returning to our main theme, however, I should like now to demonstrate that the four issues which I have described are essentially independent of each other. As an extreme case, it is possible to have a socialist state which has definite policies with respect to the amount of capital which will be accumulated and radically egalitarian objectives together with inheritance of wealth. In fact, I would argue that inheritance of wealth under these circumstances would increase the efficiency of such a state. On the other hand, it would be possible to have a completely *laissez-faire* market economy with no effort on the part of the government to affect the net rate of accumulation of capital or redistribute income in the direction of equality and, at the same time, prohibit inheritance. In this case, again, I would argue that prohibiting inheritance was inefficient. All of the other logical combinations of these factors are also possible and in all of these cases permitting inheritance is efficient. With four variables, each of which can take two values, we have a 16-cell matrix as shown in Figure 13.1.[3]

Part IV

	Inheritance		No inheritance	
	Market economy	Government operated economy	Market economy	Government operated economy
No income redistribution	A	B	A'	B'
Income redistribution	C	D	C'	D'
No income redistribution	E	F	E'	F'
Income redistribution	G	H	G'	H'

No government capital policy — rows A/B/A'/B' and C/D/C'/D'
Government capital policy — rows E/F/E'/F' and G/H/G'/H'

Figure 13.1

The eight possible combinations of the other variables with the retention of inheritance are shown to the left of the centre vertical bar and those without inheritance to the right. Each possible situation with inheritance is shown by a letter and its corresponding state without inheritance permitted is shown by the letter primed. My argument is that, by standard welfare criteria, in each case the state with inheritance is superior. A is better than A' and H is better than H'.

Before entering into the general discussion, however, I think it would be desirable to demonstrate that these four possible variables are, indeed, independent. Further, something should be said about the efficient method of administering certain types of government control. It is widely believed, for example, that a socialist economist economic policy in which the government operates the economy must, of necessity, be combined with government control of capital accumulation. This is by no means true. There is no reason why the government could not obtain its capital solely from the voluntary sale of securities while managing the rest of the economy.[4] Under these circumstances, it would be obtaining from the individuals in society information as to how much they wanted to invest, granted the physical productivity of investment at that time and using these data to obtain the optimum in amount of investment. The government itself would be deciding where the investment was to be spent.

The contrary policy—government control of the rate of capital formation without government control of the economy as a whole—is equally easy. A government could institute a subsidy for capital investment, if it thought capital investment was too low, or a tax upon capital investment, if it thought that it was too high. Note that for this purpose it would have to have some idea of what is the 'right amount' of capital accumulation, independent of the ordinary equilibrium concepts. It would be, in a sense, overriding preferences of the citizens for investment. Whether we approve of this or not, however, raises no questions as to its theoretical possibility.

Finally, income redistribution can be combined with almost any set of policies on the other variables. In general—granted that the government has some policy for income redistribution, whether from the rich to the poor from the poor to the rich or from all of us to farmers and oilmen—this income redistribution can be most efficiently managed if it is handled through direct taxes and payments rather than by attempting to change the structure of production in such a way as to bring indirect benefits and injuries to specified groups.

Let us assume that the government has some capital policy, that is, it feels that the capital accumulation which 'falls out' from the general situation including, of course, its policies in other areas is not optimal and wishes to change it. Let us assume for simplicity that it feels that more capital should be accumulated. There seems to be a widespread view that a policy of a government to increase capital investment must, of necessity, take the form of actual government management of all investment. This is untrue. Assume that people would, if left to their own devices, save 10 per cent of their money and the government, through divine guidance, knows that the correct amount is 20 per cent. One method of making this investment would be to tax the populace by 20 per cent of their income and use the money for direct government investments. A second technique would be to tax the populace some amount less than 20 per cent of their income and use the derived amount for subsidy upon new investment. A third possibility would be to tax the populace 10 per cent of their income and invest this directly in investments which, given prevailing rates of interest, are sub-marginal. If the government has infinite ability to discriminate in the size of its subsidies, it should be able to go even further than any of these three techniques and offer discriminant subsidies on specific super-marginal investments in order to obtain its total 20 per cent investment from a tax revenue well under 10 per cent.

It is, of course, possible to combine the latter three techniques in various combinations. Clearly, any one of the last three techniques or any combination of them is better than the first. In each case, the degree to which the individual is permitted to make decisions about how his income will be spent and how it will be divided between saving and investment is greater than under a direct tax-financed investment of 20 per cent. Thus, each individual in society would be better off if the first policy involving direct government management of all investment were not resorted to simply because each individual acquires some additional freedom from this decision. The gain would be particularly great for those individuals who did not wish to invest exactly 20 per cent of their income. In general, a subsidy is the most efficient method of increasing the investment of capital, if large increases are desired and, if small increases are desired, direct investment in super-marginal areas is efficient.

Note that this would be true even if we did not believe in the market economy and had a totally government-run industrial and agricultural sector. Decisions by the government as to how much should be invested would be more efficiently implemented if the individuals voluntarily buy government securities with a suitable tax or subsidy to make certain that they bought the 'right' total amount. Thus, an efficient socialist government would have (and the Soviet Union did have for many years) a market in its own bonds and would obtain the capital which is used for investment through this market. Only if the government is not concerned with providing optimal conditions for its citizens would it use its governmental powers directly to determine not only how much shall be invested but who shall invest it.

It might be thought, however, that an income redistribution programme which was radically egalitarian requires, or at least is consistent with, confiscatory inheritance taxes. This is not true. Indeed, confiscatory inheritance taxes are a bad way of equalising income. Any desired degree of income equalisation can be obtained by suitable income taxes. Since the recipients of the inheritance will receive their inheritance by what amounts to a random time-allocation, a tax which confiscates inheritances would amount to a random tax upon one particular source of income. A special tax on a single source of income combined with a general income tax is an inefficient method of equalising income. The point can perhaps best be understood if we assume that the government of the United States not only has an income tax policy aimed at certain equalisations, but has, in addition, a $5000 per year tax on economists on the grounds (quite correctly) that economists' incomes are above-average. Clearly, this combination would be a less efficient way of achieving an income equality goal than a single tax because, in some cases, the special tax would fall on people who are already not too well off. Since any desired degree of equality can be obtained through the income tax with a negative range, the addition of a special tax for this purpose in both inefficient and undesirable.

It might be argued, however, that we want not only income inequality but also a greater degree of equality in wealth. In this case, a direct equalising wealth tax would seem to be the optimal institution. Indeed a tax on one particular form of wealth is almost of necessity an inefficient way of reducing the amount of wealth inequality in society. There has been a good deal of research in attempting to determine what tax on wealth would be equivalent to a given level of death duties. These very complicated papers derive their basic complications simply from the fact that any annual tax on wealth is vastly more efficient than the death duty as a technique of wealth equalisation, and it is hard to compute the equivalent in an efficient tax for a highly inefficient tax.[5] Once again, a tax on a particular form of wealth, let us say houses, is an inefficient way of wealth equalisation. Those interested in wealth equalisation should approach the problem directly and use efficient tools, rather than indirectly through an inept set of methods.

The last few paragraphs have been devoted to demonstrating that the four variables shown on Figure 13.1 are in fact independent. They can be mixed in almost any combination. It now remains to demonstrate that the inheritance tax in undesirable. I do not propose to go through all of the eight possible cases, but I think that if I can demonstrate that the inheritance tax is undesirable in the two extreme cases—A, A', the market economy with no income redistribution and no government capital policy and H, H' the government-run economy with income redistribution and a government capital policy—I will have made my point, and may leave the filling of most of the other squares to the reader.

Let us begin with A, A'. Suppose, then, a free-market government with no capital policy and no income redistribution which is considering the imposition of 100 per cent tax on all inheritances. Let us then discuss the effect of this tax first upon the situation before some given person has died and then, secondly, after he has died. The first consequence of the enactment of such a confiscatory inheritance tax would simply be that motives for accumulating capital would be much lower than otherwise. Indeed, everyone would plan to be bankrupt on the day of their death. The market for annuities would become a very good one.[6]

Consider, then, a person who is alive, and realises that he will die. Clearly, with the confiscatory inheritance tax, he would plan to leave no estate.[7] Clearly, this person has been made worse off by the tax because he has lost one possible degree of freedom. Before the tax was enacted, he could have saved money and left it to his heirs if he wished, and after the tax he no longer can do so. This reduction in his freedon is not offset by any gain to anyone else in society.

Indeed, as we have mentioned before, this reduction in his gains from accumulating money has been used as an argument *against* inheritance taxation. Surely with 100 per cent inheritance taxation, there will be less capital investment than there otherwise would be. But, in order to make this argument, it is necessary to believe that the amount of capital accumulated under institutions in which inheritance tax is permitted is superior to that in which it is not permitted. Granting this assumption, then the inheritance tax could, of course, be offset by a suitable subsidy on investment. This subsidy would not change the tendency of people to die penniless, but it would mean that people would save more money for the purpose of buying annuities to cover their old age than they otherwise would. This situation with inheritance taxation and such a subsidy would be inferior prior to the death of some person simply because the same capital investment would be obtained as without the inheritance tax, but there would be an additional tax imposed on the general population for the purpose of paying the subsidy. Thus, the abolition of the inheritance tax would benefit the taxpayers who otherwise would be paying for the subsidy and injure no one. But all of this, as I said before, requires the assumption that we know the ideal amount of capital investment. Those people, however, who do feel that the amount of capital which would be accumulated without inheritance tax would be too small will find this point quite convincing.

But to continue with our example. Now, suppose that our selected individual dies. The state obtains no funds because he has been living on an annuity, so there is no tax receipt. The people who would have inherited the money which he otherwise would have saved are worse off than they would have been under the previous set of institutions. No one benefits. Indeed, once again, the fact that there is less capital in society might well be considered a quite general loss. I think that proponents of inheritance taxation at this point would say that the abolition of inheritance, however, *did* benefit those people who would not have received the inheritance since they are not now confronted with a wealthier person in the society. In other words, they would normally envy a man who had received an inheritance, and this is an externality which has been eliminated by the elimination of inheritance. As I pointed out above, if this is thought of as a good social reason for an institution, the appropriate institution is suitably graduated income tax or wealth tax, not an inheritance tax. For the moment, however, the society is assumed not to have a redistribution of income policy and, hence, we can assume that it is not one where jealousy of those wealthier than oneself is a dominant social motive.

Thus, we have demonstrated that A is better than A'. Our proof, however, has been a proof with respect to a confiscatory inheritance tax to which the taxpayer fully adjusts by not having any money left to tax. If we assume that the annuity market is not well enough developed so that individuals can afford to put their entire wealth into such an instrument, then the proof fails but the society is not in long-range equilibrium.[8]

It has not been proved, however, that a tax on inheritance is undesirable. Presumably, if inheritances are taxed at any rate less than 100 per cent, at least some people would choose to leave at least some money to their heirs and, hence, there is a government revenue to offset the effects of the inheritance taxation

Here, however, although we cannot prove that such taxes are unwise, we *can* prove quite readily that, if the tax is larger than that tax which brings the maximum revenue, it is unwise. Suppose, for example, that a 10 per cent inheritance tax would lead to a great many people choosing to leave money to their heirs with the result that the total tax collections were $100,000,000. On the other hand, assume that a 75 per cent inheritance tax would sharply reduce the number of people who wish to leave money to heirs so that the total income to the government was only, say, $75,000,000. The argument that we have offered so far would indicate that the first tax would clearly dominate the second. In other words, an inheritance tax in order to be even dubiously Pareto-optimal, would have to be either at that rate which maximises the return from an inheritance tax (which is, of course, not the highest possible rate) or at some lower rate.

Note that such a tax would continue to reduce the total capital available in society and, hence, if you believe that capital generates externalities, would be a dominated policy on that ground also.

We might temporarily move from square A to square E in our figure in order to discuss the capital problem a little more. Assume that the government uses the receipts from the inheritance tax, at least in part, to subsidise investment. It might be (although I doubt it very much) that it would turn out that there was some net profit; that is, that we could obtain the same net level of investment after the imposition of a joint inheritance tax subsidy on capital as we had before and still have some money left over for state use. As a judgement of the relative elasticities of the demand for savings under the two circumstances, I doubt that this would be true, but we may as well explore the possibility. If it were true, then, once again, one could say that the optimal institution could not involve an inheritance tax and subsidy which jointly were higher than needed to bring in the maximum amount of money which could be obtained by this combination of policies. It would not, of course, have to be that high.

The other possibility in square E and E′, that is, that there is an inheritance tax offset by a subsidy on capital investment which turns out to cost more than the inheritance tax brings in, is clearly undesirable. If this situation occurs, square E clearly is superior to square E′. Note that these general principles will apply to all cases where the government has a pro-capital accumulation policy. In all cases, the reasoning which we have given above would indicate that not having an inheritance tax would be superior to having one, except in those cases where maximum revenue can be derived from either the inheritance tax or the combination of the inheritance tax and the subsidy; in such cases, the tax would have to be equal to or lower than the revenue-maximising level. In other words, there will be no independent reason for restricting inheritance. We would simply be choosing a tax by much the same line of reasoning as we would choose a tax on butter.

We now, however, switch to square H, H′ where we have government which attempts to adjust capital, has an income redistribution policy (we shall assume it is an egalitarian rather than inegalitarian or horizontal income redistribution policy), and direct government control of the economy. Under these circumstances, once again, the institution of inheritance dominates the non-inheritance institution. I have previously demonstrated that it is desirable, even under these institutions, to have decisions as to who will invest the money for capital projects left to the individual citizen by way of a government bond market (which may be selling bonds at a subsidised rate) rather than having the decisions made directly by the government on both how much should be saved and who should save it. Let us, however, temporarily disregard this proof and assume that the government we are dealing with is Maoist and does not permit its citizens to acquire any kind of capital asset except small quantities of items for personal use.

The arguments for permitting inheritance of this small amount of private property are, once again, fairly compelling. If inheritance was not permitted, individuals would be well advised to rent such goods rather than purchase them. The person who did rent them rather than purchase for this reason is injured to some extent, as is, when he dies, his potential heir and no one gains from the institution.

If, however, we assume that the government with these policies does permit individuals to decide how much each one saves, then the arguments for inheritance are very much like those in the free-market system. It should be noted that, with a highly egalitarian policy and a government security as the only income-bearing asset, individuals would save not for the purpose of increasing their income in the future, but for the purpose of obtaining leisure, either for themselves or for their heirs at future times. It might turn out that this is a weak motive for saving and, hence, the subsidy on saving might have to be quite high. Still, the argument holds. Individuals before their death would be injured if they are prohibited from passing on their estate to their heirs because it eliminates one possible alternative which they might otherwise choose. Their potential heirs would be injured after their death and, assuming state annuities are available (their absence would be inefficient), no one would gain from these two changes.

We could go through all the other pairs of squares on Figure 13.1, but this would be tedious. The general principles still apply: by strict welfare economics methods, we can show that permitting inheritance of wealth is a desirably policy. Further, we can show that, although there is no reason why inheritance should be any more immune than petrol from taxes for revenue purposes, any effort to raise taxes above the revenue-maximising point is always a non-optimal policy.

NOTES

1. The point has not been made as strongly in the literature as one might expect. Nevertheless, it is contained in G. E. Hoover, 'The Economic Effects of Inheritance Taxes', 17, *Amer. Econ. Rev.* 38 (1927); and, Alvin H. Johnson, 'Public Capitalization of the Inheritance Tax', 22, *J. Pol. Econ.*, 160 (1914). Professor Johnson's article is interesting because he proposes to offset the reduction in capital by having the government invest in the capital market the full receipts of the inheritance tax. For this to work, of course, the elasticity of the 'demand for inheritance' would have to be less than one, a point which he does not emphasise.
2. Gordon Tullock, 'The Social Rate of Discount and the Optimal Rate of Investment: Comment', 78, *Q. J. Econ.*, 331 (1964).
3. In practice, of course, they can take many intermediate values, but for simplicity we will assume in each case there either is or is not a given institution.
4. Either a single general government bond or a series of different securities with different amounts of risk attached selling at different prices. Probably the former would be more efficient.
5. Cf. G. Z. Fijalkowski-Bereday, 'The Equalizing Effects of the Death Duties', 2 *Oxford Econ. Papers* (n.s.), 176 (1950); William S. Vickrey, 'The Rationalization of Succession Taxation', 12, *Econometrica,* 215 (1944); Nicholas Kaldor, 'The Income Burden of Capital Taxes', 9, *Rev. Econ. Stud.* 138 (1942), reprinted in *Readings in the Economics of Taxation*, 393, ed. R. A. Musgrave and C. S. Shoup (1959); A. C. Pigou, *A Study in Public Finance* (3rd edn., 1949), ch. 13.
6. It is of some interest that probably a good deal of current savings depends on the fact that for a variety of reasons annuities are not as widely used as they theoretically could be. A law against annuities would probably be an excellent way of increasing our investment ratio.
7. Unless, of course, he wished to make a gift to the government. Such gifts are possible without the 100 per cent inheritance tax.
8. The role of annuities or other types of income which terminate at death is so dominant in controlling the amount of savings that such institutions as the social security administration and private annuities markedly reduce total capital investment.

Part V
Problems of Poverty

14 Population Paradoxes

Discussions of optimal income distribution have always raised very difficult problems in the field of either ethics or, perhaps, aesthetics. Robert H. Strotz began a famous article by disavowing its conclusions.[1] Population theory and, in particular, the theory of the optimal population raises similar ethical and aesthetic problems. This chapter will raise even further difficulties. Like Strotz, I am not at all certain that I am satisfied with my own conclusions.

In a way, the main lesson is that certain ethical and aesthetic presuppositions which have been widely used in discussing redistribution lead to quite distressing consequences when they are applied to population theory. These results, however, in my opinion cast doubt on the initial assumptions, rather than generating an optimal population policy. In a sense, this chapter produces some paradoxes out of some rather standard assumptions as an argument against those standard assumptions. Unfortunately, I have been unable to find another set of assumptions which could be put in their place. The results, perforce, are negative: perhaps someone else will be able to build on the vacant lot.

To turn to the first of our problems, then, the starting point for modern discussions of the optimal division of income is the classic formulation of the problem given by A. P. Lerner.[2] On the rather modest assumptions of diminishing marginal utility of income and ignorance of individual utilities, Lerner demonstrated 'the maximization of probable total satisfaction is attained by an equal division of income'.[3] In my opinion, Milton Friedman was correct when he implied that people who accepted it generally were in favour of equal income distribution and accepted the argument because it led to that conclusion rather than because of its intrinsic merit.[4] I shall begin by applying Lerner's assumption to another problem, not in order to solve the other problem, but to drive another nail in the coffin of the Lerner welfare criterion. If maximising total utility is desirable, this should be true regardless of the method used to increase utility. When we turn to population problems, this criterion leads to conclusions which, in general, will be found undesirable.

Lerner assumes (in my opinion correctly) that income generates declining marginal utility. He also assumes that we cannot measure the utility of various individuals and, hence, have to assume that, if there are differences in the amount of utility that different individuals will get from a given bundle of goods or services, this is essentially a random variable. I accept these assumptions for all calculations in this chapter.[5] In general, it is obvious that an increase in population will lead to a larger total income being distributed among a larger population but with lower per capita incomes. With declining marginal utility, however, this will result in an increase in total utility over the society, up to a limit.

Consider what happens when an additional person is brought into existence. With declining marginal productivity, the marginal return on labour falls. Nevertheless, the new worker would increase the GNP in physical terms, to some extent. If we are an egalitarian society, however, there will be a transfer from other members of society to him. His appearance increases total GNP but reduces GNP per capita. The per capita incomes of the rest of society are reduced slightly, but the new citizen acquires an income he otherwise would not have and, up to a limit, the net result of this is an increase in total utility.

The limit is unfortunately reached at a very low per capita income. Consider a special case: the new individual in a very crowded society is able to produce only enough so that, if we were entirely dependent on his own resources, he would be on the boundary between misery and positive utility. Although marginal production in this society is now at this extremely low level, average production (because of declining marginal returns) is higher. There is, therefore, income for redistribution. The redistribution from the higher-income group to our new individual will lead to an increase in total utility, since on the average people are now further up their declining marginal utility slope. If we subtract from the total product that part which is necessary to keep all the population out of misery, and consider only that part that is used to generate more utility, it is clear that the more people among whom it is divided, the higher the total utility. Indeed, we can go further: the profits from redistribution are such that presumably our reference individual could produce a little less than his 'misery elimination' product, and still there would be a profit in total utility because of the better distribution of what would now be a slightly smaller cake of positive utility-generating income.[6]

Speaking for myself, I do not regard maximising total utility as a very desirable goal. Samuelson developed a somewhat similar demonstration which I would find more attractive.[7] Assume that individuals do not know what role they will play in society.[8] Under these circumstances, one can duplicate the Lerner argument for equalising income distribution without much difficulty. An egalitarian income distribution gives the highest present discounted value of lifetime income. With this interpretation, the Lerner model can again be applied to population problems.

The problem here is that if we wish to be strictly individualistic, it is necessary to consider the potential human being before he acquires any of the characteristics which he will, in fact, have in life. Only under these circumstances can it be proved that every individual has an *ex ante* probability of gaining from equalising the income distribution. It is very hard to think in these terms and, indeed, it is obvious that if we were thinking in these terms, we would have to think of how many 'potential lives' we are going to produce, since this would affect the income of individual potential lives.

I can see no reason why, in theory, we should not think of the well-being of as yet unborn individuals; it would not be the only metaphysical discussion in economics. A good many economists have discussed the well-being of future generations, which clearly involves unborn individuals.[9]

Nevertheless, it has been common in discussing population problems to consider only those unborn individuals who actually will be born. If we accept the widely-used maximum per capita income goal, then we choose from among those people who potentially could be created in the future, a number which maximises per capita return. Thus, those potential individuals are divided into two categories—those who will be given high per capita incomes and those who will be prevented from coming into existence—and we attempt to maximise the income of the former by increasing the number of the latter.

The peculiarity of this distinction among non-existent entities seems to have escaped notice. Clearly in deciding how many people are to be produced in the next generation (which presumably is what population policy is about), we are making decisions with regard to potential rather than real people. A rule of producing the maximum number who can be given a positive utility or, perhaps, maximising total utility, would seem preferable to a rule of maximising per capita income if we are concerned with the well-being of 'potential entities'. If we are not, it is very difficult to see why we should have any population policy at all.

But to leave this metaphysical issue aside, let us consider the prospects of maximising utility among a given population, whether extant or future. This given population could be either the present population or the population which generates maximum per capita income. For simplicity, let us assume it is the population that maximises per capita income, although there is no reason to believe that any existing, real-world population is of that size. Certainly, however, in such wealthy countries as the United States, Canada and Australia, the positive product of an additional member of society would be way above that needed to keep that member out of misery.

An illustrative example is shown on Table 14.1 Assume a country which has a per capita income-maximising population of 100,000 people; per capita income is $10,000. In situation II(a), II(b) and III, 50,000 people have been added to the population by birth or immigration. In case 1, the marginal return on additional effort is steeply declining, with the result that these individuals are able on the average to produce only $3000 worth of

Table 14.1

Situation	Population	Case 1 per-capita income	Case 2 per capita income	Case 2a per capita income
I	100,000	$10,000	$10,000	$10,000
IIa	100,00	11,000	10,050	14,000
	50,000	1,000	9,800	1,900
IIb	100,000	10,000	10,000	10,000
	50,000	3,000	9,900	9,900
III	100,000	7,288	9,966	9,966
	50,000	$7,288	$9,966	$9,966

real income. In cases 2 and 2a, shown in the third and fourth columns, marginal return is much more gradually declining with the result that these individuals can produce $9900 on the average. These numbers, of course, are chosen merely for illustrative purposes. Presumably in the real world, the numbers would fall somewhere between these two extremes.

It is immediately obvious that the existing population can, in fact, be benefited by an increase in population, providing only that one is willing to keep the additional people in a subordinate role. Situation II(a) shows a set of examples in which the return from the additional population is in part retained by the additional persons and in part transferred to the original 100,000 with varying increases in the income of the original population. Thus if one is attempting to maximise the well-being of the 100,000 who are the population which maximises per capita income, then retaining the population at 100,000 is not correct strategy for doing so. If, on the other hand, one has any concern at all for the 50,000 people who would otherwise be kept out of the economy—either because they are not born, or because they are now living in Ethiopia—then they benefit from being brought into the society also. The switch from situation I to situation II(a) is clearly Pareto-optimal, if the people who enter the society are immigrants from some place like Ethiopia.

If, on the other hand, we assume that we are dealing with population policy and the 50,000 people are in essence produced by a less restrictive birth control programme, then we have not made a Pareto-optimal move from situation I to situation II(a) because we have, of course, changed the population. It would, however, be clear that everyone has benefited and no one has been injured by the move. There is, of course, the possibility that the individuals in the original population might have very strong preferences for equal distribution. They might feel that the increase in their income obtained from moving from I to II(a) did not compensate them for the distaste they would feel from living in an unequal society. Note that this would have to be a pure dislike of visible inequality, rather than a charitable concern for the poor. A person charitably concerned for others would regard situation II(a) better than situation I because it does, in fact, help the 50,000. Perhaps, if we are talking not about immigration but the creation of additional people by reducing the restrictions on birth, he might be willing to argue that having zero utility is better than having a positive utility in a society in which your utility is restricted. This seems unlikely, and in any event we would wish to give the 50,000 their own choice in the matter.

Before discussing this more thoroughly, however, let us turn to II(b) and III. In II(b) we make the same assumptions about declining marginal utility of labour in the society, but assume that the existing 100,000 population will permit the new 50,000 population—whether immigrants or newly-created people—to retain the full value of the additional product. In discussion, I find that most of my friends who object to moving from situation I to situation II(a) regard situation II(b) as even worse. I assume this is because their preference function puts a high premium on equal distribution and not on helping people. Nevertheless, I see no reason why there might not be some people who prefer II(b) to II(a). Certainly, the 50,000 would.

Situation III shows the result of bringing the 50,000 in and giving them the same privileges as the original 100,000. This leads to a lower, but egalitarian, per capita income and, of course, higher total utility. Using the Lerner maximisation of total utility criterion, situations II(a) and II(b) are better than I, and situation III is better than either. On the other hand, it would, of course, be possible to produce another situation, IV, in which more people are admitted with unequal incomes and then another situation, V, in which the new income is equalised until such time as we reach the point at which the additional person did not increase total utility. Hence, if we applied the Lerner criterion, we would once again reach a society in which a mass of people live just above the misery level.

Interestingly, Lerner discusses issues somewhat similar to these in *The Economics of Control*. This is not, however, in the passage where he produces his famous demonstration of the advantages of equalising income, but far back in the book at the end of his second chapter on foreign trade.[10] Interestingly, this discussion is very largely in terms of benefiting the original inhabitants of a country, rather than maximising total utility. Although Lerner does not apparently propose a direct tax on the immigrants in order to make redistribution to the existing population, he does suggest that their presence would raise the marginal level of return on the non-labour factors of production and this would permit:

a higher social dividend to be distributed and a higher scale of living to be enjoyed by the older inhabitants or citizens who qualify for the social dividend. Those citizens with whom the immigrants compete more directly may find their *vmp* reduced more than their share of the social dividend is raised, but they could be more than fully compensated and still leave all the other citizens better off.[11]

Note that Lerner does not discuss the increased total utility which would be obtained if the individuals were permitted to migrate even under his restrictions, or the much greater increase in total utility which could be obtained if they were permitted to migrate unrestrictedly. Indeed, Lerner's only discussion of population policy indicates that the immigration of people from, say, India to the United States—which raised their utility, but which led to the population of India rising without any increase in the living standard in India—would be contrary to the 'general interest'.[12] The only argument against immigration offered by Lerner, however, is

Restrictions on immigrations are, however, very likely even in a rational and democratic collectivist economy because it is not pleasant, even if it is possible, to have a section of the population within the country discriminated against so severely.[13]

We shall discuss this point in more detail below, but note that once again the increase in total utility is ignored. Lerner would prefer Africans to starve to death quietly in The Sahel rather than live at the level, say, of $1000 per year in the United States. Lerner even objects to the wealthy countries making capital investments in the poorer countries, unless these investments take the form of gifts. Even the gifts do not seem to be intended by Lerner to be very large. He also would insist that, 'such a gift would not be expected if it would only increase population without raising standards'.[14] Once again, he pays no attention to total utility, and argues entirely in terms of more classical foreign policy goals such as 'a peaceful and satisfied world'.[15]

Lerner's argument is elaborated and made more rigorous by Leland Yeager.[16] Having presented the Lerner argument with great clarity and rigour, Yeager then sums up the arguments against permitting free immigration by saying,[17] 'To import the products of foreigners rather than the foreigners themselves provides an easy and conscience-soothing way to discriminate against foreigners by simply keeping them at a distance'.[18] This strong abhorrence of proximate inequality does not seem to be very widespread in the world today. Considerations rather like those which I have shown in Table 14.1 are presumably the explanation for the existence in many parts of the world of rules dividing the population into different groups, with one group having distinctly inferior economic opportunities. South Africa is an obvious case, but there are others. Israel, for example, appears to have such a system at the moment, although it is my impression that they acquired it by accident, as a result of military operations, and are not yet really aware of the fact that the situation exists. In any event, the immigration of Arabs to obtain the higher wages now available to them in Israel is surely very small. When the Israelis become fully aware of the situation, I would anticipate that they will change it.

Most North European countries have followed the policy of permitting the entrance of guest-workers to occupy various low-paid jobs in their society. This is rather as if we in the United States were to permit Egyptians to enter the United States, provided only that they agreed to take a restricted set of jobs where the productivity is very low. It is a situation rather like II(a). The details of the arrangement in Western Europe vary greatly and, at the moment, are in a state of flux. Indeed, one gets the impression that the West European governments may have calculated the rules improperly. It is possible that they are not by any means maximising the returns on a given number of immigrants. It is, however, clear that their institutions do lead to a society which has resemblance to our situation II(a).

There are vestiges of such a system in our immigration codes. Thus, it is not at all obvious that people find this kind of situation undesirable. If one looks round Western Europe, there seems to be no evidence that those countries which have highly developed egalitarian policies with respect to their own populations are less willing to introduce the type of situation we shows as II(a) by way of permitting guest-workers to fill the more menial jobs in their society than are less egalitarian societies. Thus, the question of whether egalitarian policies are actually motivated by distaste for inequality would seem to be answered in the negative. It seems likely that such countries as Sweden, Switzerland, West Germany and France have adopted these policies because their societies want such policies, rather than because of a desire for equality.[19]

It should perhaps further be noted that Lerner, Yeager, myself, and most readers of this chapter live in an environment in which there is a distinct class structure with widely different incomes between the two classes. The living standard distinction between the faculty and the students at most universities is an extreme one.[20] This does not seem to disturb the faculty at all. Indeed, when I talk to my colleagues about the difference between their living standard and that of the students, they normally seem to feel that it should be increased. Complaints about the makes of car the students drive are particularly common and, indeed, many faculty members seem to think that the students should be prevented from driving, or at least from parking, at all.

I began this note by remarking that I was not sure of the conclusions. In essence, what I am doing is attacking a popular set of assumptions by demonstrating that they lead to conclusions which would be widely unacceptable. Naturally, I would like now to introduce another set of assumptions (or arguments) on such problems as income distribution and optimal population that do not have these difficulties. Unfortunately I am unable to do so. Indeed, it seems to me that any discussion of optimal population must first solve the metaphysical problem of the welfare of non-existent entities. This means that we are making allocations of welfare among entities that are now non-existent with the desire of benefiting at least some of them. It is not obvious to me what criteria we should use in making such decisions.

I hope I have demonstrated in this article that maximising per capita income is not an obvious answer to the problem. Further, if we are attempting to maximise the per capita income of some particular group of non-existing entities, then in fact we can raise their income to a higher level by permitting another group, which is 'exploited', to come into existence. Since the exploited group will still have a positive utility and, hence, are better off than being left in non-existence, they also benefit by the change. This does not prove that situation II(a) is an optimal state of society; it may merely indicate that we have a very difficult problem.

NOTES

1. 'In addition to releasing other people, as usual, from responsibility for what is written here, I wish to indicate as well that the views expressed are not necessarily my own.' Robert E. Strotz, 'How Income Ought to be Distributed: A Paradox in Distributive Ethics', *Journal of Political Economy,* LXVI (June 1958), p. 189. It must be said, however, that he showed somewhat more enthusiasm for his own ideas in the controversy which followed the publication of the article. See, also, Franklin H. Fisher and Jerome Rothenberg, 'How Income Ought to be Distributed: Paradox Lost', *Journal of Political Economy*, LXIX (April 1961), pp. 162–80; Robert H. Strotz, 'How Income Ought to be Distributed: Paradox Regained', *Journal of Political Economy*, LXIX (June 1961), pp. 271–8; Franklin M. Fisher and Jerome Rothenberg, 'How Income Ought to be Distributed: Paradox Enow', *Journal of Political Economy,* LXX (January 1962), pp. 88–93. For an earlier statement of position rather similar to that of Strotz, see Milton Friedman, 'Choice, Chance, and the Personal Distribution of Income', *Journal of Political Economy* LXI (August 1953).
2. William Breit and William P. Culbertson, Jr, 'Distributional Equality and Aggregate Utility: Comment', *American Economic Review*, LX (June 1970), p. 435. This comment set off a lengthy discussion beginning with a 'Reply' by A. P. Lerner in the same issue (pp. 441–2), and continuing with Maurice McMannis, Gary M. Walton, and Richard B. Kaufman, 'Distributional Equality and Aggregate Utility. Further Comment', *American Economic Review,* LXII (June 1972), pp. 489–96; Roger A. McCain, 'Distributional

Equality and Aggregate Utility: Further Comment', *American Economic Review*, LXII (June 1972), pp. 497–500; and William Breit and William P. Culbertson, Jr, 'Distributional Equality and Aggregate Utility. Reply', *American Economic Review*, LXII (June 1972), pp. 501–2. This exchange was precipitated by Abba P. Lerner, *The Economics of Control* (New York: Macmillan 1947), pp. 20–40.

3. Lerner, op. cit., p. 29, Lerner was, of course, aware of the incentive problem. I shall, however, follow his example and ignore it here.

4. Milton Friedman, *Essays in Positive Economics* (Chicago: University of Chicago Press, 1953). Friedman's argument turns on the possibility that we might someday learn to measure utility. If we did, then the Lerner argument could lead to drastically different distribution of income.

> One could hardly take the position that analysis based on the capacity to enjoy satisfaction is relevant if it is impossible to determine an individual's capacity but irrelevant if it is possible to do so.
> (Friedman, *Essays in Positive Economics*, p. 310)

5. There is a special assumption (rarely explicitly made) which is necessary for the Lerner argument. This assumption is that total income is high enough so that it is possible to assure everyone an income which has positive utility. It is at least thinkable that there is some minimum income below which the individual is in misery and, hence, achieving a negative utility. This is not inconsistent with declining marginal utility on each unit of income. The assumption that incomes are above this level seems a fairly safe one. Even in such extraordinarily poor countries as Ethiopia or China, I doubt that there are many people whose income is so low that they are receiving a negative utility.

6. I owe the argument above to James Heade who was visiting at Virginia Tech at the time I prepared this chapter. He is preparing a rigorous presentation of the argument for publication.

7. P. A. Samuelson, 'A. P. Lerner at 60', *Review of Economic Studies*, XXXI (June 1964), pp. 369–78. For a very similar argument, see J. M. Buchanan and G. Tullock, *The Calculus of Consent* (Ann Arbor: University of Michigan Press, 1962), ch. 13, pp. 189–200.

8. In practice, genetic and family connections are such that no existing individual would be in complete ignorance. In a way, we must assume not individuals but potential individuals, i.e. future lives which are not as yet equipped with any positive characteristics which would affect their income.

9. For example, see Steven A. Marglin, 'The Social Rate of Discount and the Optimal Rate of Investment', *Quarterly Journal of Economics*, LXXVII (February 1963), pp. 95–111. I commented on this article in, 'The Social Rate of Discount and the Optimal Rate of Investment. Comment', *Quarterly Journal of Economics*, LXXVIII (May 1964), pp. 332–6, and the controversy set off has trailed through the journals ever since. Indeed, I do not believe it is yet concluded. For our present purposes, however, the specific issues in the controversy are less important than the fact that all of the participants, which included such distinguished names as Baumol and Sen, discussed the problem of the well-being of people not yet created.

10. Lerner, op. cit., pp. 364–7.

11. Ibid., p. 365.

12. Ibid., p. 364.

13. Ibid., p. 365.

14. Ibid., p. 367.
15. Ibid.
16. Leland B. Yeager, 'Immigration, Trade and Factor-Price Equalisation', *Current Economic Comment*, XX (August 1958), pp. 3–8.
17. Yeager does not discuss the prospect of determining an optimal population size by any method other than controlling immigration.
18. Yeager, ibid., p. 7. That Yeager himself may not share this value judgement is made clear by the footnote which he attaches to the end of the quoted sentence: 'This statement is meant as neither praise nor criticism of immigration barriers. Economic arguments are not the decisive ones', (p. 7, fn. 13).
19. Needless to say, I do not wish to exaggerate the degree to which such policies are genuinely egalitarian.
20. If we consider total lifetime earnings rather than the current situation, the distinction is still real, although less severe. Further, there is a large overlap.

15 The Macro Instability of the Market

In *Newsweek*, Milton Friedman once said, 'Current high interest rates offer a puzzle for which, so far as I can see, we have no satisfactory explanation.'[1] In the same article he points out that we also have no explanation for the substantially negative interest rates during most of the 1970s. In order to avoid the possibility that the reader may feel that I am going to solve Friedman's problem, I should say that I also have no explanation for either of these phenomena. The point of the chapter is not that I know why we sometimes get very large fluctuations in the market, but that if economic conditions do fluctuate on a macro scale, the market itself does not have a built-in stabilising mechanism. Specifically, I shall argue that the speculative mechanism which we tend to think of as stabilising the market doesn't work in 'macro' circumstances.[2]

Basically, the speculative mechanism cannot operate in macro circumstances for two reasons. The first is that the resources are not available. The reason they are not available has to be put down, I suppose, to a market imperfection, although in this case the imperfection is the unwillingness of the banks to make immense loans on poor security and at high risk, and that doesn't seem very imperfect to me. Secondly, there are no professional macro speculators, and the reason that there are no professional speculators is that macro fluctuations are relatively rare.

Macro economics normally is assumed to deal primarily with depressions and booms. They will be part of the subject matter of this article, but basically I am talking about major fluctuations in the economy whether they are depressions and booms, or something else. As an example, almost anyone who travelled to Europe in the 1960s noticed that the dollar was much overvalued with respect to the local currencies, and in the 1970s much undervalued. In 1982, it was, at least if my experience in Europe was correct, about accurate and the dollar not much overvalued with respect to substantially all European currencies. Why doesn't speculation straighten this out?[3]

For a more formal demonstration, consider the work of Shiller.[4] As his figures (p. 422) indicate, investors have not done a good job of discounting future income streams. The whole market sometimes offers large bargains and sometimes sells at very high prices, indeed. Further, if one assumes that individuals are concerned with capital fluctuations rather than dividends, then once again the price fluctuations are very hard to explain except on the theory that the errors are auto-correlated.

As an obvious example, the rise in stock prices during the 1920s and then their precipitate fall between 1929 and 1932 are merely extreme examples of the general phenomenon.

Having said these fluctuations are inexplicable, however, does not mean that I think that I know what the next stage will be. Currently, one can buy oil in the ground by way of buying in stock of companies which own it at less than $10 a barrel, whereas oil stored above ground costs in excess of $30. Although all the underground oil that I am discussing has actually been reached by wells and is flowing, it will, of course, take a good deal of time to get it out. Thus, we have here a judgement by the market that future prices of oil will be much lower than they are now.[5] Is this estimate right or wrong?

I don't know, but I can say that in order to bring the current prices of oil in the ground into accord with the current prices of oil in storage above ground, or even to half that price, an absolutely immense amount of speculation would be necessary. That the market does not provide this immense amount of speculation is, as I shall argue below, not necessarily explained on the grounds that all speculators believe this long-run price of oil is properly discounted at $10.[6] The phenomena cannot be explained by Michener's demonstration that the variance was regularly exceeded with random shocks.[7] His model does not involve stabilising speculation.

Let me begin my model with an elderly but extremely famous article, F.A. Hayek's, 'The Uses of Knowledge in Society'.[8] As practically all economists know, Hayek in that article points out the information economising aspect of the market in that individuals don't have to know an immense volume of technical knowledge, they can simply use prices as basic data in making their own decisions. That this is what most individuals do is, I take it, now orthodox doctrine.

There is, however, a modification. Hayek, obviously, did not mean that the individuals 'knew' the prices and simply used them in all of their purchase and sale activities. He was aware of the fact that the market fluctuates from time to time and such a model would prevent that. Further, he obviously did not mean that individuals simply accepted whatever price was offered for things that they bought and sold. He doesn't specify it, but he probably had a search procedure in mind rather like the search procedure, which has now become the standard doctrine with respect to unemployment.

Let us consider then the search theory of unemployed resources as it is applied, not strictly speaking, to unemployment although, of course, it still is important there, but to other decisions of business or for that matter individual consumption. We expect that there is not one price in the market but a spectrum of prices. Further, this spectrum will vary from time to time and, to some extent, this variance is predictable. If it were not, speculation would be impossible. Individuals making a purchase or sale decision then (whether that individual is a sales manager for a large company, a purchasing agent for another large company buying raw materials, a man looking for a job, i.e. selling his labour, or the housewife interested in feeding her family) will devote at least some effort to searching through the current spectrum of prices.

Further, that person will be, to some extent, prepared to extend the search through time, an extension which means simply waiting for a price change. Of course, the search across the existing spectrum also takes up time, but it is analytically simpler to keep the two separate. As a result of these two search activities, resources will superficially appear to be idle. In fact, they will be used in a manner which their owner thinks brings in the largest return. It is simply that this return is obtained by search activities rather than by employing them in the more conventional way.

Businessmen find this problem more difficult than most because they normally operate on quite narrow margins. The retail merchant who steadily pays ½ per cent more for his stock than his competitors will go out of business, while a careless housewife will simply feed her family a little bit worse if she makes the same error. Similarly, selling at slightly too low prices can be disastrous for a business if carried on over time.

The result is that businesses are more likely to invest resources in efforts to get good prices than are the people who are not working on such narrow margins. On the other hand, the resources invested are themselves costly and the businessman is pressed there, also.[9]

The businessman has another hazard here: he doesn't want to get the reputation of being easy, in the sense that he may purchase at too high a price or sell at too low a price. Thus, even under circumstances where he would be best advised to take a shipment of some kind of raw material at slightly a higher price than the prevailing one, he may decide to keep his factory idle and await a better price because he doesn't want to get the reputation for being a pushover. Such a reputation could be very expensive.

All of this will seem familiar to anyone who has read modern search theory, but I am changing the area in which it operates a little bit and, of course, the businessman has a somewhat different perspective than does the potential employee. Let me summarise by saying that the average businessman has an idea of what is the right price for something or other and will try to search and wait until he can get it. This idea is not held permanently, and it can change. Further, he may have an idea that prices are changing. For example, he may believe he is in an inflationary period or he may think, for one of a variety of reasons, that prices in general will fall. He takes this into account in making his decisions.

But, nevertheless, Hayek is basically correct. Most businessmen devote relatively little time to what we might call speculative activity, that is an effort to anticipate the market, to buy cheap and sell dear. A retail merchant certainly sells his product for more than he pays for it, but this is more than made up for by the various services that he performs. He would probably much prefer to be completely out of the arbitraging or speculative business but, of course, in the normal market he is forced to do at least a little of this. He must buy things at one time and sell them at another, and in most of our economy the necessary futures contracts which permit him to avoid any general market risks do not exist. Nevertheless, he puts relatively little attention to this aspect of his business if one compares it to the attention he gives to the actual technical running of the affair and tends to depend on his vague idea of market prices. To repeat, he has an idea of market prices which come partly from history and partly from various, probably not very well-thought-out or well-adjusted bits of information which he acquires in the course of his business.[10]

In a way, the businessman is depending on the division of labour, i.e. he expects the professional speculators to take care of violent price abnormalities. The first thing to be said here is that much of the economy does not have any professional speculators in it. Most manufacturing, most service trades, and even a good deal of agriculture, are carried on without professional speculation except in so far as individual businesses may expand or contract their inventories. In very large corporations it is possible that such decisions will be allocated to specialists, but in the more normal corporation they are simply made by the higher executives who have very many other responsibilities as well. Indeed, it is extremely difficult to see how even a large corporation like General Motors, which can easily afford to have specialists on this speculative activity, could maintain fluid capital large enough so that it could plan on buying its raw materials sometimes a year in advance and sometimes just when it needed them, and hold large quantities of cars during periods when it thought the market was depressed, unless these periods were quite short.

If we turn to those areas where there are professional speculators, basically the organised exchanges, the first thing to be noted is that although the speculators probably account for a very large percentage of the actual exchanges, the capital that they have in these markets is normally a very small fraction of the capital of other parties.

Take, for example, wheat. The organised exchanges are dominated, if one looks at transaction volume, by speculators whose purchases and sales are probably a very high multiple of the total amount of wheat available. If we consider the total amount of capital involved in the wheat business, however, it is obvious that these speculators hold a very small part. Indeed, the speculators normally do not actually have enough capital even to take delivery of the things which they buy.[11]

This is not only characteristic of the modern world, but it has always been characteristic. Speculation and arbitrage are economically important and have always attracted a number of very bright and aggressive merchants, but they have never been really big as a share of the total economy. This is not said in any spirit of criticism. Clearly, the net social benefit from these activities is not gigantic and it is only sensible that they have a relatively small amount of the resources, both in brains and in capital, which are available in the society. Further, the market has presumably allocated resources between speculation and arbitraging on one hand, and other activities connected with production and distribution on the other in such a way that the return in about equal in both.

In general there are a large number of different speculative or arbitraging markets, each with its own collection of specially qualified people and with its own sources of financial support. The expert in the grain market is apt to feel rather ill at ease in the London gold market. No doubt he could learn, but it would take time. Further, the person who is willing to advance funds to back the speculations of a man who has a good reputation in the Chicago pit is unlikely to fund either that man or someone else who decides to take an interest in the Singapore rubber market. All of this is as it should be. We would anticipate that there would be some people who were able to operate both in the Chicago pit and in Singapore, but the bulk of the speculators would, of necessity, be specialists. The opening-up of very large speculative opportunities in one or the other of these markets would tend to lead to some shift of resources there but not very rapidly because of the very difficult information problem, both on the part of the speculators and on the part of people who might advance them funds. This is indeed what we observe.

All of this, no doubt, is what is technically called an imperfection, but it is hard to argue that the market is not behaving well. We would like to have perfect information and perfect fluidity of resource flows, but the perfect information is clearly impossible and without perfect information perfectly fluid resource flows would do little or no good.

Let us, however, turn briefly to the nature of this speculative market. The first thing to do is to turn back to Lord Keynes and people who are in the business of guessing what other people will be guessing tomorrow, or of guessing what other people will guess other people will guess tomorrow, etc. I am not Keynesian myself, but it seems to me that in this respect he pointed towards a very important aspect of the market. It is less important for the speculator to know the actual situation of the real world as of the day after tomorrow than to know what other people, the day after tomorrow will think the aspect of the real world is. Of course, these two things are by no means unconnected, but there is also not a one to one correspondence between them. Further, the professional speculator is rather less apt to know the actual state of the world the day after tomorrow than various insiders whose major concern is not speculation but, let's say, managing a steel plant.

The speculator, of course, may have made arrangements to get information from the manager of a steel plant on, let us say, how business is going both in the steel plant and the steel plant manager's views of the steel business as a whole, but there is no reason to believe that he will be able to obtain that information at a price which would be particularly favourable to him. The insider, in a way, has somewhat better bargaining power, and even a little monopoly power, whereas there are many speculators.[12]

Under the circumstances, the speculator is apt to be very well informed about the underlying conditions, but not quite as well informed as certain people whose basic business is something other than speculation. His special advantage comes in his knowledge of the information flows through the market. If he hears a rumour today which he is confident will be a formal report tomorrow, and in the *Wall Street Journal* the day after tomorrow, the odds are very good that he can speculate effectively whether that rumour report and newspaper story are true or false. He can go in and out before the real world catches up to the information, or perhaps misinformation, in the market.

Further, Milton Friedman, in the article quoted above, refers to the 'herd mentality' of Wall Street.[13] The individual stockmarket speculator knows that this 'herd mentality' exists, that is if Wall Street thinks one thing it is apt to continue thinking it tomorrow. Since he knows that, he acts on that assumption which in and of itself pushes the herd in the direction which the herd is already going.[14]

The tendency of the speculators to go along with the general tide tends to over-correction. Thus, although we normally think of the speculators as being a stabilising force and they are, compared to a market where there are no speculators, they nevertheless may lead to the peaks and troughs of the fluctuations being more extreme than they otherwise would be. They stabilise in the sense that they round off the corners of what otherwise would be very sharp breaks, not in the sense that the extremes are necessarily eliminated.

In a way, behaviour like this is implied by the random walk hypothesis. If the market were governed by the gambler's fallacy, i.e. when it went up this automatically led to the view that it was going down, just as when red comes up on the red wheel that means black will next round, then speculators would regularly round off the peaks and troughs. The random walk hypothesis, however, implies that regardless of what the price is today it is as likely to go up as it is to go down tomorrow. The speculator must speculate on the basis of some information other than the current height of the market. This external information may indicate that the current price of the stock is inappropriate, either because the real factors are different from what the price implies, which would indicate that eventually the price will change or because there are currents of opinion in the market which have not yet been fully discounted which lead to the view that the price will change. It is the latter, I believe, that stockmarket speculators depend on predominantly, but in any event neither of these two external forces of information would necessarily lead to any flattening peaks or troughs.

All of the above description seems to indicate that there are opportunities for profits by speculators who don't behave the way I have described above. This is indeed true. These opportunities for profit, however, in general require that the 'super-speculator' be prepared to invest and hold his investment for rather a longer period of time than the speculators I have been describing. If I have some special knowledge as to what the *Wall Street Journal* will say tomorrow, I can make an immediate profit. If I think, perhaps quite properly, that the price of wheat is currently too high, although (or because) it has been rising steadily for the last three months, the odds are that if I sell short I am going to have to wait quite a while for my profit. Furthermore, unless my timing is absolutely extraordinary, I run the real prospect of running bookkeeping losses for a considerable period of time.

Catching the exact top or the exact bottom of the market is a difficult and unlikely feat. Mainly, a speculator attempting to even out the peaks and troughs would have to assume that he was buying at a point in time somewhere around the trough and selling at a point in time somewhere around the peak, but the prospect of considerable bookkeeping losses for a considerable period of time would always be there. Indeed, he could clearly exhaust his margin and thus be forced to sell and lose heavily as a result of a correct guess which was just mistimed a little bit.

The bulk of the speculators are primarily concerned with very short-term fluctuations. This implies that there is a profit to be made by longer-term speculations and this implication is one which I do not wish to contest. There is such a profit to be made and there are people making it. The problem simply is that there are not large enough resources available for speculations of this sort to stabilise the market. The remainder of this chapter is to be devoted to explaining why the resources available for this particular activity tend to be less than are needed for stabilisation. It should be emphasised at this point, however, that I have no positive reforms to offer. I am offering an explanation and not prescribing a cure.

The problem is that if there is a large fluctuation imposed on the market from some outside source, let us say a ghastly error by the Federal Reserve Board, this rather small speculative business, i.e. the specialist in speculation does not have either the expertise or the funds to deal with it. This could, of course, be the great depression of 1929–33, but it could also be a severe fluctuation in some commodity market, which is itself quite small, and speculators already in which are proportionately small. They would be both untrained and unable to get the resources to bring the thing back to a level keel. The problem is both the magnitude of the swings, together with the fact that they only occur fairly rarely.

Consider, for example, a speculator who feels that we are now in a depression, that things will get better, and hence that it is a good time to buy. He has to realise that he cannot say for certain whether we are in a depression or whether there has been a structural change which will lead to permanent lower level activities. Further, if we are in a depression, he cannot be sure whether we have reached the bottom or not, and investing before we reach the bottom may be very painful. Nevertheless, there are undeniable profit opportunities here. Note, however, that in general he would have to be prepared to hold his investment for a number of years before he sold it, the exact period depending on the size of the depression and the point in time at which he bought it. Granted the fact that the investment, like all speculative investments is risky, that means that he should discount his future profits by a fairly high rate of interest. If it is to be held for a number of years and is being discounted at a high rate of interest, then the prospective profit must indeed be very high to make this a sensible investment.

No doubt there are people who have the resources and skill, and bravery, to go in for such investments and presumably some of them make money. There aren't enough, however, to stabilise major swings. The reason here is the problem of becoming specialists in an activity that only occurs occasionally. Most of the time the market is not far enough out of kilter so that macro speculation against it is profitable. Thus, most of the time a macro speculator would either have to make a living doing something else or simply to be idle. Further, over the course of an active business life, he is unlikely to see more than perhaps five major opportunities for profit of this sort. Thus, he has little opportunity to acquire skills through practice. Further, it is very hard for him to convince potential financial backers that he has the skill since he has only fairly rare opportunities to demonstrate it. All of this is not a totally impervious barrier, but it does mean that the number of people who are making money out of macro speculation is always rather limited, and that the financial resources they can lay their hands on are also rather limited.

On the other side of the market there is, of course, the immense number of people who are engaged in business and who do not particularly want to speculate, although they are forced to some extent to do so. They have, as we said before, a vague idea of what the price should be and perhaps a vague idea of what the price will be in the near future, normally both of these are based essentially on history and a rather casual perusal of such sources of information as *The Wall Street Journal*. They are essentially specialists in other activities and cannot be blamed for not being experts in macro speculation. They also have another trait, which is in fact quite an intelligent trait but is likely to make macro drops more severe than otherwise. In times of uncertainty, and a shaky market in anything is a time of uncertainty, they are apt to feel that it is desirable to cut back on their debts and become as liquid as possible. This is not an irrational desire on their part, but it does mean that a market may be pushed down by this activity which may lead these people to even more interest in becoming liquid, which pushes the market down still further. Reverse fluctuation, when they decide that the market is stable enough so that they can reduce their liquidity somewhat, can push the market up, with the result that they find their liquidity could be reduced still further which pushes the market up still farther.[15]

Now this is not intended in any sense a criticism of these people, in the ordinary business of life, they are not professional speculators. They are behaving rationally and in the division of labour, which we have been happy about ever since Adam Smith, it is sensible for them to mind their own business and leave speculations to others. The problem is that the market does not provide for a number of macro speculators large enough to actually stabilise the macro fluctuations of the market. The reason it does not comes mainly from the fact that such macro fluctuations are not common enough so that people can be continuously engaged in that activity.

Very large amounts of capital and large amounts of skill would be necessary to counterbalance the effect of the amateur speculators, i.e. the bulk of us who are not engaged in that activity as a full-time occupation. These would have to be employed in something else much of the time and only switch over to macro speculation occasionally. Further, it doesn't really seem likely that the amounts of capital to stabilise really very big fluctuations would ever be possible. Shortly after the 1929 break, the New York bankers following in the footsteps of J.P. Morgan, got together money for the purpose of bidding up the stock market which they thought, quite properly, was too low. It turned out that they were unable to outbuy the immense number of Americans who had decided that in this time of uncertainty their accounts should be more liquid.

It seems likely that this will always be true simply because of the fact that the amount of capital invested in market activities, i.e. the literal exchange process which determines prices is always much smaller than the amount of capital, labour and skill invested in producing and distributing the commodities. If resources held by these non-professional speculators are dumped on the market, or if these people begin to buy in large quantities, the active market will be moved a long way simply because these people who are not normally a major constituent of the market actually have immensely more resources than are available to the professional speculators.

This is, of course, particularly true in that overwhelming bulk of the American markets in which there aren't any professional speculators at all. Automobiles, textiles, furniture, etc. move from raw material to the ultimate customer without ever being even nominally held by professional speculators. Adjustments of inventories by people whose main business is not speculation take the place of the speculative market and this, almost by definition, will be much less skilled than the speculative market. Further, the individual at some point in the chain between the raw material producer and the customer, who decides that the current prices are wrong and adjusts his inventory appropriately, is unlikely either to make very much profit or to make much difference in the total functioning of the market. He is better advised to improve the functioning of his factory.

So far I have said that the market has a defect in that the speculative portion of it is unlikely to level out macro swings. The question of whether we can do something about this is apt to be answered by suggesting that we have a government programme. The problem with this is that many of the macro swings have, in fact, been caused by inept government policies, and we have very little evidence that the government ever is good at flattening this kind of irregularity. I earlier remarked that it was hard for a person to get financial support on the basis of his skill at handling such markets because it is hard for him to get a reputation for having such skill, granted how rarely they turn up. The government has a well-established record of having no such skill. Under the circumstances, a government programme would probably simply make matters worse.

If we can get the government to stop imposing endogenous shocks on the market, we probably have done the most we can hope for out of government activity. There are, of course, many economists who think the market is basically quite stable and almost all major instabilities are governmental in origin. I am not convinced that this is true, particularly since they usually mean our government rather than any government, for example, Saudi Arabia, but it is fairly certain that the performance of our government, up to now, has led to considerable well-justified pessimism as to its ability to do anything about the defects I have listed above.

It is, of course, possible that some automatic rule, which would not only prevent the government from creating instability but permit it to eliminate instability originating from other sources, could be designed. Both the design and the political implementation would be very difficult, but I see no intrinsic law of nature which says it is impossible. For the time being, however, I fear that we are stuck with a government which contributes very seriously to instability and a market which is unable to correct for macro shifts regardless of their source.

NOTES

1. *Newsweek*, 21 September 1981, p. 39.
2. All of this is, of course, reminiscent of the work Leijonhufvud and Clower, my actual mechanism is different from theirs.
3. Note that the difference between tradeable and non-tradeable goods always, to some extent, explains differences of this sort. It is hard to account for reversals and large swings, however, in terms of tradeable and non-tradeable goods. Further, as a matter of fact, a lot of tradeable goods like, for example, Peugot's seem to be underpriced at the moment.
4. Robert J. Shiller, 'Do Stock Prices Move too much to be Justified by Subsequent Changes in Dividends?', *American Economic Review* (June 1981), pp. 421–36.
5. They may reflect simply a feeling that property on oil owned in the ground is insecure. Certainly, the history of oil taxes and regulations since 1973 would tend to bear that out.
6. Examples can be multiplied. For example, there is Mishkin's demonstration that over the long period speculation does not bring prices to equilibrium even if the speculation is based on correct information (Frederic S. Mischkin, 'Does Anticipated Monetary Policy Matter in Econometric Investigation?', *Journal of Political Economy*, vol. 90, no. 1 (February 1982), pp. 22–51); and the LeRoy and Porter demonstration that prices fluctuate more than present value in the stock market. 'The Present-Value Relation: Tests Based on Implied Variance Bounds', *Econometrica* (May 1981), p. 555–74.
7. 'Variance Bounds in a Simple Model of Asset Pricing', Ronald W. Michener, University of Virginia, the invisible academy, January 1981.
8. *American Economic Review* (September 1945), pp. 517–31.
9. Full-time housewives sometimes massively over-invest in an effort to get bargains. This, apparently, is due to the fact that they don't really have very much else to do and, hence, can engage in shopping as an avocation.
10. As an example of how badly informed businessmen can be, I had a conversation with the owner of a prosperous business in the Middle West who informed me that for a number of years he had been concerned about not being well enough informed about what was going on in Washington. He had, however, solved this problem by subscribing to a weekly, four page, newsletter.
11. As a vignette in the life of the distinguished economist, Armen Alchian does a certain amount of speculation and one time found himself in possession of a semi-trailer full of fresh eggs.
12. All of this is to some extent changed by the insider trading rules of current American law. In practice, however, the change doesn't seem to be very great. Henry Manne has many times explained the techniques by which insiders, in fact, make use of their inside information or trade it for suitable compensation. They don't just give it away in general.
13. Op. cit.
14. 'The mob is in the street, I must find out where it is going because I am its leader'.
15. See Dennis W. Carlton, 'The Disruptive Effect of Inflation on the Organisation of The Market', Working Paper No. 7, Program in Law and Economics, University of Chicago, for evidence of disruption of the market by a particular external cause.

Epilogue—The Grating People

Washington is the capital of the world's largest welfare state. It is also a place where the poorest people in the city are taken care of not by the welfare state, but by private charity. The same situation will be found to exist in the capitals of most other welfare states and for that matter in other cities in the United States, but I propose to confine myself to Washington because I know more about the situation here.

The exact number of 'homeless' or 'hungry' is not known.[1] This is particularly true because whenever anything is done which improves the status of such people their numbers increase. This is not intended in any sense as a criticism of them. It is however, obvious that if you set up a soup kitchen which provides free if rather bad meals, you must expect that not only people who have nothing to eat will turn up at that soup kitchen, but a certain number of people who before it opened were feeding themselves badly, and doing badly in most other aspects of life, will decide to take the free food and use their small income for other things. The same is of course true of free shelter.

This has been a problem with charitable provisions from earliest times. Further, it is a problem which I do not know any way of curing and which doesn't bother me particularly. Those people whose incomes are so low that they patronise the church groups which provide free meals and free shelter in Washington, seem to me people who are in need of help. I would, in general, prefer that the help be given in a more efficient way than providing them with free meals or shelter, but that does not mean that I resent their taking advantage of the meals and shelter. The problem that I am concerned with is why this condition persists. Why doesn't the welfare state take care of these people?

It is not that they are inconspicuous. *The Washington Post*, a couple of winters ago, published a picture on its front page of one of these people lying on a grating and literally covered with snow. He was directly across the road from the White House, and it was clear they thought this was a terrible situation. Indeed, they may have exaggerated the desperation of his position. I don't think he was cold, as the snow was on the outside of a sort of tent that he had constructed. They had, however, no suggestions whatsoever as to what should be done about him. They simply took the view that it was a bad idea, and vaguely implied that President Reagan was responsible. They did not suggest that their readers send in contributions which they could use to take care of the matter; Mrs Graham, the owner of the *Post*, who is wealthy enough easily to take care of all of the present numbers of grating people in Washington, did not offer to do so; and, last but not least, and most mysteriously, they did not criticise the government welfare agencies for not rescuing this man.

It has to be said that most of these people are indeed somewhat difficult to deal with. They are often mental cases, who have difficulty making any kind of social contact with other people; they have difficulty negotiating even with civil servants; and they tend to fight with each other if brought together in aid shelters. Still, it is possible to help them and, indeed, there are a number of voluntary charities in Washington which do so. Further, these voluntary charities are quite skilful at coercing the federal and local government into giving them funds which they use to supplement their private charity.

Why, however, do we observe this matter simply being left to these private charities? To put the matter at its crassest and most imperialistic, why do the welfare state bureaucracies not take advantage of this opportunity to expand their appropriations and scope of activity by asking Congress to fund a special programme for this purpose? Why doesn't *The Washington Post* suggest it? I understand why the current voluntary agencies don't directly demand a government programme. After all, this would lead to unemployment for their own personnel. But I would think they would at least be pushing for government grants large enough to permit them massively to improve their current charitable activities.

None of these things is happening. And frankly, I don't understand why not. Well-intentioned, charitable people should be trying to get government aid for these people. Crass selfish bureaucrats should be trying to get aid for these people and well intentioned intellectuals or for that matter, imperialistic intellectuals such as the staff of *The Washington Post,* should be pushing for such government programmes, yet we observe that none of these things are happening.

There are of course, individuals, including a certain number of people from all of the categories I've listed above, who are making charitable gifts to help these people, sometimes making considerable personal sacrifice. Nobody seems to feel that a major government programme, or for that matter even a major charitable drive to help them is justifiable. In keeping with what was said above, I don't understand why not.

One of the themes of this book has been that we have a lot of puzzles in the field of charitable activity. From my standpoint, this is the most recent one that I have encountered and in many ways the most puzzling, possibly one of the readers can solve the problem.

1. After an exhaustive and careful study, the government department of Housing and Urban Development found that the number of homeless was between 192,000 and 586,000. *A Report to the Secretary on the Homeless and Emergency Shelters*, HUD Office for Policy Development and Research, 1 May, 1984.

Index

210